# CLASSICAL THEORIES OF INTERNATIONAL RELATIONS

**St Antony's Series**
Series Standing Order ISBN 0 333 71109 2
(outside North America only)

You can receive future titles in this series as they are published by placing a standing order.
Please contact your bookseller or, in case of difficulty, write to us at the address below with
your name and address, the title of the series and the ISBN quoted above.

Customer Services Department, Macmillan Distribution Ltd
Houndmills, Basingstoke, Hampshire RG21 6XS, England

# Classical Theories of International Relations

Edited by

**Ian Clark**
*Department of International Politics*
*University of Wales*
*Aberystwyth*

and

**Iver B. Neumann**
*Head of Foreign and Security Policy*
*Norwegian Institute of International Affairs*
*Oslo*

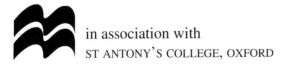

in association with
ST ANTONY'S COLLEGE, OXFORD

Published in Great Britain by
**MACMILLAN PRESS LTD**
Houndmills, Basingstoke, Hampshire RG21 6XS and London
Companies and representatives throughout the world

A catalogue record for this book is available from the British Library.

ISBN 0–333–65066–2 hardcover
ISBN 0–333–74646–5 paperback

Published in the United States of America by
**ST. MARTIN'S PRESS, INC.,**
Scholarly and Reference Division,
175 Fifth Avenue, New York, N.Y. 10010

ISBN 0–312–15931–5 clothbound
ISBN 0–312–21926–1 paperback

Library of Congress has cataloged the hardcover edition as follows:
Classical theories of international relations / edited by Ian Clark
and Iver B. Neumann.
p. cm. — (St. Antony's)
Includes bibliographical references and index.
ISBN 0–312–15931–5 (cloth)
1. International relations—Philosophy. I. Clark, Ian, 1949– .
II. Neumann, Iver B.
JX1395.C54 1996
327.1'01—dc20
95–51279
CIP

Selection and editorial matter © Ian Clark and Iver B. Neumann 1996
Chapters 1–12 inclusive © Macmillan Press Ltd 1996

First edition 1996
Reprinted 1997, 1999

This book is printed on paper suitable for recycling and made from fully managed and
sustained forest sources.

10  9  8  7  6  5  4  3  2  1
08  07  06  05  04  03  02  01  00  99

Printed and bound in Great Britain by
Antony Rowe Ltd, Chippenham, Wiltshire

# Contents

# Foreword

During his time at Oxford University, 1986–89, John Vincent offered a course on classical theories in international relations which his students tended to see as the perfect forum for what he himself always referred to as the conversation about international relations. When his own spoken part in this conversation was cut short by his much too early death in 1990, it struck me that one way of continuing the conversation would be to fashion a book around his course syllabus. On the bus back to St Antony's College from a commemorative service in his honour held by the LSE I mentioned this to another of his former students, Geoffrey Wiseman. Together we contacted a number of John's students and colleagues. The current volume has grown and developed from this original idea.

First drafts were presented at a panel organised by Timothy Dunne at the British International Studies Association's annual conference in Swansea, January 1992. At this time Geoffrey Wiseman had to withdraw from the project due to other commitments, and Ian Clark kindly stepped in as co-editor.

A number of other people have offered advice and assistance along the way. The editors are grateful to the many people who have played a part in bringing the project to fruition. It is hoped that, in its small way, it will stand as another tribute to John Vincent's powerful influence upon all who had the good fortune to encounter him.

Iver B. Neumann
Oslo

# Notes on the Contributors

**Ken Booth** holds a personal chair in the Department of International Politics, University of Wales, Aberystwyth. He has been Scholar-in-Residence at the US Naval War College, Senior Research Fellow in the Centre for Foreign Policy Studies, Dalhousie University, Canada, and Visiting Fellow, Clare Hall, Cambridge. His books are *Contemporary Strategy: Theories and Policies* (co-author), *Navies and Foreign Policy, Soviet Naval Policy: Objectives and Constraints* (co-editor), *American Thinking about Peace and War* (co-editor), *New Thinking about Strategy and International Security* (editor) and *International Relations Theory Today* (co-editor). His latest book, edited with Steve Smith and Marysia Zalewski, is *International Theory: Positivism and Beyond.*

**Ian Clark** is a Professor of International Politics in the University of Wales, Aberystwyth. Previously, he was Deputy Director of the Centre of International Studies, University of Cambridge. Since 1996, he has also been an annual Visiting Professor in the Graduate School of Economics and International Relations, Catholic University of Milan. His many publications include *Limited Nuclear War* (1982), *Waging War: A Philosophical Introduction* (1988), *The Hierarchy of States* (1989), *The British Origins of Nuclear Strategy (co-author)* (1989) and *Nuclear Diplomacy and the Special Relationship: Britain's Deterrent and America* (1994). His most recent work is *Globalization and Fragmentation: International Relations in the Twentieth Century* (1997).

**David P. Fidler** is Associate Professor of Law at Indiana University School of Law, Bloomington. He is co-editor with Stanley Hoffmann of *Rousseau on International Relations* (1991). Many of his articles combine international relations theory and international law, including 'Caught Between Traditions: The Security Council in Philosophical Conundrum', *Michigan Journal of International Law* (1996), 'Challenging the Classical Concept of Custom: Perspectives on the Future of Customary International Law', *German Yearbook of International Law* (1996), and 'LIBERTAD v. Liberal Theory: An Analysis of the Helms–Burton Act from within Liberal International Relations Theory', *Indiana Journal of Global Legal Studies* (1997). His forthcoming book *International Law and Infectious Diseases* will be published by Oxford University Press.

**Andrew Hurrell** is University Lecturer in International Relations and Fellow of Nuffield College. He is currently Director of Graduate Studies in International Relations at Oxford University. His major interests include international relations theory and the international relations of Latin America, with particular reference to the foreign policy of Brazil and US–Latin American relations. His publications include *The International Politics of the Environment* (co-editor with Benedict Kingsbury) (1992), and *Regionalism in World Politics* (co-editor with Louise Fawcett) (1995). He is currently completing a research project on Dimensions of Inequality in World Politics.

**Benedict Kingsbury** is Professor of Law at New York University Law School. Previously he was Professor of Law at Duke University and University Lecturer in Law at Oxford University. His publications include *Hugo Grotius and International Relations* (ed. with Hedley Bull and Adam Roberts, 1990), *The International Politics of the Environment* (ed. with Andrew Hurrell, 1992) and *United Nations, Divided World* (2nd edn, ed. with Adam Roberts, 1993). A New Zealand citizen, he specialises in international law and human rights, and writes also on the connections between international law and international relations.

**Andrew Linklater** is Professor of International Relations at Keele University and Dean of Postgraduate Affairs. He has published *Men and Citizens in the Theory of International Relations* (1982, 1990), *Beyond Realism and Marxism: Critical Theory and International Relations* (1990) and *The Transformation of Political Community: Ethical Foundations of the Post-Westphalian Era* (1998). Current research interests include the relationship between critical theory and the English school.

**Richard Little** is Professor of International Politics in the Department of Politics at the University of Bristol. Before moving to Bristol, he taught at the Open University and Lancaster University. His recent publications include *Perspectives on World Politics,* co-edited with Michael Smith, and *The Logic of Anarchy,* co-authored with Barry Buzan and Charles Jones.

**Cornelia Navari** is Senior Lecturer and Director of the Graduate School of the Department of Political Science and International Studies at the University of Birmingham. She has edited *The Condition of States* (1991) and *Chatham House and British Foreign Policy during the Interwar Period* (1994). Her work on the history of thought includes 'Hobbes and the Hobbesian Tradition in international Thought', *Millennium: Journal of*

*International Studies,* Vol. 11, No. 3 ; 'The Great Illusion Revisited: The International Theory of Norman Angell', *Review of International Studies* (1989); and 'David Mitrany and International Functionalism', in D. Long and P. Wilson (eds), *Thinkers* of *the 20 Years Crisis* (1995).

**Iver B. Neumann** heads the section for foreign and security studies at the Norwegian Institute of International Affairs, Oslo but is presently on leave working in the Planning Staff of the Norwegian Foreign Ministry. He earned his doctoral degree at St Antony's College, Oxford, in 1992. His books are *Russia and the Idea of Europe, 1800–1993: A Study in Identity and International Relations, Regional Great Powers in International Politics* and *The Soviet Union in Eastern Europe, 1945–89* (edited with Odd Arne Westad and Sven G. Holtsmark). His forthcoming book from Minnesota University Press is *Uses of the Other: The 'East' in European Identity Formation.*

**Martin C. Ortega** is Lecturer in Public International Law and International Relations at the University of Salamanca. He is currently on leave for three years as a Research Fellow at the Institute for Security Studies of the Western European Union in Paris. He was senior associate member of St Antony's College, Oxford. His works include *La legitima defensa del territorio del Estado* (1991) and *Hacia un gobierno mundial* (1995).

**Andrew Walter** is Senior Lecturer in International Relations at the LSE and previously was Lecturer in International Relations and Fellow of St Antony's College, Oxford. He has held a number of visiting Professorships. His Publications include *World Power and World Money* (1993); 'Regionalism, Globalization, and World Economic Order' in L. Fawcett and A. Hurrell (eds), *Regionalism in World Politics* (1995); 'Globalization, Corporate Identity, and European Technology Policy', *Journal of European Public Policy* (1995); 'The United States and Western Europe: The Theory of Hegemonic Stability' in N. Woods (ed), *Explaining International Relations Since 1945* (1996). He is presently working on a book on the international politics of capital mobility.

**Jennifer M. Welsh** is a graduate of St Antony's College, Oxford. She worked as a consultant at McKinsey's and now runs her own company, 'd-code', and teaches part-time in peace and conflict studies at the University of Toronto. Her previous positions include: Cadieux Fellow with the Policy Planning Staff, Ministry of Foreign Affairs, Canada;

Lecturer, McGill University; Jean Monnet Research Fellow, European University Institute; and Lecturer, Central European University. She has published *Edmund Burke and International Relations* (1995).

**Howard Williams** is Professor of Political Theory in the Department of International politics at the University of Wales, Aberystwyth. He has published numerous books including *Marx* (1980), *Kant's Political Philosophy* (1983), *Heraclitus, Hegel and Marx Dialectic* (1988), *Concepts of Ideology* (1988) and *Political Theory in International Relations* (1991); He has edited *Essays on Kant's Political Philosophy* (1992). His most recent works are *Political Theory and Limits of International Relations* (1996) and, as co-author, *Francis Fukuyama and the End of History* (1997).

# 1 Traditions of Thought and Classical Theories of International Relations

## Ian Clark

The division of thought about international relations into various, and often conflicting, traditions is virtually the hallmark of the classical approach to the subject. Drawing its strength from the self-styled timeless dialogue about the nature of international society, this conception of international theory has made its distinctive contribution by presenting sundry visions of international life around which prominent historical writers have coalesced and on the basis of which antinomies with other writers have been created. At a stage in the theory of international relations when the validity of such all-encompassing intellectual schemes and the notion of political theory outside historical time are both being increasingly challenged, it is not surprising that the respectability of the very idea of a tradition of international thought should be open to renewed questioning. Is there then a place for the tradition in theoretical reflections about international relations?

It is one of the great paradoxes of the subject that Martin Wight, the foremost presenter of international relations in the form of various traditions of thought,[1] should also have been the writer to express greatest scepticism about the existence of a body of international theory at all.[2] Is it not fundamentally contradictory that there can be traditions, implying some continuity of social practice and of intellectual heritage, within a realm of theorising, the existence of which is itself in doubt? This chapter will deal with the place of traditions in international theory, with the costs and benefits of so approaching the subject, and finally with the role of 'traditions' in the expanding agenda of contemporary international theory. In short, it will seek to explore the degree of continuity and discontinuity between the classical and the 'non-traditionalist' writers and to offer some suggestions about a possible synthesis between the two.

Wight's disclaimers about whether we might accurately make reference to a body of international theory derived from his doubt that there was a thematically coherent set of writings on international relations in any way comparable to the political theory of the state: the former was not concerned with the 'good life' and was little more than the occasional contemplation of the scattered remnants left over when the latter task had been duly completed. Political philosophers had seldom been directly interested in international relations as such.[3] The objection is not dissimilar to Walker's more recent complaints that '[i]nternational political theory has become the taken-for-granted silence against which the political theory of the civil society has come to be heard'[4] and that international theory has thereby developed as a 'tradition by negation'.[5] Conceived in these terms, it is all the more remarkable that Wight should have outlined traditions of international relations at all since they were anything but part of the mainstream. The point is echoed in Mayall's observation that '[s]ince the 17th century Western political theory has been predominantly concerned with the justification of authority and the basis of civil society. This preoccupation has notoriously confined the consideration of international relations to the margin of the Western philosophical tradition.'[6] If valid, this restates the query as to whether such marginalised fragments of thinking warrant the prominence, and the possibly artificial coherence, that their grouping into traditions seems to accord them.

And yet a presentation of the history of international thought in terms of a number of traditions remains closely associated with the classical approach, or with the 'English school' of international relations. While common acceptance of such traditions is not a focal point of unity for that school, its concentration upon international society, and the degree of order within it, lends itself readily to a formulation into traditions.[7] So much is this so that there have been recent attacks, not simply upon the disparate traditions, but upon their overweaning dependence upon the central concept of international society itself. '[T]he tradition of international society, as outlined and defended by the classical school,' in the words of one critic, 'is ultimately incoherent.'[8] Despite this, the embedded sympathy with the Wightian tripartite categorisation into Realists, Rationalists and Revolutionists is fully revealed by the effort made by subsequent writers to locate members of the English school within these traditions. Not surprisingly, there has been much interest in arguing where Wight himself had his intellectual home. Wight occasionally made teasing suggestions which implied his Rationalist credentials, as in his comment that Rationalism 'is a road on which I suppose all of us, in certain moods, feel we really belong'.[9] But later judgements have been more mixed. Alan James was in no doubt that 'Wight falls unambiguously into the category which is widely termed …realist.'[10] Bull's judgement was more qualified. He thought Wight belonged with the Rationalists but that it would be wrong to force him into that particular pigeon-hole. Rather, Wight stood outside the three traditions, 'embodying in his own life and thought the tension among them'.[11] Others have thought it safe to label him a 'neo-Grotian' because he did not share the natural-law foundations of Grotius's thought.[12]

Similar disagreements about the location of Hedley Bull have been a prominent feature of the attempt to assess Bull's contribution to the field. Robert Gilpin unhesitatingly regarded him as 'one of the foremost proponents of realism.' Hoffmann, more diffidently, thought him 'close to realism' but displaying significant points of disagreement with some of its tenets. Finally, Vincent pronounced Bull to be 'four-square in the Grotian or rationalist tradition'.[13] Such is the hold that the classification has that, it would be seem, we cannot truly assess the members of the English school without finding their assigned place within it.

## THE TAXONOMY OF TRADITIONS

How should such traditions of thought be identified and categorised? Much of the literature has been content to concentrate on a dualistic division into Utopianism and Realism, an approach given definitive expression by E. H. Carr.[14] Wight himself acknowledged that such a simple dichotomy was peculiarly fashioned by the 'diseased situation' in post-appeasement Britain and post-isolationist America but, otherwise, was too constricting and inadequate to comprehend the richness and texture of international thought.[15] Nevertheless, the quest for parsimonious clarity has encouraged others, including the present author, to force a reluctant motley of thinkers into twin Procrustean beds. For this they were justly chastised by John Vincent. 'Unlike Julius Caesar and graduates of the London School of Economics, who think in threes', he wrote with impish good humour, 'Ian Clark thinks in twos...'[16] More recently, the preference for a twofold scheme of traditions has re-emerged but is incarnated in communitarianism and cosmopolitanism, rather than in Utopia and reality.[17] Meanwhile, Steve Smith, while not quite addressing traditions of international thought as such, tends also to see a bifurcation in international theory: 'the fundamental normative issue in the subject', he writes, 'is the conflict between foundationalism and anti-foundationalism'.[18]

Yet others have discerned a broader range of still-discernible traditions. Overly constrained by a simple duality, Donelan offers us a quintuple arrangement into Realist, Historicist, Rationalist, Fideist and Natural Law traditions.[19] The narrower the focus, the greater the number of such traditions. In a recent collection on international ethics, the editors are able to identify twelve separate traditions for inclusion. But while each such botanic specimen is distinct, the collectors sensibly warn that they 'are interdependent, overlapping, and historically entangled perspectives on a common body of experience'.[20] Whatever the virtues of such heterogeneous schemes, however, the proliferation of categories carries the risk, noted by Dunne, that the 'coherence of the original traditions has been displaced by a Babel of contending voices'.[21]

Despite these competing taxonomies, Wight's tripartite division into Realists, Rationalists and Revolutionists sets the terms of reference for most discussions.[22] Even Wight, however, was to subdivide his categories at various times and to insist that traditions of international thought could be organised into 'three, *at least three*, coherent patterns of thought'.[23] While so much of his work was devoted to the elaboration, restatement and refinement of various dimensions of this fundamental framework, his intent throughout was equally to intermingle the three traditions rather than to keep them starkly apart. It is a brave, and utterly candid, academic who can conclude a series of lectures devoted to identification of these patterns by admitting, disarmingly, that 'there has been a confluence, a convergence, if not to say a confusion of traditions'.[24]

What is the intellectual content of these individual traditions? There is an identity, formally, among the procedures in all three, although obviously the substantial content varies from one to the other. As Hedley Bull summarised the situation, each tradition 'embodied a description of the nature of international politics and also a set of prescriptions as to how men should conduct themselves in it'.[25] Each tradition analytically explores facets of the same interconnecting series of questions, each emphasising the aspects that most directly concern its own separate agenda. These problems pertain to whether or not there is an international society and, if so, what its essential characteristics might be; the relationship between the state and that wider society; and the place of the individual human being within the national and international context.

The Realist tradition is identified with Hobbes, or with Machiavelli whom Wight considered 'in a real sense the inventor of Realism'.[26] It denies the existence of an international society, depicting international relations as being in a pre-social state of nature which is equivalent to a state of war. In this situation, the state is master of its own fate and, in turn, depends upon the *virtù* of the statesman. It is through 'the personal creativity of a strong leader'[27] that the state's external security is to be guaranteed and its national interest unerringly perceived. The most important theoretical consequence of this analysis is that it is power, enshrined in the state, that determines all normative categories: 'power', Wight wrote, 'is anterior to society, law, justice and morality'.[28]

From this description, certain prescriptions follow inevitably. The state is not enjoined to observe a common morality because no such universal order exists. Rather the task of statesmanship is to protect the insular political order of the state from the anarchic seas which surround it. The accepted currency in this trade is power, and foreign policy is primarily devoted to the manipulation of power balances to maximise the state's security interests. Such order as exists in international relations is fragile and temporary and must be understood against a background of the constant potentiality for warfare.

The Rationalist dissents from key elements of this analysis. In associating this tradition with Grotius, Wight used it to identify the social and institutional basis of international relations such that it makes sense to speak of an existing international society. States shares common interests and cooperate in their achievement. Even if the international society is imperfect, it does exist and, to the extent that international relations is a state of nature, this is an already sociable condition.[29] It is a 'true society, but institutionally deficient; lacking a common superior or judiciary'.[30] There is, though, cooperation and it is manifested in the institutions of international society such as diplomacy and international law. Even war is an institution of international society because the principal function of international law is to regulate, and not to outlaw, this particular activity. It is in this regard that Bull, classically, dismissed the relevance of the domestic analogy because war points to the distinctiveness of international society, rather than representing its anti-social nature.[31] In brief, international relations is characterised by shared rules and norms, reflecting a 'solidarist' conception of society of the kind that underlay much of Grotius's thinking.[32]

The mode of behaviour appropriate in this context is markedly at odds with Realist prescriptions. Preservation of the bases of international society becomes itself a principal task of statesmanship, and customary behaviour allows for the development of sufficient trust for genuinely cooperative approaches to emerge. However, despite these sharp contrasts, the Realist and Rationalist traditions converge in that they are both essentially statist analyses of international relations.[33] It is in this regard that the Revolutionist tradition is marked off as being radically different from the other two.

Revolutionism's initial image is of an incipient or immanent world community which goes beyond the society of states. Its fundamental constituents are human beings rather than the 'contracted' states through which they have contingently given political expression to their interests. This tradition is identified with Kant, albeit that his thought was suffused with an ambivalent mixture of statist and cosmopolitan elements.[34] At base, however, it is a conception which emphasises a world society of individuals beholden to a universal moral order. In the centrality which it commits to the moral freedom and autonomy of the individual, it is ultimately corrosive of inter-*state society* and envisages its final supercession. Such a tradition brings together thinkers that the earlier-presented duality tends to keep apart. For Wight, Rousseau and Kant are bedfellows because modern Revolutionism dates from the French Revolution and 'Kant was the funnel through which the intoxicating alcohol of Rousseau was poured into the veins of international society'.[35]

## TRADITIONS OF THOUGHT: A CRITIQUE

The dominant question within the classical approach has been how best to categorise the traditions of thought: for those critically outside such a procedure, the question is whether any such attempt is desirable in principle. In this section, the merits of presenting international relations theory through the medium of such traditions will be debated.

The case for doing so is seldom set out explicitly but rests upon certain simple and readily accessible assumptions. The first is the most basic. It is that international relations deals with relatively few canonical problems that are sufficiently constant to be conveyed in terms of an ongoing tradition of reflection. Basic questions about international society, the state and the individual are inseparable from any theorising about international relations and structure our key responses to the field. This is what international relations theory *is*, and as the range of answers to these questions is inherently limited, they can usefully be identified and clustered in categories sharing common characteristics. Taxonomising is a means to an end, however, rather than an end in itself. Its assumption is that 'the truth about international politics had to be sought not in any one of these patterns of thought but in the debate among them'.[36] Analysis into discrete traditions is thus but a preliminary step towards a more complete synthesis of the subject's central characteristics.

Secondly, it is the function of these traditions to identify certain permanent normative orientations. It matters decisively to any discussion of international relations whether there is an international society, whether the state is the sole or supreme repository of moral value or whether, analytically, priority should be assigned to the individual's rights and duties.

Recourse to the device of the tradition simply lends coherence to a debate that is already structured by these choices, and the function of scholarship is to make these orientations as explicit as possible.

Thirdly, appeal to a tradition of thought is regarded as a potent safeguard against the *hubris* of the present. As an antidote to the temptation to regard the world's present problems as unique, or susceptible to an infinity of choice as regards their solution, the notion of a tradition fixes politics in history. The problems of each age represent no more than variations on the same central themes. Consequently, we can take advantage of the collective wisdom of the ages since it has something to say about today's preoccupations. Indeed, in the Burkean sense, we are duty-bound to engage in such a dialogue because we are but temporary custodians of a society itself shaped by traditional concerns.

Finally, to say that it is appropriate to exploit the wisdom of the ages is not by itself to vindicate its structuring into traditions. Few would deny the value of studying past political theory in context: many would object to organising it in such a way that it is distorted to meet present moods and needs and so that it closes off other intellectual options. What the tradition adds to the study of past thought is a constant point of reference against which change can be measured; in the context of which elements of continuity can be explored, but certainly not assumed nor revered; and against which critical questions can be asked about why certain traditions of theorising have developed, been brought into scholarly focus or come to be considered more important than others which have not found a voice. In short, the concept of a tradition has an important role to play even in the most inhospitable surroundings of contemporary 'anti-traditional' theory.

If the case for employing traditions has been mostly implicit, the critique of the traditions has become much more explicit in recent years. The objections raised can be considered in ascending order of importance.

The first is a group of criticisms that seems more concerned with the manner in which the project is executed than about its fundamental validity. In part, its anxiety is that the quest for traditions inculcates a fetish for categorisation for its own sake: the history of thought becomes subordinate to discovering the pigeon-hole in which any particular writer most appropriately belongs. In these terms, it would be a limited and artificial exercise. But surely this is not the object of the exercise: the categories are means to a more intelligent framework of discussion and not ends in themselves. Indeed, Wight himself was fully aware of this danger and insisted that '[c]lassification becomes valuable... only at the point where it breaks down'.[37] Similarly, we can give short shrift to the worry that the paradigmatic writers do not fit conveniently into their own traditions. Was Grotius a Rationalist, or Kant a Revolutionist, and so on. The traditions are not straitjackets and complex and subtle thinkers should not be constrained by them. This is all the more so because there is intermingling among the traditions themselves, sharing as they do some characteristics in common.[38] Nor is it an objection that the traditions of thought identified are misconceived because they represent western traditions of thought alone. While there is force to the complaint, it raises no objection in principle to the procedure but merely points to the unrepresentativeness of the selection of writers, a defect that can be rectified.

Much more fundamental is the criticism that the construction of traditions of thought is itself an essentially illegitimate scholarly procedure because it makes untenable assumptions about the nature of political language. Historians of ideas, and notably Quentin Skinner, deny the notion of a timeless language and concepts in terms of which a trans-historical dialogue can take place. Political language is rooted in its own context and it follows that the creation of a tradition across time must, by its nature, be a fabrication which is insensitive to the nuances of the distinctive ages and concerns which are said to give rise to it. Rob Walker gives edge to this critique in lamenting the treatment of such writers as Thucydides, Machiavelli, Hobbes and Rousseau:

> In place of a history of political thought is offered an ahistorical repetition in which the struggles of these thinkers to make sense of the historical transformations in which they were caught are erased in favour of assertions that they all articulate essential truths about some underlying and usually tragic reality: the eternal game of relations between states.[39]

This is not far removed from Rennger's objection to other forms of reification in that 'the so-called "tradition" of international society is in fact a scissors-and-paste construct taken from a wide variety of past traditions'.[40] What we end up with is not a clearly considered concept of international society but little more than a 'guardian angel',[41] giving comfort if not scholarly illumination. A postmodernist analysis simply gives a twist to this, given its preoccupation with the indeterminacy of meaning and with 'how, in history, meaning is imposed, put into question, reinterpreted, and fixed anew'.[42] Without such an appreciation, we do not realise that a tradition is no more than 'the ebbtide of philosophy'.[43] Such a conception also alerts us to the danger that the framing of a tradition implies a story with a beginning and such a 'practical convenience is always liable to turn into a powerful myth of origin'.[44]

Thirdly, the construction of theoretical traditions is condemned for encouraging intellectual conservatism and for closing down the agenda.

The framework of thinking fostered by these traditions favours the posing of certain issues and stifles the consideration of others. Again, Walker is the most articulate and penetrating representative of this tendency. Writing of the Great Debate between realism and idealism, he levels a charge of even wider significance:

> As roles in a manichean theatre, these terms have served primarily to close off serious discussion in a manner that has helped to insulate the discipline of international debate ever since. Rather, the categories of realist and idealist ... should be understood as the primary forms in which the basic assumptions governing the study of world politics have been left to congeal, requiring little further exploration.[45]

This is the key danger, that the agenda itself is set and left to ossify. In short, the question that must be faced in any investigation into the validity of the classical traditions-of-thought approach to theory is whether it has indeed inhibited discussion of issues that do not fall within the mainstream of these particular traditions. In short, have other traditions been strangled at birth and is it the proper task of theory to embark on a quest for 'lost traditions'?[46]

The nature of this critique is similar in principle to Steve Smith's questioning of the competing theoretical perspectives in international relations. Despite the 'liberating' intentions of the framers of that other trilogy – Realism, Pluralism and Structuralism – the scheme becomes 'another gatekeeping device for maintaining the status-quo'.[47] Likewise, while the presentation of three traditions seems to offer a liberal spectrum of choice, it may serve instead to eliminate options: we have a freedom of choice but only from within the menu on offer. Reification thus occurs at two levels. The individual traditions become single constructs, as in the case of Realism, where internal 'polarities and contradictions' are concealed by appeal to 'a single tradition ... located somewhere among the classic texts'.[48] The spectrum of traditions becomes a second reification, constraining the range of discussion to that which is encompassed by its intellectual boundaries.

The validity of these sundry criticisms very much depends upon the questions thought to be raised by the 'traditional' approach. Narrowly conceived as a stock set of reflections upon individual, state and international society, as if these were themselves timeless and unchanging concepts, the points are all well taken, as is the danger that such a framework of thought directs our thinking too rigidly along predetermined paths. However, if it could be argued that the traditions can be adapted to raise a wider series of questions, not just about the content of 'traditional' thought but about their scope as well, and so on to more basic reflections about the very purposes and nature of international theory, then they might yet be integrated into the contemporary 'anti-traditional' agenda.

## TRADITIONS AND CONTEMPORARY THEORY

Wight sought at one point to add further clarity to his three traditions by suggesting that Realism, Rationalism and Revolutionism were identified, respectively, with accounts of international relations in sociological, teleological and prescriptive terms.[49] This raises a fundamental issue. Should the three traditions be regarded, narrowly, as aggregations of political thought on the international, national and individual dimensions of human activity? Alternatively, and more broadly, does the arrangement into three traditions provide us with a set of intellectual tools for exploring the nature of theory itself and a self-questioning basis for exploring the relationship between the theory and practice of international relations? Posed in other terms, how useful is Wight's tripartite constellation in probing the kind of issues that currently beset major areas of contemporary international theory?

Does Wight's choice of the three terms, 'sociological', 'teleological' and 'prescriptive', permit an extension of enquiry beyond the traditional concerns of classical theory? The question can be answered with a hesitant, but modestly positive, affirmative. The choice of these terms by Wight indicates a lurking agenda behind the one more usually identified with his name. Why should Realism be identified with a sociological approach? It might with greater force be argued that Rationalism's focus on the norms, practices and institutions of international society sat more comfortably with such an understanding. Equally, Kantian Revolutionism might more appropriately have the title of 'teleological' bestowed upon it. And is it not the case, as Bull pointed out, that all three traditions are prescriptive? One is left to wonder, then, what precise significance attaches to Wight's identification of his traditions in this way.

In context, it would seem that Wight's characterisation of Realism as being, above all, sociological must refer to a positivist methodology: Realism's central, and convenient, assumption is that it describes an extant world 'as it is in reality'. To this extent, the world of power politics is no figment of the conceptual imagination: 'To use the word Realism implies an affirmation about what is real, what is reality'.[50] By extension, and in his logic *a fortiori*, Ashley feels entitled to see neorealism as 'theory of, by, and for positivists'.[51] Realism may then be described as sociological in the specific sense that the techniques and assumptions of positivist sociology are appropriate instruments for laying bare the essentials of the world of international relations: it is based on inductive experience of the world and is happy to regard theory and practice as distinct categories.

Wight's attribution of the teleological approach to Rationalism is more difficult to comprehend. Wight concedes that in their theory of history, Rationalists are 'cautious and agnostic' and assume no immanent design nor invincible progression towards a foreordained goal. It is in the much more limited sense of a residual faith in the instrument of reason itself that any teleology resides in human affairs:

> Both in its Christian and in its secular form, the Rationalist tradition appeals to reason. It affirms that besides being a sinful, pugnacious and irrational animal, man is also rational, and through his reason he can attain a considerable degree of success in adjusting his political and social arrangements.[52]

The question which this, in turn, raises is whether the teleology that Wight perceives as part of Rationalism is simply a characteristic of an analytic category, in terms of which international relations might be understood, or whether this teleology is itself part of the historical process. It was on this basis that Jones early speculated about Wight's traditions representing a dialectic with Rationalism as the development, and progressive synthesis, of the other two. Significantly, in such a conceptualisation, the dialectic 'is inside international society' and not simply a set of categories outside it.[53] Such a view was later refuted as an accurate portrayal of Wight[54] but it is revealing to note that, implicitly, what was being touched upon was the relationship between theory and practice of international relations and the epistemological separation, if any, between the two.

The assignment of the term 'prescriptive' to the Revolutionist tradition in particular, if questionable, can at least be understood within the terms of Wight's own argument. While it can be demurred, with Bull, that *all* three traditions are prescriptive, Revolutionism is explicitly and distinctively so, and in the very special sense that it accepts a different account of the relationship between theory and practice. It is because the two are deemed to be inextricably linked that Wight can regard this tradition as epitomising the prescriptive or, in alternative terminology, as being written in the imperative mood: what is true in theory stands as an injunction to action.

These themes are not pursued to any great extent in Wight's work but are suggestive of a broader agenda which is similar to that predominating in much of contemporary international theory. What this indicates is that Wight's traditions might be represented not simply as traditions of thought about the nature of international society, but rather as traditions of thought about the nature of theory itself. In this repackaged form, the classical traditions do indeed address the present theoretical agenda.

It would be inappropriate at this point to offer a comprehensive overview of the issues currently preoccupying international relations theory.[55] Hopefully, however, not too much distortion is entailed by mentioning a few highlights. In sum, as has been recently stated, the last decade has witnessed a prominent resurgence of 'second order or meta-theorizing' by which is meant a quest for understanding of world politics which proceeds 'indirectly by focusing on the ontological and epistemological issues of what constitute important or legitimate questions and answers for IR scholarship'.[56]

Many of the concerns of this 'second order' revival have been generated in international relations by their importation from cognate disciplines such as philosophy and social and political theory.[57] The disenchantment with the assumptions of positivism, symbolised by the work of Richard J. Bernstein,[58] and the more general percolation of ideas from sociology, semiotics, literary studies and political theory has spawned attacks on traditional conceptualisations in international relations from a variety of post-positivist directions, such as critical theory and postmodernism. Each of these challenges, whatever the intellectual merits of the exotic 'epistemological flora and fauna'[59] it brings to the field, has contributed to a radical polarisation of international relations, the sad hallmark of which has been a failure, or unwillingness, to communicate between competing schools. The danger is that we are now witnessing the rigidification of two new traditions, each diverse within itself, but rendered asunder by incompatible 'second-order' assumptions about 'the social construction of meaning, the linguistic construction of reality, and the historicity of knowledge'.[60]

Are there links between Wight's traditions and the contemporary debate about the nature, types and purposes of theory? What is so striking about the work of some contemporary anti-traditionalists is their penchant for discerning tripartite classifications of method and approach. Most interesting of all is perhaps the recent work of Andrew Linklater. He begins his discussion with the Wightian taxonomy and pronounces the three traditions to be based, respectively, on their primary concerns with power, order and emancipation.[61] Having done so, he correlates the developing debate about international relations with earlier debates in sociology and presents a second triumvirate – positivism, hermeneutics and critical theory. These, in turn, are identified with Habermasian 'knowledge-constitutive interests', such that positivism reflects a technical interest in controlling behaviour, hermeneutics a practical interest in maintaining social consensus and critical theory a cognitive interest in emancipation.[62] Thus Linklater weaves a rich tapestry into which are interwoven three separate strands, each in turn combining three colours (power/order/emancipation; positivism/hermeneutics/critical theory; control/consensus/freedom). Finally, each of these is associated, more or less implicitly, with Realism, Rationalism and Revolutionism. Realism is a 'scientific' theory of international control; Rationalism is a 'cultural' theory of how international society functions; and Revolutionism is an assertion of the autonomy of the individual by a theory of action. Above all, Linklater insists that the traditions disagree not merely 'about the empirical nature of world politics' but also about 'the nature of international theory' and about the 'relationship between theory and practice'.[63]

The most revealing adaptation of the Wightian formula wrought by Linklater is his identification of Revolutionism with critical theory and his belief that the three traditions represent a qualitative progression with critical theory (or Revolutionism) emerging as the dialectical synthesis and superior form of the preceding two:

It suggests that realism, rationalism and revolutionism (for which critical international theory will be substituted below) form a sequence of progressively more adequate approaches to world politics. If this is so, a theory which analyses the language and culture of diplomatic interaction in order to promote international consensus is an advance beyond a theory of recurrent forces constituted by an interest in manipulation and control. And an account of world politics which seeks to understand the prospects for extending the human capacity for self-determination is an even greater advance in this sequence of approaches.[64]

Lest it be objected that Linklater is forcing a correspondence that does not exist, it does seem that in opening the deeper issue about the nature of theory itself, he is doing no more than rendering explicit what is implicit in Wight's characterisation of Revolutionism as being prescriptive. Indeed, elsewhere Wight himself had already described Revolutionism in terms that reinforce the parallel with the key assumptions of critical theory when he analysed it in the following terms: 'the Revolutionist condemns the existing system of power by a standard external to that system of power but drawn from within the political category. He resembles the Realist in finding the ultimate meaning within the realm of politics ... it is politics which prescribe human goals, the right of moral judgment and duty of action'.[65] Few critical theorists would dissent overly much from such a depiction of their stance.

If the equation between critical theory and Revolutionism is tenable, might it not be equally acceptable to extend the agenda of Realism and Rationalism in similar ways? Thus, as already indicated, Wight's Realism is but an invitation to engage in a 'second-order' debate about the appropriateness of a notion of knowledge as separate from, but truly reflective of, an extant reality of international relations. Likewise, Rationalism serves as coded expression for a discussion of the nature of how societies are constituted, how they maintain themselves and of the extent to which they are 'self-interpreting' organisms. Thus conceived, we have a ready transcription of many of the issues on the contemporary meta-theoretical agenda.

Others seemingly stand much further removed from Wightian principles and classifications. Der Derian, while confessing reluctantly to acceptance of the plausibility of a 'tradition' in international relations, then makes clear that the task of theory is most assuredly not to wallow in the self-perpetuation of such schemes but rather 'to understand *why* a particular tradition develops in a specific historical moment, *how* it makes the world intelligible, the *source* of its persuasive power, and the cost of an intellectual tradition which outlives its heuristic value'.[66] Elsewhere, he espouses the concept of genealogy, rather than of tradition, the former serving as antidote to the latter in that it helps explain why particular traditions solidify as they do.[67] It might be fair to conclude, in the light of these admonitions, that Der Derian sees the traditions as part of the problem of, rather than as part of the solution to, the understanding of international relations: they are an integral part of the subject matter rather than autonomous intellectual schemes which can bring enlightenment to us as observers.

But the temptation to formulate clusters of thought is irresistible even to the hardened sceptic, and Der Derian presents contemporary discussions of international theory, not as traditions, but as what he more coyly refers to as 'three rivulets leading away from the Enlightenment tradition'. He consolidates his thinkers into a unitary body of 'post-rationalist' thought. We have, in effect, a separate post-Enlightenment tradition, itself divisible into three categories.

In which directions do these rivulets flow? The 'post-classicists' build on existing theorisation but cease to privilege 'Western, rationalist, analytical' work at the expense of 'multicultural, revolutionist, critical texts'. The 'post-Marxist' tributary flows in a direction which 'resituates human agency through critical theory'. And 'post-structuralism' challenges 'totalising, universalist discourses'.[68] Evidently this is *not* a back-door reinstatement of Wight's trichotomy. But, while remaining agnostic about the merit of the individual rivulets mapped out by Der Derian, one is left to wonder whether it is quite necessary to present them collectively as a tradition *de novo*. Instead, if Wight's scheme is regarded in the above expanded form as a series of debates, both about the nature of international society but also about the nature of theorising in this realm, it might well suffice as a vehicle for raising the issues which 'post-rationalism' considers to be pivotal. It is not clear what essential elements of the debate need be left out of account by such a procedure. If positivism, hermeneutics and critical theory can be encompassed within the expanded trilogy, as Linklater suggests, is this not an adequate meeting-ground for Der Derian's writers as well? The Traditions are Dead: Long Live the Traditions.

## REVIVING THE TRADITIONS

How might such a project be carried forward? Might not the traditions, suitably reconceived, serve as a starting-point of unity rather than as a source of division? As indicated, this requires that they be represented not simply as substantive claims about the existence, nature or absence of international society but also as methodological strategies for asking questions about the nature of theory, about its functions across time and about its relationship to the practices of international relations itself. Walker seems temperamentally well-disposed to such an endeavour. In offering an alternative reading of the significance of Machiavelli's writings, Walker suggests that reflecting upon 'the identification of Machiavelli with claims about a tradition of international relations theory is to begin to see how it might now be possible to think otherwise: to use references to a tradition not as a legitimation of reification and closure, but as a source of critical opportunity'.[69] Thus in the very act of undermining a traditional interpretation, Walker tacitly accepts that traditions are an important part of the theoretical project, partly as schemes of theoretical understanding but also as part of the total web of international relations that needs explaining. The very reification of traditional patterns of thinking, and their entry into the cultural practice of the field, endows them with a reality which the theorist cannot ignore.

For there to be fruitful engagement with the traditions, they must be moved beyond competing portraits of an extant world. They must be understood to pose questions about the kind of knowledge to which we might aspire in international relations and what the purpose of such

knowledge might be. They must explore the tensions between the traditions viewed as constellations of ideas that structure choices over time and
the rediscovery of the contextual and historical bases of ideas. Above all,
they must be understood as devices for opening up the subject to critical
examination and not as a set of definitive answers which close the field
down. Wight's characterisation of his traditions as representing the sociological, teleological and prescriptive dimensions of theory may be a faltering approximation to this agenda but, suitably transcribed, this tripartite
scheme may prove as useful a Wightian legacy as the Realism,
Rationalism and Revolutionism with which his name is more commonly
associated.

## NOTES

1. The lecture notes on this are now happily available in M. Wight,
   *International Theory: The Three Traditions*, ed. Gabriele Wight and Brian
   Porter (Leicester: Leicester University Press, 1991).
2. 'Why is there no International Theory?' in H. Butterfield and M. Wight
   (eds), *Diplomatic Investigations* (London: Allen and Unwin, 1966).
3. By employing his own definitions and terminology, Jackson has demonstrated that Wight was, in fact, very much engaged in international theory
   directed to the 'good life'. R. H. Jackson, 'Martin Wight, International
   Theory and the Good Life', *Millennium*, Vol. 18, No. 2, Summer 1990.
4. R. B. J. Walker, 'Realism, Change and International Political Theory',
   *International Studies Quarterly*, Vol. 31, No. 1, March 1987, p. 69.
5. R. B. J. Walker, *Inside/Outside: International Relations as Political Theory*
   (Cambridge: Cambridge University Press, 1993), p. 37.
6. J. Mayall (ed.), *The Community of States* (London: Allen and Unwin, 1982).
7. See e.g. Roy E. Jones, 'The English School of International Relations: A
   Case for Closure', *Review of International Studies*, Vol. 7, No. 1, Jan. 1981,
   p. 3; P. Wilson, 'The English School of International Relations: A Reply to
   Sheila Grader', *Review of International Studies*, Vol. 15, No. 1, Jan. 1989,
   p. 55.
8. N. J. Rennger, 'A City which Sustains All Things? Communitarians and
   International Society', *Millennium*, Vol. 21, No. 3 Winter 1992, p. 366.
9. *International Theory*, p. 14.
10. Alan James, 'Michael Nicholson on Martin Wight: A Mind Passing in the
    Night', *Review of International Studies*, Vol. 8, No. 2, April 1982, p. 118.
11. 'Martin Wight and the Theory of International Relations', in Wight,
    *International Theory*, p. xiv.
12. A. Claire Cutler, 'The "Grotian Tradition" in International Relations',
    *Review of International Studies*, Vol. 17, No. 1, Jan. 1991, p. 53.

13. See chapters by Gilpin, Hoffmann and Vincent in J. D. B. Miller and R. J. Vincent (eds), *Order and Violence: Hedley Bull and International Relations* (Oxford: Oxford University Press, 1990), respectively pp. 120, 13–14 and 41.
14. *The Twenty Years' Crisis* (London: Macmillan, 1939).
15. *International Theory*, p. 267.
16. Review of *Reform and Resistance in the International Order*, in *Survival*, May–June 1981, p. 138.
17. Two recent books have utilised this categorisation for discussing normative theories of international relations: C. Brown, *International Relations Theory: New Normative Approaches* (Brighton: Harvester Press, 1992); J. Thompson, *Justice and World Order* (London: Routledge, 1992).
18. S. Smith, 'The Forty Years' Detour: The Resurgence of Normative Theory in International Relations', *Millennium*, Vol. 21, No. 3, Winter 1992, p. 505.
19. M. Donelan, *Elements of International Political Theory* (Oxford: Oxford University Press, 1990).
20. T. Nardin and D. R. Mapel, *Traditions of International Ethics* (Cambridge: Cambridge University Press, 1992), p. 20.
21. T. Dunne, 'Mythology or methodology? Traditions in international theory', *Review of International Studies*, Vol. 19, No. 3, July 1993, p. 307.
22. The categories are outlined in M. Wight, 'An Anatomy of International Thought', *Review of International Studies*, Vol. 13, No. 3, July 1987; *International Theory*, passim.
23. Wight, 'An Anatomy', pp. 221–2, emphasis added.
24. *International Theory*, p. 265.
25. Bull, 'Martin Wight and the Theory', p. xi.
26. *International Theory*, p. 16.
27. This is the description of Kissinger's realist theory offered by M. J. Smith, *Realist Thought from Weber to Kissinger* (Baton Rouge: Louisiana State University Press, 1986), p. 199.
28. 'An Anatomy', p. 222.
29. 'An Anatomy', p. 223.
30. *International Theory*, p. 39.
31. H. Bull, *The Anarchical Society* (London: Macmillan, 1977), pp. 46–50.
32. B. Kingsbury and A. Roberts, 'Introduction' in *Hugo Grotius and International Relations* (Oxford: Oxford University Press, 1990), p. 8.
33. Bull, *Anarchical Society*, p. 26.
34. A. Hurrell, 'Kant and the Kantian Paradigm in International Relations', *Review of International Studies*, Vol. 16, No. 3, July 1990.
35. *International Theory*, p. 263.
36. Bull, 'Martin Wight and the Theory', p. xvii.
37. *International Theory*, p. 259.
38. *International Theory*, p. 158.
39. R. B. J. Walker, 'History and Structure in the Theory of International Relations', *Millennium*, Vol. 18, No. 2, Summer 1989, p. 172.
40. 'A City which Sustains', p. 363.
41. F. Halliday, 'International Society as Homogeneity: Burke, Marx, Fukuyama', *Millennium*, Vol. 21, No. 3, Winter 1992, p. 438.

42.  Richard K. Ashley, 'Living on Border Lines: Man, Post-structuralism, and War' in J. Der Derian and M. J. Shapiro (eds), *International/Intertextual Relations* (Lexington, Mass.: Lexington Books, 1989), p. 283.
43.  J. Der Derian, 'Introducing Philosophical Traditions in International Relations', *Millennium*, Vol. 17, No. 2, Summer 1988, p. 190.
44.  Walker, *Inside/Outside*, p. 27.
45.  Walker, 'History and Structure', p. 167.
46.  Der Derian, 'Introducing Philosophical Traditions', p. 190.
47.  S. Smith, 'The Forty Years' Detour: The Resurgence of Normative Theory in International relations', p. 494.
48.  Walker, 'Realism, Change', p. 70.
49.  *International Theory*, p. 24.
50.  *International Theory*, p. 16.
51.  Richard K. Ashley, 'The Poverty of Neorealism', *International Organization*, Vol. 38, No. 2, Spring 1984, p. 248.
52.  *International Theory*, p. 29.
53.  Jones, 'The English School', p. 11.
54.  S. Grader, 'The English School of International Relations: Evidence and Evaluation', *Review of International Studies*, Vol. 14, No. 1, Jan. 1988, p. 34.
55.  For surveys of recent developments, see Y. Lapid, 'The Third Debate: On the Prospects of International Theory in a Post-Positivist Era', *International Studies Quarterly*, Vol. 33, No. 3, Sept. 1989; J. George and D. Campbell, 'Patterns of Dissent and the Celebration of Difference: Critical Social Theory and International Relations', *International Studies Quarterly*, Vol. 34, No. 3, Sept. 1990; and J. George, *Discourses of Global Politics: A Critical (Re)Introduction to International Relations* (Boulder, CO: Lynne Rienner, 1994).
56.  Alexander Wendt, 'Bridging the Theory/Meta-Theory Gap in International Relations', *Review of International Studies*, Vol. 17, No. 4, Oct. 1991, p. 383.
57.  The most accessible presentation of much of this material is to be found in M. Hollis and S. Smith, *Explaining and Understanding International Relations* (Oxford: Oxford University Press, 1990).
58.  *The Restructuring of Social and Political Theory* (Oxford: Blackwell, 1976).
59.  Hayward R. Alker, Jr, 'The Humanistic Movement in International Studies: Reflections on Machiavelli and Las Casas', *International Studies Quarterly*, Vol. 36, No. 4, Dec. 1992, p. 348.
60.  David Campbell, 'Recent Changes in Social Theory', in R. Higgot (ed.), *New Directions in International Relations? Australian Perspectives* (Canberra Studies in World Affairs No. 23, Dept of International Relations, ANU, Canberra, 1988), p. 45.
61.  A. Linklater, *Beyond Realism and Marxism: Critical Theory and International Relations* (London: Macmillan, 1990), p. 8.
62.  *Beyond Realism*, p. 9.
63.  *Beyond Realism*, p. 10
64.  *Beyond Realism*, p. 10.
65.  *International Theory*, p. 105.

66. 'Introducing Philosophical Traditions', p. 190.
67. J. Der Derian, *On Diplomacy: A Genealogy of Western Estrangement* (Oxford: Blackwell, 1987).
68. 'Introducing Philosophical Traditions', pp. 191–2.
69. *Inside/Outside*, p. 31.

# 2 Hobbes, the State of Nature and the Laws of Nature

## Cornelia Navari

That philosophical doctrines speak differently to different ages is nowhere more apparent than in the intellectual fortunes of Thomas Hobbes. In the seventeenth century, he was considered a 'hobbist', a libertine and free thinker, so much so that even Locke, who held much in common with him, avoided any mention of his doctrines. (The seventeenth century would have also scorned the notion that he was a philosopher of order, seeing in his doctrines the roots of sedition and disorder.) By the eighteenth century, he had risen to the level of Filmer and Rousseau and was honoured as the precursor of Pufendorf. He was 'discovered' in his own right towards the end of the century by the English philosophical radicals, notably Bentham, who admired not so much the method or premises as the break with natural law and the robust concept of a rationally directed sovereign will. But he only really came into his own during the second half of the nineteenth century, largely because he provided the foundations, and many of the categories, for Austin's legal positivism, and support for the theory of the untrammelled rights of Parliament. By its end, he was being read as an authority on the requisites of political institutions as they had come to be understood under Austin's influence; that is, legal perfection and the importance of clear delegations of the sovereign authority. But it was a short-lived glory, as theories of untrammelled sovereignty came increasingly under attack. In the twentieth century, his method of founding an anti-foundational political science has become grist to the mill of analytical philosophy and his contractarianism the subject of efforts to locate contractarianism on firmer, in some cases naturalistic, in other cases rationalistic, foundations.

It is to the twentieth century, particularly its latter half, that we owe yet another Hobbes, the international relations Hobbes. Scarcely mentioned in this context previously except as the disavower of the possibility of an international law, he has been discovered by the twentieth century as the preeminent theorist of the anarchical condition and a theorist of war. Appeals to Hobbes became commonplace in American realist writing

20

during the late 1940s and early 1950s, where the Leviathan was used to provide a theoretical grounding for approaching foreign policy in terms of prudential laws and practices and to defend a rational choice approach to the understanding of international relations. Above all, it became the source for theorising a 'security dilemma'.

This essay will not seek to argue that some of these uses are more legitimate than others (although my own analytical preferences will be signalled). Its concern will be rather to map the internationalist Hobbes, to demonstrate the range of uses to which he has been put and to account in some measure for this superficially unlikely emergence. (After all, Hobbes wrote almost nothing about international relations.) In the course of doing so, I will occasionally distinguish between international relations uses of Hobbes and proper Hobbes scholarship. On the one hand, Hobbes's incorporation into discussions of contemporary international problems has created a small body of commentary on his categories from the perspective of interstate relations; on the other, the body of contemporary writing directly analysing Hobbes is immense and has produced many new understandings of his work. These two bodies of scholarship seldom meet, but there are points at which they are addressing similar questions, notably the status of the state of nature and the question of moral possibilities in a state of nature. Hobbes's state of nature teaching has been of particular interest to recent Hobbes scholars, as has the nature of morality in a state of nature, and the conclusions of Hobbes scholars on these questions must be of interest to students of international relations. I shall, therefore, indicate where some modern Hobbes scholarship has served to, in some cases, illuminate, in other cases solve, some international relations puzzles.

## HOBBES AND THE IDEALISTS

The first point to make about the contemporary reception of Hobbes is that, while generally associated with twentieth century political realism, he was not merely a realist rediscovery. Indeed, his first strong appearance in the twentieth century was as part of a revised idealist programme. The work to which I primarily refer is Collingwood's *The New Leviathan*, which first appeared in 1942, a conscious imitation in purpose as well as structure of Hobbes's main political treatise. In purpose, it was to build up an inner portrait of man on which was to be founded a new understanding of the requisites for a proper civic order, and which was to correct the idealist understanding of man and society which had dominated the first half of the century. In structure it imitated the Leviathan in establishing, first, the idea of a civic society, and then an idea of a rightly ordered civic society, and, like Hobbes, it also distinguished them. Collingwood modelled *The New Leviathan* in its four sections on Hobbes's treatise, beginning with man, then the political life, then the requisites of the well-ordered political life, then the kingdom of darkness.

This structure was not accidental. Idealist thought rested on assumptions concerning the developmental potential of man; idealists believed in moral progress, sometimes receding but still moving upwards, essentially through an education programme inculcating duty to others and an increasing sense of social responsibility. Man's perfectibility had, in turn, underlain their hopes for the creation of more perfect social orders. Idealists had also sourced the Nazi appeal in some base psychological or cultural instinct, and they were seeking for an understanding of that instinct upon which to more firmly base the political order. Collingwood first turned to Hobbes, he tells us, for a different, more tempered picture of man, a portrait in which moral progress was not to be taken for granted and in which evil proclivities were allowed to exist. He also sought for a political theory and a theory of civic association which encompassed man's dual nature. This, among modern thinkers, Hobbes seemed to provide.

Second, there was a revised understanding of historical progress and its attendant conditions. Consistent with their ideas of moral progress, idealists had tended towards an historical evolutionism in which civilisation succeeded barbarism and in which there could be no reversions, an understanding of social progression into which fascism, the 'new barbarism', fitted with difficulty. Hobbes had, however, little idea of historical progression. Instead, he presents us with synchronic alternative conditions, of state and state of nature, conditions which are analogues and opposites, each capable of being transformed into the other if correct understanding of man's situation were not present. Collingwood used Hobbes to underpin a view of civilisation as fragile and conditional, one in which, if right thinking were not present, the Christian Commonwealth could revert to a Kingdom of Darkness. What he sought from Hobbes was an understanding that civilisation and barbarism are only in part historical processes, succeeding one another; that they are also conditional processes, ever present within one another and capable of being transformed into one another. It was an appeal to the consciousness of the subject to understand the factors making for civilisation, and not to take them for granted.

The third area of illumination concerned the fact that it was 'precisely the agents of this longed for safety that are the chief authors of the evils for whose ending we have made them'. Collingwood believed that fascism and Nazism, horrible as they were, were not entirely aberrations of the modern condition and that they had something to do with what has since become known as 'the Enlightenment project'. That project has often been dated from Hobbes, seen as the first Enlightenment man in his efforts to devise a political order on entirely rationalist foundations. If the new idealists gained from Hobbes support for a more rounded understanding of human nature, they also sought from him an understanding of the limitations and the dangers of a purely rationalist view of political order.

Hobbes also became a referent point for the analysis of human transformations under autocracy. Ernst Cassirer, in *The Myth of the State*, used Hobbes as an example of the pure theory of subjugation, noting that, in Leviathan, 'the social will has become incorporated with the ruler of the state'. Were this to occur, however, he would give up himself, for if 'a man could give up his personality he would cease being a moral being'. 'There is no pactum subjectionis, no act of submission by which a man can give up the state of a free agent and enslave himself. For by such an act of renunciation he would give up that very character which constitutes his nature and essence: he would lose his humanity.'[1] According to Cassirer, it was their self-enslavement that had demoralised the German people and that had allowed them to participate in Nazi atrocities.

Hobbes, then, appeared to offer insights not only into the fragility of civilisation but into the nature of barbarism, into why fascism had beguiled and how it had transformed the desire for a stable social order into a monstrous perversion. More particularly, he offered lessons in the dangers of attempting to construct political orders on purely rationalist and contractarian foundations. Robert Kraynak, who has offered one of the most insightful analyses of Hobbes as the philosopher of the freed mind, concluded his essay with praise for those who embrace neither dogmatism nor scepticism, 'nor that hybrid monster of the Enlightenment, dogmatism built on radical scepticism', and recognise that 'the human soul needs theoretical detachment and divine illumination to be complete'.[2]

## HOBBES AND THE REALISTS

If the idealists sought from Hobbes material for a revised and strengthened idealist programme, the realists aimed to bury idealism entirely. That they should have deployed Hobbes for this task is not, however, as self-evident as recent portraits of Hobbesian realism may lead us to suppose. There were other varieties of social theory upon which they could, and indeed did draw. The choice of Hobbes was connected to the particular nature of the challenge that Idealism posed to Realist political doctrine.

To comprehend the difficulty, we should note that international idealist thought had no single root but rather was linked to and embedded within several distinct modes of social comprehension, which together dominated the latter nineteenth and the early part of the twentieth century. There was not only Hegelian philosophical idealism but also Social Darwinist and evolutionist thought, in its progressive Spencerian aspect, as well as Durkheimian functionalism. These tides of thought tended to cross, as well as to draw upon, one another, supporting internationalism in a variety of ways. In Spencer's schema, for example, society was pictured to be in a condition of simultaneous differentiation and integration; that is, splitting and specialising, while also unifying at more complex levels. It was also portrayed as naturally progressing towards more integrated and coherent social forms, including international forms. English Hegelians, for their part, were not sociologically inclined, but they were historically inclined, and T. H. Green, Bosanquet, Bradley and Ritchie tended to absorb evolutionary categories, and to argue that the unifying process of individuals in organised wholes was progressive. They further maintained that this progressive movement might eventually supersede the state, producing a form of Hegelian internationalism, albeit with more emphasis on ethics than sociology.[3] For its part, Durkheimian functional sociology, which became very prevalent after the turn of the century, made its way easily into Hegelian thought, especially Durkheim's distinction between organic and mechanistic social forms, a typology in which the organic society was presented as the more modern or advanced; and in turn it also deeply influenced the non-Hegelian utilitarian thinkers, such as Angell and Hobson, who became outright functionalists. Finally, idealist thought was also highly dogmatic in spirit, not least of all because of its links to, and invasion by, a doctrine of Christian immanentism. Christian idealists were not naive as to the schisms that might cut across society. These were generally seen, however, as proceeding from a lack of social and personal development. Moreover, it was deemed the work of the higher social orders to bring enlightenment to the less advanced, essentially through establishing and supporting such progressive endeavours as the League of Nations, while encouraging social progress from within.

Power was represented as an extremely negative quality in all of these world-views. In Durkheimian analysis, for example, power or subordination, either through religious conformity or main force, was the mark of the mechanistic and not the organic society, and social control which depended on coercion was strongly represented as the mark of the less functional social order. In Spencerian evolutionism, the higher order was marked by the increasing eschewing of conflictual modes for the resolution of the problems of social life; it was the lower order which depended on coercion. Equally, for the neo-Hegelians, humanitarian ethics, including arbitration of conflict within federal forms, presented itself as the antithesis of power relations. There was also a horror of power as the antithesis of Christian teaching, at least the teaching of the gentle developmental Christ of immanentist theology. Other Christian imperialists tended to interpret the uncooperative subjects of Empire as wily orientals who had to be suppressed, but this said little of the relations between the major western European states. Some Christian idealists did believe in a fighting Christianity, but this was not the stance of the majority in the League of Nations movement, and gave rise to those confusions between pacifism, pacificism and collective security which had so dogged prewar internationalism.

Given the pervasiveness of these views, those seeking to legitimate the use of power for political ends had certain rather limited choices. One of these was to set power within a Christian frame of reference where it might appear as a necessary evil, and its use justified in terms of a bastion against greater evil. We may call this the Augustinian move, and it was the one taken by Niebuhr.[4] Another was to secularise the world in some way, to remove it from the progressive and sacramental and to return it to a form of liberal humanism, in which power could be related to a cycle of civic virtue and decay, the Machiavellian move and the one taken by Herbert Butterfield and also E. H. Carr. The third was to neutralise all states, by providing an entirely objective, abstract picture of likely outcomes in positions of uncertainty, and in which power could be presented as a rational exercise of the rational human will in the face of uncertain prospects; this we may call the Hobbesian move.

I should not like to suggest that one can strictly divide realists among these schools. In fact, most of the Realist literature which emerged during the late 1940s and early 1950s tended to draw on all of them in a somewhat haphazard manner. But the Hobbesian elements are usually placed in a particular way; they tend to appear early on in Realist works and take the form of first principles or axioms, establishing the foundations for the generally Machiavellian prudential or Augustinian dutiful recommendations which then ensue. (Hence, the tendency of critical theorists currently firing at Realism to aim especially at Hobbes.)

At one level, it is easy to see where the Hobbes appeal lay. It appeared scientific and rational, and appealed to the growing positivist spirit of the time. It also appeared politically neutral, since it called for a suspension of judgement among alternative claims and tried to lay a foundation for no more than a minimal state of security. Above all, it treated all antagonists as equal in moral status, and was hence and somewhat paradoxically, most congenial to the liberal mind. Arnold Wolfers, describing the mechanics of what was to become known as the security dilemma, noted almost in passing that the 'vicious circle' theory 'makes statesman and people look less vicious than the *animus dominandi* theory'.[5] Of all the doctrines mentioned above, a Hobbesian understanding of relations between states most appealed to Western liberal sentiment, since it treated both the West and the Communist powers as of equal status, enmeshed within the same dilemma, and the dilemma as the problem, not the intentions of either side. Of course, there is nothing very liberal about Hobbes's picture of human nature; it is a mechanistic picture of desires and aversions. But in the highly dogmatic and ideological atmosphere of the late 1930s, a dogmatism which appeared ready to reemerge after the experience of national unity during the war, its neutral scientism had much to recommend it.

But I would like to suggest that there were also deeper reasons for the Hobbesian appeal, connected to a rough parallelism or analogy between the project Hobbes set for himself, and to which his state of nature teaching was essential, and the situation in which the realists found themselves in the late 1930s and 1940s.

Let us recall that Hobbes in the seventeenth century, like the realists in the twentieth century, was facing a situation of intense ideological conflict, in Hobbes's case conflict not merely among the advocates of various religious traditions but arising also from individual illuminism. Hobbes, moreover, wished these various advocates to see, in the strong sense of enlightenment, that their present avowals were forms of untestable assertion, acts of mere faith, which were moreover placing them in a situation of extreme danger, that of losing their lives. So, too, did twentieth-century realists regard idealism in the atmosphere of the build-up to the war, as blind faith without regard to consequences. Finally, there was his method to this end, which was to attack the essentially *ideological* quality of these views. In essence, Hobbes divested his subjects of their ideologies, or preconceived wisdoms, by delegitimating them. He asked his audience not to listen to received wisdom and to see all claims of this sort as simple aspects of desire, inducing a moral scepticism. (E. H. Carr was to make a similar move via Mannheimian sociology. By forcing his subjects to historicise and conditionalise their deeply-held beliefs, he placed them in a condition of scepticism concerning their ultimate validity.) He then placed these divested creatures in a state of nature, and asked them to receive, with their now illuminated or enlightened minds, the rational lessons of ones in such a situation. The result is something in the nature of a self-evident proposition.

The 'security dilemma' is the modern application of Hobbesian logic to international relations. The notion of a security dilemma was the invention of the determined anti-idealist, John Herz, and an important weapon in the battle to establish an ascendancy over idealism; and, in developing it, its designer drew heavily and consciously on Hobbes.

Wherever such anarchic society has existed – and it has existed in most periods of known history on some level – there has arisen what may be called the 'security dilemma' of men, or groups, or their leaders. Groups or individuals living in such a constellation must be, and usually are, concerned about their security from being attacked, subjected, dominated or annihilated by other groups and individuals. Striving to attain security from such attack, they are driven to acquire more and more power in order to escape the impact of the power of others. This, in turn, renders the others more insecure and compels them to prepare for the worst. Since none can ever feel entirely secure in such a world of competing units, power competition ensues, and the vicious circle for security and power accumulation is on.[6]

Whether Hobbes succeeded in laying a purely rationalist foundation to the necessity of a Leviathan (in terms of international relations, the necessity of a security system) has been a subject of debate among analytical philosophers, who point to the confusion between theorems and axioms. On the other hand, the post-Hegelian natural-law theorist, Howard Warrender, maintains that Hobbes does succeed, but that he built on natural-law, not rationalist, foundations. For his part, Kraynak believes that Hobbes succeeded only too well in historical and political terms: he traces the origins of totalitarianism to Hobbes's theory that the will of the one be dissolved in the will of all, and attributes the success of totalitarianism to a successful Hobbesian parlay. If we adopt Kraynak's criteria of political effect in the world, then the strategy was clearly successful in terms of political realism; the notion of a security dilemma swept the literature of international relations during the Cold War years and helped lay the foundations for the 'liberal realism' of the United States foreign policy establishment of the 1950s and 1960s.

Beyond these initial moves to legitimate recourse to power, the question of how to apply Hobbesian principles to international relations is a somewhat perplexing one, and the common reading of his dicta uncongenial to the liberal spirit. At one level, they point to a realm of continuous endangerment with no obvious solution at the international level. It is fairly clear that Hobbes expected hostility to be the normal relations of states, unless there were a combination or threat which held groups of states together (but which lasted only so long as the threat lasted), and that interest, interpreted as the desires and aversions of Sovereigns, could be the only cement to those alliances. It is uncertain whether such innate postures of hostility would be nuanced in a behavioural sense, a distinct possibility, sufficient to change the picture. For example, it is certainly clear that states go from 'amity to enmity', in Arnold Wolfers' terms, and that the behaviour of states towards one another varies over time: amity and enmity were the categories developed by Wolfers to provide a Realist explanation as to why all states did not display hostility *inter se* all the time.[7] But, as has been pointed out, Hobbes in his historical as well as theoretical writing described the state of nature in different ways at different times. This fact cannot be used to challenge the basic logic of the argument.[8] It would depend on how we account for the amity, whether it is a happy coincidence of shared interests, and likely to change as interests change, or whether it is sufficiently 'overdetermined' by such long-term structural features that it is unlikely to change. Nor is such amity collectivised; that is, all states do not share such common interests all the time, nor are they all placed structurally in a happy situation of cooperation.

A second Hobbesian insight concerns the behaviour of the rational egoist within the context of the security dilemma, an insight developed by games theory. Here, the conclusion of a good deal of the rational choice literature is that states are bound to get themselves into prisoners' dilemmas, i.e. in the good Hobbesian spirit, cooperation among rational egoists is not enough to save them from the rigours of the state of nature. Whether this dilemma is unavoidable has served to produce a lively literature: Isabel Hungerland has suggested that reiterated games plus communication can produce cooperation, if not world government.[9] But the point remains a serious one for those who put their trust in the rationality of the actors, the Machiavellian move. Hobbes holds very emphatically that Machiavellian prudence, endlessly adjusting itself, cannot succeed in producing peace, stability, security or order, an insight which one eminent realist, Clausewitz, suspected might indeed be true and who wrote a whole tract trying to save war.

That Machiavellian prudence may not be enough to achieve security is well illustrated in the rational deterrence literature. The hypothetical science of strategic studies is the closest analogue to Hobbesian political science. It pictures rational incrementalisers; it also pictures them in aggregation, driven by the endless dynamics of the security dilemma. Both Rapoport and Wohlstetter made it clear early on in the consideration of the modalities of deterrence that the outcome of such aggregated behaviour is all too likely to be war, including nuclear war, and that, in order to secure stability, states needed some kind of second-strike capability.[10] As Alan

Ryan has pointed out, a second-strike capability is like the Leviathan, a guarantee that if we are killed nonetheless the aggressor will not get away with it, and that he will suffer unacceptable costs for his attempted pre-emption.[11] This is what the Leviathan is intended to produce – a certainty that the transgressor will pay for his transgression. It is this Leviathan-like function which guarantees some stability, not rational prudence. Those who are inclined to absorb Hobbes into the Machiavellian tradition should especially take note of this analogue.

These arguments illustrate the complexity of Hobbes's lessons for international relations: that besides sourcing the security dilemma, and providing a most compelling justification for a politics of power, Hobbes also provides among the most powerful arguments for the necessity of escaping it. But equally, it is not clear how one can devise an exit on Hobbesian premises. It is not mere fancy that has led scholars to devise world government schemes from Hobbesian premises, nor that in doing so they have had to attack the problem of the prisoners' dilemma. Hobbes tried at the individual level precisely to construct such a dilemma, but at the level of the state, he appears to have condemned us to remain within it.

One way out of this dilemma, for those who take Hobbesian premises seriously, is to deny that the prisoners' dilemma problem exists, or to affirm that it can be overcome. Let us return to the work of Hungerland, noted above. She maintains that the essential element in the hypothetical conception of prisoners' dilemma is the lack of communication between the prisoners: one of the reasons that they cannot escape their choice dilemma is that they cannot speak to one another, nor communicate their intentions. She maintains, however, that such a condition does not maintain between states; that they can communicate intention; and that communication plus learning, through reiterated games, can produce more desirable outcomes. In this theory, states can learn, and can adjust their behaviour accordingly, to avoid zero-sum outcomes.

While this dispenses with one of the problems, however (and it is not clear that it does so dispense with it), it does not give us an idea of what form the second-strike or international Leviathan is to take, nor the tasks it must perform. According to Hobbes, Leviathan is to be understood as a legal agency, not merely as any form of security system. It is for the security of the laws that men give up their liberties. What sort of legal agency is it possible to imagine as arising between states?

Hobbes does, of course, give us a certain confidence in the notion of the enlightened actor who understands how civilisation can descend into barbarism. This confidence comes from his own certainty that he has produced a persuasive argument which can appeal to Everyman and, by extension, to Every State. But this Everyman must be understood in a certain way: it is a behavioural sort of Everyman, a mechanistic creature driven only by appetites, a sort of computing machine whose judgement is 'but the last act of deliberating'. Ryan describes him as a Skinnerian man, and sees the contemporary behaviourists as Hobbes's closest modern counterparts.[12] Hobbesian man is a creature without consciousness, beyond the experience of appetites and aversions.

Nowhere is this more clear than in Hobbes's account of war. Hobbes is usually considered to have provided a graphic picture of the 'war of all against all', but in fact accounts of this war occupy no more than a few lines in the *Leviathan*. (Is it part of the persuasiveness of his argument that we feel there must be more?) Moreover, these are synthetical accounts, the accounts of a political scientist, weighing up costs. Hobbes's natural man does not experience war; we have no Hobbesian account of what it feels like to be in war or to face the ever-present possibility of death. To gain this sort of understanding, we need a different sort of literature entirely, literature such as Crane's *The Red Badge of Courage*, or Tolstoy's *War and Peace*, where we experience, through the consciousness of the participant, his experiences. But it is equally the case that Hobbes does not want us to have this sort of experience, because this sort of experience may lead us to the opposite conclusions from those towards which he wants to push us. We may wonder whether we would have acted like the young soldier, or whether we would have been more heroic; we may be attracted to the idea of war as a testing ground of the self, or as a test of the virtues. To individualise war is also to offer the real picture of contingency and opportunity which real war is: we might get away with it; we might achieve our individual desires and hopes. Hobbes is trying to abstract from all this to produce a picture of aggregate effects, not of individual effects, to produce a picture of overall losses, not of the possibility of individual gains, which a real picture of real war might indeed reveal.

But this also means that there are inherent limitations to the persuasiveness of Hobbes's argument. To buy it, we must be willing to forget ourselves.

The likelihood of self-forgetfulness was rated rather high during the 1950s, with the announcement that we had reached the 'end of ideology'. Integral to the end-of-ideology thesis was the postulate that modern citizens had become sceptical of the politics of ultimate ends and were willing to suspend belief to the point of creating all sorts of rational contracts. This is a condition of which Hobbes would have approved. By now, however, we should know that this sort of thing does not work for very long, and that modern society is also rather intensely given to its own forms of individual and collective illuminisms. Oakeshott, in his introduction to the *Leviathan*, points out the work to be done relating Hobbes to Hegel, the latter the theorist of the individual as but a moment in the life of the nation and an advocate of the doctrine that individual death might indeed have a meaning.[13] There is also evidence that Hobbes did not buy it. Professor Watkins has put forth an extremely interesting reading of Hobbes where he points out that there are in fact two different versions of the cement of Leviathan. On the one hand, there is the rational contract, worked by rational men who can foresee the aggregative effects of their self-directed and solipsistic interaction; on the other hand, there is the Leviathan as an organic body, a collective self, to be accomplished by social control and censorship.[14] The latter is a totalitarian vision, to be sure, but what it indicates in this context is that Hobbes had certain reservations about the ability of man to sustain a purely rational commitment to self-abnegation and the coercive legal order.

To this dilemma there have been two proposed solutions. One, the liberal solution, is to use Hobbes to support a doctrine of national liberalism. In this doctrine, warm feelings are engendered towards the political order through a quest for perfection at home, in which liberalism is made the subject of ongoing discussion by liberals as to its best form, a discussion within which Hobbes's recipe for the good state, for example, can be found wanting. This public realm is at the same time endangered by international relations and needs protection, as demonstrated by the Hobbesian logic of states. This is the move taken by Kenneth Waltz in *Liberal Legacies* where he both defends the liberal quest within society and yet also paints a picture of a liberalism not for export, and a liberalism in need of defence, on Hobbesian grounds. But in this solution, there are no guides to international behaviour, besides, perhaps the unsatisfactory Machiavellian prudential. Over the second move we might pause longer. This move aimed to turn Hobbes's Laws of Nature from general guides to right reason on the part of individual Sovereigns into the basis for a form of moral and ultimately legal order between them.

## THE LAWS OF NATURE

Since Hobbes was recovered in the context of an attack on idealism, the first generation of contemporary realists generally ascribed to Hobbes a distinction between ethics and law, paralleling the positivist legal reading, and stressed the weak status of Natural Law, or the rational ethical precepts Hobbes presents in his account of Natural Law, as a guide to international behaviour. Some indeed went further, following Geoffrey Goodwin in maintaining that, if the state of nature were as Hobbes described, then moral considerations must be literally absent in the relations of states. But modern Hobbes scholarship does not support such a reading. If Hobbes is seeking for, as noted above, a rationalist and anti-foundationalist Enlightenment understanding of the political condition, then of course the state of nature is not value-free at all; it is infused with a moral message which it itself carries: Rely on yourself and on experience, think things through. It is a form of persuasive argumentation which appeals to inner experience and self-knowledge. Kraynak has gone further, arguing that the Laws of Nature are vital parts of Hobbes's argument; and that, far from wishing to free his subjects from them, Hobbes's state-of-nature teaching aims to give his rational precepts added persuasiveness. He maintains that it is the Laws of Nature, visible, knowable and obliging even in the state of nature, which link the prudence of the subject with the obligation towards contracting.

For other international relationists, the existence of such Laws of Nature, or precepts of right reason, derived from a few simple axioms concerning human nature, were attractive in another sense: as dictates which might appeal to Everyman. As universalisable precepts, they seemed capable of tying the use of power to some non-ideological moral standard, and to promise that even in a state of nature of states, that is, among sovereigns, some type of morality or perhaps moral dicta were possible. In simple terms, they offered a moderated exit from the Hobbesian dilemma, and a guide to just ends and means in the use of power. The English school in international relations has particularly seized upon Hobbes's Laws of Nature as a method of mediating between the necessity of self-defence and the requirements of laying some kind of philosophical foundation to international cooperation. Hedley Bull, in a rather elegant argument which incorporates Hobbes into the Machiavellian tradition, nonetheless notes the possibility of moral rules in the state of nature.[15] It is in this spirit that, recently, Howard Williams has derived a set of injunctions to state behaviour drawn from Hobbesian criteria.[16]

Of course, such injunctions as may be derived from Hobbes's Laws of Nature are formalistic, but they are not intended, as Arnold Wolfers observed in his treatment of moral philosophers, to guide foreign policy-making. Rather they are intended to sketch the value choice in the face of the world, the predispositions to behaviour. Moreover, there are good reasons why contemporary political philosophers looking for such a standard might be drawn to Hobbes. First of all, Hobbes insists that the Laws of Nature do compel *in foro interno*; they are, in other words, genuine obligations, albeit imperfect. Secondly, they have an essentially rationalist foundation. Third, they are clearly ethical propositions, connected with sociability and the good life. This fusion of the rational and the ethical which Hobbes attempted, together with their status as injunctions upon the Sovereign, even if imperfect obligations, provides a standard beyond desire and aversion for directing behaviour.

The question of whether Hobbes is deriving an ought from an is, or whether there are hidden oughts in the argument, has excited a lively debate among Hobbes scholars, and one which has significance for international relations in its various treatments of the Laws of Nature. Warrender and Taylor sought to argue that he was doing both and that his argument had escaped neither value-ladenness, which is unarguable, nor some pre-existing foundationalism. This argument was intended to demonstrate that the ambitions Hobbes had set for himself were unfulfilled, in Warrender's case as a preliminary to reabsorbing Hobbes back into the natural law tradition and demonstrating the continued vitality of that tradition. Warrender's aim was to incorporate Hobbes back into the natural law corpus, but without abandoning the contractarian elements, fusing both into a theory of obligation.[17] Watkins has disagreed with Warrender's reading and relates Hobbes's instructions more to the diagnoses of a doctor, a strongly prudential set of instructions. Here, a kind of morality may be present, in the doctor's obligation as a doctor to diagnose the situation properly. But it is not clear that the doctor's advice constitutes a moral obligation on the patient to follow it. The third way out of this puzzle is that of Barnouw who relates Hobbes' theory to a set of compelling analogies which act convincingly upon the mind; they are part of the art of political persuasion.[18] In yet another reading, we are invited to consider them a form of moral necessity, akin to the *grundnorm* of legal necessity of Kelsen. In this reading, they are the logically necessary foundations for the condition of peace, something akin to the categorical imperative, or what is required for the civic life, and also the moral life, to be lived at all.

The choice of diagnosis has obvious implications for the status of Hobbes's Laws of Nature and the degree to which they may be presented as compelling guides to international behaviour. As laws of nature in Warrender's sense, they speak to us directly, in the form of the normal or natural way of going on, and from which proper laws might be derived. In the form of prudential rules, however, they have no more status than any other rules of prudence; that is, no obligation ensues from the recommendations of a doctor, and the diagnoses are changeable according to the conditions of the time. In Barnouw's formulation, on the other hand, they are part of the art of persuasion, part of the rhetorical skills with which the philosopher enters the public realm; in other words, they belong to the realm of the political, and are only convincing so long as the analogies stick in the mind. As a form of Kelsenian *grundnorm*, however, they depend on our accepting a logic-of-laws type argument. The essential question here, however, is not how we should read Hobbes, but the rather more important one of the founding of public values.

We might, of course, return to the contractarian basis of Hobbes's argument for generating a notion of international society. Hobbes maintained that it was on the basis of contract, finally, that social peace was arrived at, and contractarianism presents itself as deontological. Hobbes also allowed that there were natural contracts, including contracts among Sovereigns in the form of confederacies and alliances to defend themselves in times of war, and that these were binding, in reason. Hobbes provides a defence of such contracts in Chapter XV, based on the Laws of Nature. Murray Forsyth has used them to identify an intermediate condition, in between the raw state of nature of individuals and the true civil society, a condition made up of the alliances and confederacies of states and quasi-states in which there remains a *ius belli*, but which is exercised jointly. His analysis elicits a more moderated picture of the state of nature of states than is usually derived from Hobbesian premises.[19] Even here, however, we have to answer the question from whence the obligation derives and the validity and duration of such contracts.

There seem to be two sorts of natural contracts: contracts of prudence and contracts of fear. The first are intended to forestall a predicted or expected outcome; the second are what would be more accurately described as contracts of subordination. Contracts of prudence would seem to arise on the basis of a rational understanding of what we wish to avoid, and are based on reason and will; contracts of fear hold from the more emotive desire to avoid death. The argument that neither represents a true civil contract has been used to emphasise not merely the instability of such contracts but also their moral nullity. If a Hobbesian reading might support the first, however, I do not think it supports the second, and the first proposition also needs qualifying. On the stability of contracts in a state of nature, research seems to indicate that it is when contracts are changeable that they are more likely to be entered into, and that contracts are least likely to hold in war; that is, they are least likely to be the escape from the ultimate condition.[20] With regard to their moral nullity, first, Hobbes tells us that, in a condition of instability it is better that contracts be kept – this is a rationally generated premise. Secondly, there is the inviolability of promises; Hobbes maintained that promises should be kept, even to robbers, until the state so released a man. Finally, there is Kraynak's argument, which sees the Laws of Nature as the link between the prudence of the subject and the founding of the contract. Kraynak's argument, applied to international relations, does show how the precept *pacta sunt servanda* might be grounded in a Hobbesian theory.

Whether a moral obligation is thereby created is, however, another question. Jean Hampton has distinguished between the self-interested act and the exchange of obligation. Only the latter, she maintains, creates a promise and, in the act of creating a promise, also creates a foundation for morality. Her argument denies that Hobbes aims to create this kind of contract, since the Hobbesian contract is among the citizens, and it is not clear that they are promising one another anything. A Lockean contract, on the other hand, is in the nature of an exchange between the rulers and the ruled, in which reciprocal promises are made. The latter contract, she maintains, does create a set of distinctly moral, as opposed to merely prudential, obligations.[21]

When we apply this distinction to international relations, we get some interesting results. There are many types of contracts in international relations, and they are constructed on different bases and do different things. Some, such as the GATT, set the rules for an enterprise, and are not really exchanges of obligation, while still other treaties are exchanges of a sort, but may not involve promising. A treaty which stipulates that you allow me to put in a base and I allow you to buy my weaponry is a form of exchange, but it is not clear that a promise is entailed. Yet others such as NATO are exchanges of obligation with promises entailed; in the NATO treaty, each promises to defend the other. According to Hampton's criteria, it is only really the latter sort of contract which would create a moral and hence obligatory basis.

If I might be allowed to bracket this rather large question, there remains a strong argument that the Sovereign is bound by the Laws of Nature in reason (an argument which Hobbes supports) and, moreover, that he is more likely than individuals to be able to keep his promises (which Hobbes might also support). First, no one in the state of nature would, with his enlightened mind, contract to establish other than a Sovereign so bound. The contractors should in reason insist that the rules establishing and empowering the Sovereign they have set over themselves must be such as to encourage forgiveness, conciliation, in so far as it is possible, and generosity. Above all, they would insist that he be equitable and treat the most powerful in the same way as the most humble. There would, in reason, be a strong inclination to institutionalise natural justice, as an attribute of the public power. Theodore Waldman makes the point that Hobbes's theory is a theory of how to generate a public person;[22] we may suppose therefore that the Laws of Nature are intended to point to the substance of that public person's persona.

Now, once this Sovereign or public person is established on such a basis, it could be argued, the conditions are there for such predispositions to peace to be generalised among Sovereigns so endowed; that is, they would share such qualities as being peace-loving, generous and tolerant. (Here, of course, we are envisaging the tolerant and not the totalitarian image of the Hobbesian sovereign; it does make a difference. Hence, the question of the totalitarian nature of Hobbes's teaching is just as crucial for international relationists as for those trying to ground liberal theory.) Of course, the anarchical condition is not thereby done away with; states still quarrel. But they inhabit the same meta-world of public values and they speak the same language. Nor is this a trivial sense. James Mayall has noted the difference between just differences among states and radical differences, and Fred Halliday has recently pointed out that one way of comprehending a society of states is to comprehend a world of similar states.[23] The equivalent would be the Benthamite world of equal utility seekers. Bentham did not do away with war in his world, but imagined the limitations that would be imposed on their mutual relations by each state considering all other states as utility seekers, equal to itself.

There is also another point; Sovereigns like their subjects in a state of nature do not escape from the conditions of nature. This may be a rather different nature experientially from that suffered by individuals; Sovereigns experience internal stability which creates some ability to calculate their own and others' power. Nonetheless, they too must face a situation of the war of all against all; they too face the prospect where the unregulated quest for the optimum on the part of all like agents is likely to produce losses all around. In the strategic literature, this is generally called escalation; that is to say, that condition where the best is what everybody wants, but which threatens to end in a no-win situation. This produces a strong incentive to auto-limitation and to the reception by the illuminated mind of the message, Think Again.

Even if we accept this, however, we still have a problem: these are at best predispositional inclinations or meta-laws; these are not laws, in the sense of a clear determination of behaviour in a specific situation, and they do not establish a Rule of Law. If this is what those building on Hobbes's Laws of Nature think they may be achieving, they had better think again.

One of the most illuminating treatments of the question appears in Oakeshott's essay on *The Rule of Law*, an essay of clear Hobbist inspiration.[24] Oakeshott distinguishes between a rule of prudence or instruction, an ethic and a conditional qualifier to behaviour. In his view, a law is neither an instruction, nor is it an ethic, even when that ethic has been specified in a policy declared by a government. A law is a specific qualifier to behaviour, a rule on how we go about seeking our ends. In this view, predispositions alone do not and cannot create laws, nor do policies. To become laws they must be turned into behaviour-qualifying rules. Such rules, moreover, are created by legislative authorities, not by ethical philosophers. Equally important, in Oakeshott's view, is some adjudication procedure; according to Oakeshott, the rule of law requires not merely a specified law-maker, but courts where the general rule can be applied to the specific case. These stand as criteria of real law, and general predispositions would need these added qualities to qualify as real law. General ethical dicta which float about, even if they have a quasi-legal form, as for example international law, do not constitute a legal code.

The other difficulty with grounding a theory of international obligation on a Hobbesian contractual basis relates to the equality argument. One of the strongest bases in reason for prudential behaviour of the kind recommended by Hobbes, and for keeping contracts, was his insistence, the anti-Machiavellian argument, that men in nature were sufficiently equal to ensure that none could prevail on their own or even in a combination. But Rousseau has pointed out the problem of simply transferring this argument to the level of the state: 'for if men in nature are equal, the state not being bounded by natural limitations can grow so as to dominate the rest'. In other words, if we limit Hobbes's argument to its purely rationalist basis of self-interest, we cannot generate from it even a prudent self-limitation at the international level. It is for this reason that notions of a public good keep reappearing in international relations literature, and why the Machiavellian option keeps recurring in Realist literature, since its republican foundations do lay out a notion of the *salus publica* for the sake of which selfish or self-interested behaviour must occasionally be put aside.

## HOBBES AS LEGAL THEORIST

Hobbes's legal ideas were very rich, and his analysis of the state conceives it as a legal apparatus. I have written in another place about the status of *Leviathan* as a legal treatise which distinguishes between different kinds of legal phenomena and its application to international relations,[25] but it is worth reiterating some of those points here.

In the first instance, Hobbes distinguished between dictates of reason and prudence on the one hand and the civil laws on the other, and he provided a coherent set of conditions under which the civic laws gained their legal quality. In the second place, he related them through the notion that the natural laws, including the ability to fulfil our obligations, were only recoverable within the framework of the civil laws. (It was this link which was intended to provide the real linchpin to the argument for contracting.) Finally, there was the link between the framework of the civil laws, sociability and social life generally; notably, that it was the establishment of a coherent legal order, and respect for that order, which allowed for social life as we recognise and value it.

Hobbes's legal distinctions have served many purposes in modern international theory. They are used extensively in the modern analysis of international organisations to discuss the locus of authority within them; they are central props in the analysis of international law. They help us understand the different force of Security Council as opposed to General Assembly resolutions, and why Security Council resolutions have the status they do. Hobbes as a constitutional theorist may also be deployed to construct constitutional comparisons of different sorts of international organisations, using the criteria Hobbes developed for the state. Hobbes was among the first to distinguish the law-making, law-executing and law-adjudicating power; and we may apply these distinctions to international organisations, measuring them by the different capacities or qualities in respect of each that they display. This rather old-fashioned type of constitutional analysis or typology has the virtue of differentiating between international organisations and illustrating the complexity of modern organisational development. It also serves to break up the rather static and over-simplistic view of international relations as a state of nature which a too-earnest usage of Hobbes has tended to create.

There are also Hobbes's political definitions as they may be applied to the deployment of force; the distinction, for example, between 'hostility' and 'punishment', or between authorised and unauthorised troop deployments. Or, in the status of utterances, between the ideological, the normative and the authoritative. Or, in the exercise of power, between influence and authority. Paul Wilkinson uses what are essentially Hobbesian criteria to distinguish between terror, the organised use of force for a political purpose, and random violence. These sorts of distinctions provide us with a vocabulary for speaking about and distinguishing a variety of international as well as domestic phenomena, and they are all of Hobbist inspiration.

## CONCLUSIONS

What can be said about a thinker in whom can be found the origins of both totalitarianism and liberalism; who can be used to defend absolute sovereignty and yet also be used to justify its abandonment into a theory of world government; who can be used to sustain a natural law reading of obligations and yet blow it apart; who can be at once the theorist of international anarchy and also the compelling theorist of the necessity of international order? Some of these tensions may be understood better if we remember Hobbes's project, which was to free his subjects from pre-ordained, and contending, authorities and yet also to tie them down to Authority. This involved him in creating a set of categories which would at once liberate the subject from a previous set of mental directives, ethical views, customs or tradition, while creating a set of neutral imperatives which could then act upon the freed consciousness to create a set of rational imperatives to behaviour which could be grasped by the rational, because now freed, mind. Hobbes's writings are in consequence a bit like Puchala's elephant; depending on what you touch, your view will be different. But Hobbes did have a system and his various theorems are related. Accordingly, the picking and choosing must be done with some care, at least if the result is to be declared Hobbist.

The first of these is the abstract rational aggregative actor set within a number of ideal typic contexts. It is against the spirit of Hobbes to overly clothe the actors. They are simple calculators who may be convinced to abandon much that they hold dear because their logic tells them that unless they do so they are bound to lose it anyway, and in frightful circumstances. We must also understand that Hobbes's rational sceptic is an ideal type; that human beings may be persuaded to see themselves in this light some of the time but, in the Hobbesian understanding, not all the time. Accordingly, we may be able to seize those moments of enlightenment to get them to write their contracts and agree some basic rules of the game, but, in the Hobbesian understanding, such moments are unlikely to last and the agreements they produce will have to be supported by institutional contexts which operate coercive mechanisms.

A second Hobbesian understanding is with the nature of those coercive mechanisms. Hobbes draws our attention to the stability and certainty produced by rigorous expectations of behaviour; that such an action will be followed by such an outcome. A Hobbesian understanding of international relations ought to be infused by an appreciation of reliable sanctions, as well as of clearly formulated undertakings to which those sanctions will apply.

A third Hobbesian understanding concerns what Walzer has called rough justice. International authorities may not represent the perfection of liberal understanding – the Security Council may not be perfectly representative. That, however, is not what is important about them, nor what we should be looking for when we construct or reform them. Rather we should be looking for the ability and courage to mobilise force in defence of agreed undertakings.

As moral theorist, Hobbes is likely to appeal most to the exhausted: Save yourself from death. The problem with Hobbes is that we are absorbed into the maw of Leviathan without thereby escaping death. There is also the morally unsatisfactory situation of inhabiting one moral world within the state and yet another outside. Above all, Hobbes is a desperate sort of utilitarian. He draws on the extremities of experience and seeks to create fairly minimal conditions of security. He is not likely to appeal to those who have warmer ideas of justice.

## NOTES

1.  *The Myth of the State* (New Haven: Yale University Press, 1946), pp. 174–5.
2.  Robert P. Kraynak, *History and Modernity in the Thought of Thomas Hobbes* (Ithaca: Cornell University Press, 1990), p. 216.
3.  See esp. David Boucher, University of Swansea, 'British Idealism, the State and International Relations', unpublished paper; Lord Haldane's 'Higher Nationality: A Study in Law and Ethics' is a good example of how Hegelians could foresee the growth of a worldwide sense of obligation, and D. G. Ritchie in 'War and Peace', *International Journal of Ethics*, XI (1900–1) displays a particularly vivid account of progressive integration from the clan to the international community.
4.  See, esp. Roger Epp, 'The "Augustinian Moment" in International Politics', International Politics Research Papers, No. 10 (University College of Wales, Aberystwyth, 1991).
5.  Arnold Wolfers, *Discord and Collaboration* (Baltimore: Johns Hopkins, 1962), p. 84.
6.  'Idealist Internationalism and the Security Dilemma', *World Politics*, 2, 2, 1950, pp. 157–80.
7.  'Amity and Enmity Among Nations', in Wolfer's *Discord and Collaboration* (Baltimore: Johns Hopkins, 1962).
8.  François Tricaud, 'Hobbes' Concept of the State of Nature from 1640 to 1651: Evolution and Ambiguities', in *Perspectives on Thomas Hobbes*, ed. G. A. J. Rogers and Alan Ryan (Oxford: Clarendon Press, 1988).
9.  'Hobbes and the Concept of World Government', in *Hobbes: War Among Nations*, ed. Timo Airaksinen and Martin Bertman (Aldershot: Avebury, 1989).
10. A. Rapaport, *Fights Games and Debates* (Ann Arbor: Michigan University Press, 1957) and A. Wohlstetter, 'The Delicate Balance of Terror', *Foreign Affairs*, January 1958, reprinted in *Problems of National Strategy*, ed. H. Kissinger (New York: Praeger, 1965).

11. 'The Nature of Human Nature in Hobbes and Rousseau', in *The Limits of Human Nature*, ed. J. Benthall (London: Allen Lane, 1973).

12. 'The Limits of Human Nature', op. cit., p. 9.

13. The Introduction has been reprinted, with several other essays, in Michael Oakeshott, *Hobbes and Civil Association* (Oxford: Basil Blackwell, 1975); for an essay relating Hobbes to Hegel in the consideration of war, which well underlines the distinctions, as well as the way in which war and the state can make sense of individual death, see Philip Windsor, 'The State and War', in *The Condition of States*, ed. Cornelia Navari (Milton Keynes: Open University Press, 1991).

14. *Hobbes' System of Ideas* (London: Hutchinson University Library, 1965).

15. Hedley Bull, 'Hobbes and the International Anarchy', *Social Research*, 48, 4, 1981, pp. 717–38.

16. Howard Williams, *International Relations in Political Theory* (Milton Keynes: Open University, 1992), pp. 62–6.

17. Howard Warrender, *The Political Philosophy of Hobbes: His Theory of Obligation* (Oxford: Clarendon Press, 1957); Warrender stresses that Hobbes's theory is, above all, a theory of obligation, and he, like Kraynak, sees the Natural Laws as vital parts in the construction of that theory.

18. Jeffrey Barnouw, 'Persuasion in Hobbes's *Leviathan*', *Hobbes Studies*, 1, 1988, pp. 3–25.

19. 'Thomas Hobbes and the external relations of states', *British Journal of International Studies*, 5 (1979), pp. 196–209.

20. See Raymond Cohen, *International Politics: The Rules of the Game* (New York: Longman, 1981), pp. 22–30.

21. Jean Hampton, *Hobbes and the Social Contract Tradition* (Cambridge: Cambridge University Press, 1986), esp. pp. 138–47.

22. 'Hobbes on the Generation of a Public Person', in *Thomas Hobbes in His Time*, eds R. Ross, H. W. Schneider and T. Waldman (Duluth: University of Minnesota, 1974); Waldman stresses that the Laws of Nature are guides to the sovereign in the conduct of domestic, as well as foreign affairs.

23. James Mayall, 'The Variety of States', in *The Condition of States*, ed. Cornelia Navari (Milton Keynes: Open University, 1991), pp. 44–60; Fred Halliday, 'International Society as Homogeneity: Burke, Marx, Fukuyama', *Millenium, Journal of International Studies*, 21, 3, 1992, pp. 435–62.

24. In *On History and Other Essays* (Oxford: Blackwell, 1983), pp. 119–63.

25. 'Hobbes and the "Hobbesian Tradition" in International Relations', *Millennium, Journal of International Studies*, 11, 3, 1982, pp. 203–22.

# 3 Grotius, Law, and Moral Scepticism: Theory and Practice in the Thought of Hedley Bull

Benedict Kingsbury[1]

Hugo Grotius (1583–1645) was accorded a prominent position in the canon of that approach to 'classical theories of international relations' developed by Martin Wight, Hedley Bull, and others in the British Committee on the Theory of International Politics – an approach that was both the inheritance and the legacy of the much-missed R. J. Vincent.[2] Wight posited a 'Grotian tradition' of thought, which he used in counterpoint with other traditions (Machiavellian/Hobbesian, Kantian) to elucidate important problems in international relations.[3] Bull adopted from Wight much of the language of the three traditions, while pointing explicitly to their limitations, but Bull's systematic rigour caused him to distinguish sharply between the writings of Grotius and the tenets of a 'Grotian tradition', and he was decidedly cautious as to the senses in which any such *tradition* could usefully be said to exist.[4] Bull more than Wight produced analyses of particular works of Grotius intended to demonstrate, quite apart from any connections with 'neo-Grotians' or a 'Grotian tradition', their intrinsic interest for modern students of international relations. In these various enterprises Wight and Bull were influenced by the varying but increasing interest in Grotius among international lawyers from about the middle of the nineteenth century,[5] and especially by the efforts of Van Vollenhoven and Lauterpacht in the wake of the two world wars to expound a 'Grotian tradition' of international law for the twentieth century.[6] This chapter deals with aspects of Bull's use of Grotius, focusing in particular on Bull's reluctance to follow Grotius's views on the nature of law and on the possibilities of moral commitment in the face of the challenge of moral scepticism.

Writing about Grotius in international law and relations has treated Grotius primarily (although not exclusively) through analysis, against the background of his biography and the history of his period, of a small though important subset of his extensive oeuvre. Vastly the most important of these has been *De Jure Belli ac Pacis* (*On the Law of War and Peace, JBP*), completed in 1624 and first published in 1625. That *JBP* received significant attention is evident from the numerous subsequent editions (Grotius himself worked on editions published in 1631, 1632, 1642, and 1646) and translations,[7] although a comprehensive study of its intellectual impact has not yet appeared. Grotius also had an impact on contemporaries and subsequent generations through *Mare Liberum* (*Freedom of the Seas*), which was published (anonymously at first) in 1609, apparently with a view to providing juridical support for positions taken by Grotius's patron Oldenbarnevelt in the domestic and international political manoeuvring leading to the 1609 truce between the United Provinces and Spain.[8] The main lines of *JBP*, and the entirety of *Mare Liberum*, were anticipated in *De Jure Praedae* (*The Law of Prize*) (*JP*), written in the period 1604–6 as a work of legal advocacy connected with the seizure by a vessel of the Dutch East India Company (the VOC) of the Portuguese carrack the *Catharine*. Because *JP* was substantially unknown until the rediscovery of the manuscript in 1864 and its publication four years later,[9] *JP* had little direct impact on the development of ideas, although it has attracted considerable scholarly attention as evidence of Grotius's thought in the milieu of the period, and it is of great value in understanding the structure and arguments of *JBP*.

The work of Quentin Skinner, J. G. A. Pocock, Richard Tuck, and others of the *historiens historisants* represents a methodological reproach both to the decontextualised analysis of historic texts of Western political theory, and to loose assertions about the existence of 400-year traditions of thought. These writers have sought to locate each author in close intellectual context, recovering the normative vocabulary available to the author from earlier writings then accessible, tracing the author's intellectual formation and inheritance, and connecting the author's texts with the political, theological, social, and intellectual debates or circumstances that seem to have affected them.[10] For the *historiens historisants*, as Pocock once put it, 'history of theory cannot be written as that of a dialogue between figures in a canonical tradition' – the organisation of history into a canonical dialogue is to reduce history to historical drama, in which the canonical actors are isolated in each other's company and can be interacting with each other only in accordance with the ideal of the author.[11] The canonical dialogue may be theory, but it is not history of theory. 'The text as the theorist reads it is not the same things as the text as event, or part of an event, reconstituted by historians. If the historian must abstain from deconstructing the theorist's encounter, the theorist must abstain from trying to reconstruct history.... If the two are combined, the result must be pseudohistory, myth-as-history, or Popperian historicism.'[12] For a historian of the Pocock/Skinner school, Grotius 'demands assignation to contexts: to his own, which we must recover if we are to understand him, and to our own, in which we must read him if we are to interpret him.'[13]

The 'recovery' of Grotius's context, assuming such a project is intelligible after its confrontations with critical theory, must be a highly specialist enterprise.[14] The recent specialist contributions concerned with the assignation of Grotius to his own context have added a great deal to the understanding of Grotius advanced by Bull, but it will be argued that they do not undermine the basic tenets of his interpretation. One approach to the problem of understanding Grotius in his own context is represented by Peter Haggenmacher's examination of the major 'international' texts, *JP* and *JBP*, by reference to patterns of ideas discernible in a vast range of prior texts – not all of which Grotius had necessarily read even at second hand. Haggenmacher argues that Grotius represents the culmination of a long tradition of writing on just war in which scholastic authors, especially the Iberian *seconda scholastica*, were of central importance. Haggenmacher's thesis that *JBP* is only a book about *justitia belli*, and that it contains no recognisable system of 'international' law in any modern sense,[15] is a sharp challenge to much of the received wisdom about the place of Grotius in a Grotian tradition of international law, not least the major premises of Van Vollenhoven and Lauterpacht.[16] The attack this thesis makes on anachronistic readings of Grotius does not apply to Hedley Bull, who did not treat Grotius as a general theorist of international law, and indeed (for quite independent reasons) eschewed any modern use of Grotius's account of the normativity of law and morality.

The *historien historisant* Richard Tuck has begun – as have, in different ways, other historians such as C. G. Roelofsen – to place works such as *JP* and *JBP* methodically in the structure and evolution of Grotius's thought as represented in his writings on theology, political church/state issues, Dutch and comparative constitutionalism, and Dutch law, taking account of the currents of ideas with which he was imbued and the context of particular controversies in which he was engaged or interested.[17] Tuck's rich and detailed work analyses Grotius as an opponent of the moral relativism inherent in the scepticism of Montaigne, and as laying foundations for a new science of morality or modern natural law leading to Pufendorf and above all to Hobbes.[18] It will be argued that this account is important in helping to fill in – or perhaps to shore up – the under-specified or inadequate foundations on which Wight and Bull built the solidarist theory of international society.

The assignation of Grotius to modern contexts has been greeted with scepticism by specialists on Grotius where – as is not uncommon in works on the 'Grotian heritage' or the 'Grotian tradition' – Grotius is utterly displaced from his own context.[19] As Haggenmacher points out, the clichéd but heavily-subscribed internationalist account of Grotius confronting the emergence of separate sovereign states from the wreckage of the medieval order, and heroically staving off lawless chaos by formulating a comprehensive legal order of interstate relations based on mutual respect and equality of sovereign states, 'utterly fails to give a correct idea of Grotius's real endeavour and accomplishment'.[20] (In mitigation, some of the internationalist references to Grotius scarcely claim to be more than purely emblematic, conveying little beyond a spirit or sense long received into the culture and lexicon of legal internationalism, as in the notion of a 'Grotian moment' of opportunity for transformation popularised by Richard Falk and endorsed by Boutros Boutros-Ghali.)[21]

If modern international relations writers have often not met the first part of Pocock's challenge, it is notable that writers such as Tuck, Haggenmacher, and Roelofsen have been cautious in responding to calls for explicit assignation of Grotius to 'our own context'.[22] Beyond the truism that everyone writing about the past necessarily by that act connects the past to the context of the present, the explicit projects of theorising about the present and future of international relations through reflection on distant texts or perceived traditions have been left by historians of ideas (with notable exceptions, such as Isaiah Berlin) to specialists in contemporary international law and international relations. Hedley Bull sought to understand Grotius in historical context while connecting him to issues confronting modern international relations theorists. While Bull refers frequently to Grotius or Grotian positions in developing his theory of order and justice in international society, he also chooses *not* to incorporate important elements of Grotius's thought dealing with the normative system of law and the possibilities of overcoming moral scepticism. In these respects Bull did not seek to assign Grotius to any contemporary context, and perhaps believed that as to these matters such an assignation was impossible in a world so different. The reasons for and implications of these fundamental differences between Bull and Grotius are considered later in this chapter.

## GROTIUS AND BULL ON THE NATURE AND ROLES OF LAW

For Grotius, law provided both a language and a mechanism for the systematic application of reason to problems of social order and conflict. It is possible to read *JBP*, as Pufendorf did, as the application to law and morality – and through these to society – of the new scientific methods associated with Francis Bacon. Not only is the scheme one based on reason, but its major component, the law of nature, is a dictate of right reason (*recta ratio*).[23] In these senses Grotius is a rationalist, and he has been much admired for his apparent commitment to bringing the violence and injustice of international affairs within the domain of reason.[24] It is not accurate to describe Grotius as a rationalist in the Cartesian sense: he professes an intention to emulate the approach of geometricians,[25] but he does not seek to maintain a truly 'mathematical' scheme in *JBP*,[26] and the rationalist/empiricist dichotomy does not shed much direct light on the contemporary interest of international relations writers in Grotius. Martin Wight's use of the term 'rationalist' to describe the Grotian tradition is puzzling in so far as he intended it to identify a fundamental break with the Hobbesian and Kantian traditions: in a broad sense the international relations ideas of Hobbes, Grotius, and even Kant are all 'rationalist'.[27]

The structure of *JBP* makes plain Grotius's most central concern, the regularisation and control of social conflict.[28] The book is organised around questions bearing on just war: who may be a belligerent, what causes of war are just, doubtful, or unjust, what procedures must or should be followed in the inception, conduct and conclusion of war. War is understood broadly, as coercive conduct. The formal scheme extends to war involving parties other than states or sovereigns, although the greater part of the material deals with public war. Grotius makes a major contribution to the just war tradition in attempting to state exhaustively the grounds for waging a just war, so that wars waged on other grounds are unjust or at least of doubtful justice. He contributes also by his commitment to extending the ambit of just war from issues about the parties and causes of war, to issues relating to the conduct of war, a major theme of Book III of *JBP*. Bull was undoubtedly right to identify the relation of war to justice, and the control of war, as the core of the Grotian conception.

Haggenmacher goes beyond this interpretation, arguing that *JBP* is a preeminent book about the *justitia belli* – that it is indeed the crowning achievement of the scholastic just war tradition – but that Grotius had no vision of 'international law' in the sense that the concept was subsequently to be understood. By 'international law' Haggenmacher intends a body of rules, comprising an autonomous and homogeneous juridical sphere, having as its specific object the whole of the relations among a limited group of subjects of law, and of which the law of war is merely one special part.[29] He argues that no one had such a view until after the publication of *JBP*, although he accepts that such a conception began to crystallise very shortly afterwards, and was evident already in Hobbes's *De Cive* (1642, which Grotius had read by 1643)[30] and in Zouche's *Iuris et Iudicii Fecialis* (1650). The passages in *JBP* – and particularly in the Prolegomena, which were written at the end with the benefit of an overview of the text – often cited as evidence that Grotius had a concept of international law in such a modern sense, are analysed by Haggenmacher as consistent with Grotius's just war scheme but fortuitously capable of having modern concepts read back into them. This applies, for example, to the opening passages of *JBP* (Proleg. 1 and 2) in which Grotius refers to the need to systematise '[t]hat body of law ... which is concerned with the mutual relations among states or rulers of states whether derived from nature, or established by divine ordinances, or having its origin in custom and tacit agreement',[31] and to the importance of 'a knowledge of treaties of alliance, conventions, and understandings of peoples, kings, and sovereign nations ... in short, of the whole law of war and peace'. Abstracted from context these appear to promise a recognisable notion of international law, but they are explained by Haggenmacher simply as mapping the range of controversies with which a comprehensive theory of just war must deal.[32]

Haggenmacher argues that *JBP* manifests not a concept of international law, but of extra-national law – that is, the law applicable outside the bounds of the municipal law of any particular polity.[33] Grotius was conversant with the distinction between *jus inter gentes* and *jus gentium*, but Haggenmacher's view is in accord with Grotius's consistent position in *JBP* that the erection of civil authority within a polity has the practical effect of transforming the legal regime – for example, subjects are generally expected to tolerate even unjust laws emanating from their properly constituted sovereign.

Haggenmacher's thesis is radically opposed to anachronistic readings of subsequent ideas back into Grotius, but it is clear that Grotius transmitted and systematised many ideas that were to remain important as international law developed, and that the appreciative reception of *JBP* had a significant influence on the way in which structures and inchoate ideas in *JBP* became part of the emerging subject of international law. In conformity with Haggenmacher's general approach, however, it is possible to identify at least five central concepts of modern international law that are not to be found – certainly not in anything resembling their high modern forms – in *JBP*.[34] First, Grotius's account of sources is a theory of sources of law in general rather than a specific hierarchy of formal or material sources of the types found in modern international law. Grotius discusses in systematic fashion the law of nature (divided in *JP* into primary natural law, common to all beings, and secondary natural law, applicable only to humans through the power of reason), divine volitional law, and human volitional law (ranging from the power of the paterfamilias or the slave-owner, through the *jus civile*, to the *jus gentium*).[35] In *JBP* he indicates that both divine positive law and the *jus gentium* are in effect subordinate to natural law, although the actual use of these different sources in relation to particular substantive issues of law is much more variable than this simple formal hierarchy implies.[36]

Second, Grotius does not have a closely defined concept of 'the state' in the senses subsequently developed in Western legal theory. Civitas, respublica, populus, regnum, and imperium are all used in *JBP* in ways that touch on the modern concept of 'state', but only 'civitas' is defined, and Grotius does not employ a taxonomy that feeds into later analytic usages.[37]

Third, Grotius does not have a theory of subjects of law of the sort that became a central feature of theories of public international law, although he applies law to a range of sovereign and non-sovereign entities (including individuals).

Fourth, while Grotius does have a concept of sovereignty – 'That power is called sovereign whose actions are not subject to the legal control of another'[38] – he does not systematically distinguish the legal personality of the sovereign state from that of the ruler or other governing power within the state,[39] and so does not present a theory of state responsibility in the modern sense.

Fifth, Grotius has no general doctrine of the equality of sovereign entities.[40] *JBP* itself makes clear that his world was one of vast differences in political systems, power, values, and units of authority, with individuals and political units existing in numerous different legal relations with one another.

Hedley Bull independently reached similar conclusions about characteristics of the thought of Grotius (conclusions he applied also to Vitoria, Suarez, Gentili, and Pufendorf): the values of international society were Christian, even though social bonds extended to non-Christians; membership of the society was not clearly defined and was not based on a notion of 'state'; the most significant source of obligations was natural law; the international society was predicated on universalist assumptions more than on a conception of separate sovereignties (let alone equal sovereign entities).[41] Bull's assignation of Grotius to his own context carefully avoids anachronisms which have beset some internationalist writing on Grotius. In dealing with the assignation of Grotius to contemporary contexts, Bull rightly emphasised that the positions of Grotius and of the twentieth century neo-Grotians are quite distinct. Grotius stands at the birth of international society and is rightly regarded as one of its midwives. For him the terminology of a universal state is what is still normal, and the language of international relations can only be spoken with an effort. The neo-Grotians, however, have three more centuries of the theory and practice of international society behind them; their novelty lies not in moving away from the domestic model in international relations, but in moving back towards it.[42]

The possibilities of connecting Grotius to current concerns arise for Bull not through attribution to Grotius of later ideas he didn't have, but through recognition that Grotius engaged thoughtfully with recurrent issues in ways that made it possible for subsequent readers to connect the open structures of Grotius's thought with their contemporary concerns. These open structures are sometimes described in terms of Grotius's 'ambivalence',[43] but this suggests a rather simple indecision across dualities which does not capture the best elements of Grotius's writing. The dichotomised image of many modern problems – for example, the perceived opposition in theories of sources of law between natural law and positivism – has made 'ambivalence' the major strategy of reconciliation. Where such narratives have prevailed, challenging or reproducing this ambivalence has come to seem a dominant motif of international law scholarship. For those committed to such a narrative of international legal history, Grotius and Grotianism have come to stand for both the challenging and the reproduction of such 'ambivalence', or, in the same way, for pragmatism or eclecticism.[44] On the issues he addresses, Bull's approach to Grotius is much more subtle than standard 'ambivalence' narratives.

Bull said very little, however, about Grotius's concept of law or the importance of particular legal concepts in the scheme of Grotius's thought. He recognised, of course, that the works of Grotius with which he was principally concerned are juridical, and that legal reasoning is central to the purposes and system of *JBP. JP, Mare Liberum*, and *JBP* are couched as expositions of law, even if the doctrine is often more open-textured, the sources and evidence less tight than in works by Grotius on other aspects of law, particularly *Inleidinge tot de Hollandsche Rechts-Geleerdheid* (*Introduction to the Jurisprudence of Holland*). Bull and Wight both numbered many international lawyers in the ranks of Grotians, and recognised a broad correspondence between the professional exposition of international law and adherence to the 'Grotian' tradition.[45]

Yet several features of Grotius's legal thought germane to international relations issues are scarcely mentioned in Bull's extensive and careful treatment of Grotius. The first and perhaps most significant of these omissions is Grotius's central role in the transformation of *jus* from an essentially objective character to the subjective character embodied in the modern idea of rights.[46] Grotius was not the first to see the idea that *jus* might be something a person *has* rather than something an action or state of affairs *is*,[47] but his contribution to developing and transmitting this idea was of great importance in the natural rights tradition.[48]

Second, Grotius's theory of moral action is one in which legal rights play a central part in defining what is required, permissible, or impermissible; but it is not exhausted by his account of perfect rights. The idea of imperfect rights, and the propriety of pursuing these without legal entitlement to their vindication, is emphasised repeatedly; this socially beneficial theory of morality in society was further developed by Pufendorf as the distinction between perfect and imperfect duties. The law of love, as Grotius calls it, is important to the scheme of *JBP*.[49]

Third, Grotius was deeply committed to constitutionalism, expending vast amounts of intellectual and political energy on historical and comparative constitutional analysis bearing on Dutch constitutional controversies,[50] and the subordination of religious to secular authority as a means of protecting liberty against religious extremism.[51] He was at the same time opposed to any general right of resistance to subjects confronted even with tyranny, which was one of the grounds for Rousseau's bitter denunciation of him, and caused Lauterpacht much agony.[52] Grotius was a theorist of liberty based on active rights, although not a theorist of liberalism.[53]

Fourth, *JBP* is about disputes – represented above all as lawsuits.[54] Recourse to a lawsuit is required where possible.[55] War – whether public or private – is the extension of a lawsuit.[56] As Schneewind puts it, 'If we ask why the project of the Grotians was to establish a law-like code of morals [and hence eventually to undermine the role of virtue], the answer must be that they took the central difficulties of life to be those arising from disagreement – disagreement involving nations, religious sects, parties to legal disputes, and ordinary people trying make a living in busy commercial societies. It is not an accident that the very first word in the body of Grotius's text is "controversiae".'[57] As is to be expected in a book about the law of disputes, a considerable part is devoted to legal procedures.

For Grotius, law played a range of important roles – normative, communicative, procedural – in the ordering of society. Elucidating these roles was an important task of the theorist, and entailed intimate connections of theory and practice. By contrast, Hedley Bull's treatment of international law is not probing, and shows little interest in the foundations or the normativity of law. The reasons for this have some parallels with Bull's treatment of morality and ethics (discussed below), and will be considered further in the concluding section.

The general function of law in Bull's theory was astutely summarised by John Vincent:

> The function of international law in relation to international order, according to Bull, was not itself to produce it, as some progressivist thought asserted, but to identity the constitutive principle of the political organization of humankind – the society of states; then to state the basic rules of coexistence between them; and then to provide a language in which their formal relations could be carried on.... The interest in international law, then, was not for what it was, but for what it signified. It provided evidence for existence of society, not the reason for its existence. It was in this regard a very useful instrument for Bull, locating society like a miner's lamp locating gas: *ubi societas ibi jus est.*[58]

In unpublished lectures on international law, Bull adopted Oppenheim's division of international lawyers into natural lawyers, positivists, and 'Grotians', a group concerned with both natural and voluntary or positive law.[59] Oppenheim's purpose was to chronicle the laudable rise of positivism, and Bull's own analysis of international law adopts a number of positivist tenets, drawing heavily on the thought of Bull's teacher H. L. A. Hart.[60] One of Hart's central concerns was the analytic separation of law and morality. Bull devotes curiously little attention to arguing for this separation, which he endorses by implication, but he argues strongly for distinctions between law and political assertions and between law-as-fact and social values. Law must be clearly separated from these varieties of non-law: 'if international lawyers become so preoccupied with the sociology, the ethics or the politics of international relations that they lose sight of what has been in the past their essential business, that is the interpretation of existing legal rules, the only result must be a decline in the role of international law in international relations'.[61] In Bull's terminology, 'Grotianism' or 'neo-Grotianism' among international lawyers referred to solidaristic tendencies to find new sources of law in order to evade the requirement of sovereign consent; extend the range of subjects of international law beyond states; and promote the triumph in war of the party representing the just cause.[62]

Bull does not construct an extended argument as to *why* international lawyers should adhere to positivist premises, but he is committed to the view that international law is separate from but validated by practice, and to the position that international law can be based only on express or tacit consent – that is, on genuine consensus. This position was at variance with that of Martin Wight, who observed in answer to the question 'why must agreements be observed?' 'Utilitarian that reasons may be adduced as the sources of authority for this principle, but the oldest and profoundest answer is that the observance of agreements represents an ethical norm; it conforms to an inherent standard of justice.'[63] This is virtually a paraphrase of Grotius.[64]

The vast gulf between the positions of Bull and Grotius on law is equally evident with regard to morality. For Grotius law and morality are parts of a single whole, and are both normative and central, while for Bull law and morality are to be kept separate, and the spheres of both are confined.

## GROTIUS, BULL AND MORAL RELATIVISM

Twentieth-century proponents of a 'Grotian tradition' have seen Grotius as a hero in the perennial confrontation with doctrines of 'reason of state' exemplified by the writings of Machiavelli.[65] At the beginning of *JBP* Grotius lists possible objections to his enterprise, the first of which is represented by a saying from Thucydides 'that in the case of a king or imperial city nothing is unjust which is expedient', to which for good measure Grotius added an excerpt of the Athenian position in the Melian dialogue.[66] In a general way the reading of *JBP* as a humanist constitutionalist rejection of *ragion di stato* and *raison d'état* is justified. Grotius reflects an awareness of reason of state positions, and assigns a not-insignificant role to expediency or interest (*utilitas*).[67] Whether the approaches Grotius reacted against were strictly those of Machiavelli is another matter.[68] The 'big picture' of an opposition between Grotian and Machiavellian conceptions tends to a reductionism which misses much of what is important in the system of Grotius's thought, and overlooks the fruitful possibilities of reading Grotius as responding to a different type of scepticism.

Tuck makes a stimulating case for retrieving a long-submerged view that Grotius sought to respond in *JBP* (as earlier in *JP*) to a particular form of sceptical challenge that had become increasingly influential in the two or three decades before he wrote *JP*. This was the moral relativist position of Michel de Montaigne and Pierre Charron. 'Grotius and his successors were responding to a straightforward pre-Humean moral scepticism, which simply pointed to the multiplicity of beliefs and practices around the world, and concluded that there were no common moral beliefs and hence nothing stable upon which to build a universal ethics.'[69]

Grotius's express acknowledgement of a concern with moral relativism is very limited. In *JBP* Grotius chooses the second-century BC Greek sceptic Carneades as representative of a particular objection he must confront.[70]

> Carneades ... was able to muster no argument stronger than this, that, for reasons of expediency, men imposed upon themselves laws, which vary according to [peoples'] customs, and among the same peoples often undergo changes as times change; moreover that there is no law of nature, because all creatures, men as well as animals, are impelled by nature toward ends advantageous to themselves; that, consequently, there is no justice [justitia], or, if such there be, it is supreme folly, since one does violence to his own interests if he consults the advantage of others.

Building a picture of the development of humanist thought and Grotius's likely reception of it, Tuck interprets this passage, together with the structure of Grotius's positive argument for natural law, as indicating that 'for "Carneades" one should in effect read "Montaigne" or "Charron"'.[71] For the purposes of this chapter, the most persuasive – and significant – aspect of this interpretation is its coherence in explaining elements of the foundations and methods of Grotius's system, particularly with regard to his approach to natural law.

This interpretation of Grotius was in part suggested by Pufendorf and mapped out by Barbeyrac, the influential French translator of Grotius and Pufendorf.[72] In an essay attached to his 1709 translation of Pufendorf's *De Jure Naturae et Gentium*, Barbeyrac argues that the enterprise of Grotius, as of Selden, Hobbes, and of course Pufendorf himself, was the elaboration of a science of morality, and that it was calculated to refute the scepticism represented by Montaigne and Charron without seeking to re-establish (on a scientific footing) Aristotelian ethics.[73] For both Pufendorf and Barbeyrac, Grotius was the first to understand natural law as a modern science. For Grotius, as for Pufendorf, natural law is the dictate of right reason.[74] Grotius asserts that the law of nature could be proven by either of two means: *a priori*, 'by demonstrating the necessary agreement or disagreement of anything with a rational and social nature', and *a posteriori* (as a matter of probability if not absolute certainty), by showing what is believed to be the law of nature 'among all nations, or among all those that are more advanced in civilization'.[75] This sidesteps at least one of the methodological objections of Montaigne, that there is not even one rule of the supposedly firm and immutable natural law 'but is contradicted and disowned, not by one Nation only, but by many. And yet this same universal Approbation is the only probable Mark, from which they [natural lawyers] can argue, or infer, any Laws at all to be natural.'[76] As to the content of the natural law, Grotius's innovation was to base his system on the natural urge of all humans for self-preservation.[77] For Tuck, this is the crucial insight in responding to moral relativism, for even the sceptics, in their philosophy for living, accepted that self-preservation was a necessary and proper basis of action. The exact connection and balance in *JBP* between self-preservation and the appetite for society as motivating forces and foundations of natural law are matters on which opinions differ – *JP* is clearer in positing a series of rules of natural law which follow from self-preservation, whereas the *appetitus societatis* plays a more prominent role in *JBP*. As Tuck states his case: 'Grotius had one central and simple idea: that precisely because scepticism was a theory about the route to wisdom, a theory which presupposed that wise men were primarily concerned with protecting themselves from harm, sceptical ideas could be restated in the language of natural rights and duties.... The fundamental character of these rights and duties also meant they could play the role of cross-cultural universals, an Grotius himself seems to have been principally interested in this aspect of them'.[78]

Tuck suggests that the Pufendorf/Barbeyrac interpretation was lost in the rewriting of the history of modern philosophy occasioned by Kant's innovations – and that the overdue retrieval of this interpretation shows Grotius to be the most creative and original thinker in the development of the new moral science represented by 'modern' natural law, even while Hobbes was the deepest and most acute thinker on problems of moral relativism as on the foundations of Enlightenment political thought.[79] Whether or not all of these bold assessments are justified,[80] the reading of Grotius as mounting a methodical defence against moral relativism provides a revealing counterpoint to the position of Hedley Bull on the central problem of whether it is possible to ground principles of international morality – or international law – other than by reliance on express agreement.

The whole tradition of thought about the existence and nature of an 'international society' comprised primarily of states bound together by common rules and institutions – a tradition Bull labelled 'Grotian' in the broad sense – represents one pattern of approaches to this issue.[81] Within this pattern is a set of solidarist approaches, labelled by Bull 'Grotian' in the narrow sense, including: solidarity in the enforcement of law;[82] understanding war as an act of law enforcement legitimated or delegitimated in any particular case by its service or disservice to the interests of international society;[83] basing international law on some conception of right – or on the solidarity or consensus of international society – even in the absence of express consent and even if empirical behaviour is inconsistent with the putative rule.[84] While Grotius can certainly be described as a theorist of 'international society' in the broad sense, although he was by no means the first such theorist, he did not envisage a society of states in what was later termed (rather unhelpfully) the 'Westphalia' model,[85] and he said little or nothing about such institutions as international conferences, the balance of power, special responsibilities of particular categories of power, or permanent international organisations. The extent to which he espoused a 'solidarist' vision of such a society is much less certain, as Bull recognised.[86] Grotius's positions on such solidarist themes as the consequences of the justice or injustice of a war for the rules concerning its conduct and the position of neutrals,[87] intervention in 'civil' conflicts or against tyrants,[88] and the enforcement of law by third parties generally,[89] are all complex and often difficult to reduce to rules of decision.

Bull embraced the notion that there exists an international society of states, and he was not necessarily hostile to some tenets of solidarism as aspirations for the future, but he argued strongly that a circumspect pluralist conception of what was presently possible in international society was preferable to a solidarist conception it was not (yet) in a condition to bear. In 'The Grotian Conception of International Society' he set up the pluralism of Oppenheim against the solidarism he attributed (albeit with careful qualification) to Grotius, precisely in order to attack neo-Grotian solidarism as premature. *The Anarchical Society* posits an international society – of states – founded on minimal solidarism and an overlay of pluralism. Unsurprisingly, this work has been criticised as lacking a theory of ethics and as offering inadequate accounts of the place of ethics and of ethical evaluations in world politics.[90] This is not to suggest that Bull himself was oblivious to such issues – several of his other works attest to his abiding interest in such problems.[91] The criticism directs attention to the nature of the theoretical enterprise Bull saw himself as undertaking in *The Anarchical Society*: a largely non-normative analysis of how order is achieved or might differently be achieved, in which norms are for the most part derived from practice, presumed to rest on consent, and reported as facts. As Ian Harris points out, this line of criticism does not apply (at least not at a basic level) to *JBP*. Grotius's system of natural law yields a series of ethical norms suitable for prescribing and evaluating conduct. In particular cases, these are supplemented by other sources of normative standards that are, as a practical matter, not simply 'voluntary'. It is true that Grotius does not deal satisfactorily with many issues confronted by other theorists: the nature of political obligation;[92] an account of practical action, which is necessary to make a system of moral norms into a system of ethics;[93] the problem of self-judging, expounded by Hobbes;[94] the 'nature' and proofs of human nature; the vast range of epistemological problems which occupied many of his successors. Nevertheless, Grotius has a foundational moral theory applicable to individuals and to units of authority that does not depend on particular religious belief. In this respect *The Anarchical Society* departs radically and deliberately from the method of Grotius.

That Bull did not equate Grotianism with commitment to a theory of universal morality or ethics may be interpreted simply as a manifestation of positivism, but a more plausible explanation is hesitancy as to the possibilities of grounding a moral theory in the face of apparent diversity of practice.[95] Grotius himself presents two different methods of grounding natural law, although the first is hierarchically superior and is the only one on which Grotius ultimately relies. The first and pre-eminent method for establishing the system of natural law is through reason applied to nature. Second, he grants that practice plays a significant role, both as a foundation for *jus gentium*, and more importantly as evidence for the law of nature, which for many practical purposes can be demonstrated *a posteriori* by empirical evidence. Generality of practice is confirmation, at least, of the rectitude of results reached by reason. Thus consensus and practice are relevant. Pufendorf and other naturalists follow only the first of these methods; Bull follows only the second.

Pufendorf takes a much more robust line than Grotius against sceptical arguments. He dispenses with *jus voluntarium* as a major source of law, and renounces reliance on *a posteriori* means of proving the law of nature (in correspondence he criticises Grotius for allowing any role to customary practices as evidence of the law of nature).[96] He grants the objections of Montaigne to the notion of law based on the consent of all nations, citing the impossibility of gathering evidence as to the practices of different peoples, the inevitability of many divergences in such practices, the relativity and self-judging character (and therefore the uselessness) of proposals by any people to designate other peoples as 'Barbarians' whose practice can be discounted on grounds of lack of civilisation, the tendency of many peoples to behave less well to strangers and downright badly toward enemies, and the general problem that 'the Number of Fools far exceeds that of wise Men'.[97] This is one of the strongest naturalist repudiations of consensus as a basis for establishing the law of nature.

Bull's approach follows a dominant modern pattern, by which consensus and validation through practice are the *via media* between contemporary moral scepticism and emancipatory or prescriptivist approaches. The consensus method of grounding normative positions is used consistently by Bull, and has been treated as one of the hallmarks of modern 'Grotianism'.[98] On one view such consensus may be established by bare agreement, as exemplified by the works of David Gauthier.[99] On another view, consensus must be more deeply rooted in social practice and values.

Martin Wight inclined to the Burkean view that common morality depends upon generation of a deep moral community through shared interests and through a long experience of shared culture, history, and patterns of religious thought. Thus Wight opined that the discovery and cultivation of political morality – an ethics in the political realm that is more than simply the personal honour of individual leaders or the practice of expediency – seemed to be 'peculiarly related to Western values'.[100] Bull did not dismiss the Burkean element of this view, although he was much more ready than Wight to see the possibilities of culturally-rooted consensus on political and moral values globally and in different regions.[101] He believed that the continued viability of the states system and of international society depended 'on maintaining and extending the consensus about common interests and values that provides the foundations of its common rules and institutions', and that in the face of the vast extension of European international society and the rise of the non-European world relative to Europe, international society could survive only if a common moral and political culture deeply rooted in different societies grew up alongside the common diplomatic and intellectual cultures of the elites.[102]

That Grotius represented and embodied a sense of continuity in European culture, combining Greco-Latin learning with humanism and pious Christian ecumenism, seems likely to have appealed to Wight's deep-seated disposition toward a Burkean or Rankean connection between international relations and the depth of historical and cultural community. The deep permeation of religious elements in Grotius's thought may also have appealed to Wight's own religiosity, whereas Bull professed himself uneasy about religious derivation of any modern theory of international relations, and believed international society must become inclusive and less Western. In addition to his explicit reliance on the Divine Will and Christian ethics, Grotius frequently uses argumentative structures and metaphors derived from Christian theology even in discussion of apparently secular legal issues.[103] (Similar religious patterns can be traced in modern international law more generally.)[104] For Grotius religion is important within the polity, but its function as a bond and motivating force is even greater in the broad human society beyond the civil polity.[105] Grotius's philosophical eclecticism is equally evident in his commitment to unity across the theological divides in Christendom.[106]

Parallels are readily drawn between Grotius's consensus-based arguments for unity in Christianity and his arguments for a universal law of nature.[107]

## CONCLUSION: BULL, THE GROTIAN TRADITION, AND THE CONNECTION OF THEORY AND PRACTICE

In the scheme of *JBP*, law and morality are inseparable although not identical. Both are immanent in nature and accessible to human reason. The methods of Baconian science are applied to both, and Grotius's derivation of natural law in *JBP* equally grounds morality and law. His position in *JP* that natural law is just because it is willed by God is transformed by the time of *JBP* to the position that even God cannot change natural law.[108] Law and morality have many of the same sources in common. The further rules obligatory for Christians are rules of morality and of law – the same is apparently true for Jews as recipients of the Mosaic law and other rules of religious obligation. Law is not, of course, co-extensive with morality. Natural law does not cover all of morality, and must be supplemented by the 'law of love'. Human law may purport to conflict with natural law, and may in practice bear on conduct even though theoretically in Grotius's scheme it is invalid to the extent of the inconsistency.[109]

In Grotius's scheme, law and morality are of major importance as normative systems. They are manifested to a significant extent in practice, but are not ultimately dependent on practice. They are causally relevant to the conduct and evaluative behaviour of individual actors. All of this is consistent with features of the Grotian tradition noted by Bull: the importance in international society of moral and legal restraints; the connection of international politics to arrangements of constitutional government; the recognition of both the existence and the complexity of moral problems.[110]

The extent to which Grotius had been influenced by Bacon and the kinds of ideas about to be popularised by Descartes is difficult to assess. Philip Allott argues that Grotius's relation to practice is that of an 'ironic empiricist', describing historical practice empirically, distilling norms from it faithfully, but aware that in purporting to describe reality he is also making it, and that in making it he should be guided by what is accessible to him through right reason. Whether or not Grotius had a methodological self-perception of this type, such readings of *JBP* have long been part of the Grotian tradition. The possibilities of the social construction of reality are bounded – by norms, history, facts, as well as the limits of concepts and imagination. The theorist unmindful of reality as society sees it contributes little, but the theorist is not simply in the business of detached description. The engagement with reality must be humble. As Wight suggested, Rationalists have a 'conception of politics as the field of the approximate and the provisional'.[111]

Bull ascribed much of Grotius's influence on both thought and action to his combination of visionary ideas and practical engagement, including a willingness to give 'some play to the interests that were predominant in seventeenth-century Europe even while condemning others'.[112] Wight and Bull both exhibited a sustained interest in the thought of practitioners of international relations: Wight's list of 'Grotians' thus included Burke, Gladstone, F. D. Roosevelt and Churchill. Bull's writings point to careful thought with regard to his own position on the complex connections between theory and practice. Linklater rightly if somewhat too simply summarises this position as a middle ground, refuting the scepticism of realism about the possibility or importance of norms as causes of practical change, conscious of the importance of norms in maintaining and deepening international society, but sceptical of revolutionist or critical proposals that theorists should themselves be committed to the realisation of liberation through the power of theory to effect transformation.[113]

In his understanding of the relations between practice and theoretical inquiry in international relations, Bull, like Wight, adhered for the most part to a Grotian position. The system of the three traditions can itself be understood as a tradition of enquiry in the sense outlined by Alasdair MacIntyre: 'a coherent movement of thought ... in the course of which those engaging in that movement become aware of it and its direction and in self-aware fashion attempt to engage in its debates and to carry its enquiries forward'.[114] The trialectic is itself a kind of Grotian solution by Wight, carried forward by Bull, to the theory practice/problem – a reproduction of the relations between a society and a practice of thinking about, and social criticism in, that society.[115] The method of the trialectic is itself a Grotian method – adherents of the trialectic method see themselves as both standing outside the three traditions and as themselves having a standpoint and hence being open to analysis by the same method. In Linklater's terms, they recognise that reality must be theorised (in this case by using a trialogue), and that the theory of competing conceptions is itself part of the practice, but purport mainly to discuss what is, and only occasionally to venture remarks on what ought to be, what the ideas of an improved practice of international relations should consist of. As Grotius seems to have recognised, the choice of method must itself be a normative choice. Bull stated his choice: 'I believe in the value of attempting to be detached or disinterested, and it is clear to me that some approaches to the study of world politics are more detached or disinterested than others. I also believe that inquiry has its own morality.'[116] The higher value of adherence to these criteria, combined with inability to ground law and morality in international relations on any basis other than consent or consensus, led Bull to depart from Grotius on two of the most fundamental aspects of Grotius's thought.

For Grotius and for Bull, the great problem of theory and of practice is controlling the constant menace of war. Hobbes has much in common with Grotius: although Grotius holds a somewhat more positive view of human nature resulting from its social element, he does not accept Hobbes's war of all against all, and he sees possibilities for amelioration of war through law and morality.[117] Hobbes's statement of the problems of human nature, authority, and war is starker, and the implications for international relations are bleak.[118] For Bull, as for many other theorists, Grotius has much to offer, but in the pluralist modern world theories of law and morality as normative constraints threaten to get dangerously ahead of the greatest practical problem of international relations, which is to cope with and eventually to move beyond the world according to Hobbes. The method of inquiry, the engagement with practice, the possibilities of amelioration, may all be 'Grotian', but in this Western theory Hobbes poses the single greatest problem.

## NOTES

1. Special thanks to Philip Allott, Ian Clark, Andrew Hurrell, Lewis Kornhauser, and Liam Murphy for helpful discussions of ideas in this chapter.
2. John Vincent's principal work dealing specifically with Grotius – undertaken with characteristic generosity of spirit to help bring to completion a project initiated by Hedley Bull – is 'Grotius, Human Rights, and Intervention', in H. Bull, B. Kingsbury, and A. Roberts (eds), *Hugo Grotius and International Relations* (Oxford: Oxford University Press, 1990), p. 241.
3. The approach is elegantly employed in 'Western Values in International Relations', in Herbert Butterfield and Martin Wight (eds), *Diplomatic Investigations* (London: George Allen & Unwin, 1966), p. 89. The most wide-ranging use of these approaches is Martin Wight, *International Theory: The Three Traditions* (a manuscript based principally on influential lectures given in the 1950s, edited by Gabriele Wight and Brian Porter and published in 1991, 19 years after the author's death, by Leicester University Press). See also Martin Wight, 'An Anatomy of International Thought',.

*Review of International Studies* 13 (1987), p. 222. Wight acknowledged the artificiality of approaches based on traditions and their interplay – see e.g. 'Western Values in International Relations', p. 90 – but he was disposed more to experiment with sub-traditions or alternative traditions than to question the basic approach.

4. Bull, 'The Grotian Conception of International Society', in Herbert Butterfield and Martin Wight (eds), *Diplomatic Investigations*, p. 51; Bull, *The Anarchical Society: A Study of Order in World Politics* (London: Macmillan, 1977), esp. ch. 2; Bull, 'The Importance of Grotius in the Study of International Relations', in *Hugo Grotius and International Relations*, p. 65. For Bull's comments on Martin Wight's use of traditions of thought, see 'Martin Wight and the Theory of International Relations', *British Journal of International Studies* 2 (1976), p. 101.

5. The renewal of international legal interest in Grotius from about the middle of the nineteenth century is exemplified by the treatment of Grotius in Henry Wheaton, *History of the Law of Nations in Europe and America* (New York: Gould, Banks & Co, 1845); Baron Carl Kaltenborn von Stachau, *Die Vorläufer des Hugo Grotius auf dem Gebiete des Ius naturae et Gentium sowie der Politik im Reformationszeitalter* (Leipzig: G. Mayer, 1848); Pradier-Fodéré's French translation of *De Jure Belli ac Pacis* (3 vols, Paris, 1865–7); the obeisances paid to Grotius in conjunction with the 1899 Hague peace conference, as to which see e.g. the introduction to A. C. Campbell's 1901 English translation of *De Jure Belli ac Pacis* (Washington: M. W. Dunne, 1901); Jules Basdevant, 'Hugo Grotius', in A. Pillet (ed.), *Les fondateurs du droit international* (Paris: V. Giard and L. Brière, 1904); Lassa Oppenheim, *International Law*, vol. 1 (London: Longman, 1905); the Carnegie Endowment's reprint of the 1646 edition of *De Jure Belli ac Pacis* in 1913; and the deluge of material published around the time of the tercentenary of *De Jure Belli ac Pacis* in 1925.

6. Cornelis van Vollenhoven, 'Grotius and Geneva', *Bibliotheca Visseriana* 6 (1926), p. 1; 'The Framework of Grotius' Book De Jure Belli ac Pacis (1625)', *Verhandelingen der Koninklijke Akademie van Wetenschappen*, Afd. Letterkunde, 30 (1931); 'Grotius and the Study of Law', *American Journal of International Law* 19 (1925), p. 1; 'Het Theorema van Grotius', in *Verspreide Geschriften* vol. 1 (The Hauge: Martinus Nijhoff, 1934), pp. 461–8; Hersch Lauterpacht, 'The Grotian Tradition in International Law', *British Year Book of International Law 1946*, p. 1.

7. Jacob Ter Meulen and P. J. J. Diermanse, *Bibliographie des écrits imprimés de Hugo Grotius* (The Hague: Martinus Nijhoff, 1950).

8. Roelofsen, 'Grotius and the International Politics of the Seventeenth Century', in *Hugo Grotius and International Relations* (1990), pp. 109–12. Elements in the VOC encouraged publication of *Mare Liberum*, although Grotius's text also provided a basis for arguments inconsistent with the VOC's interest in establishing monopolies in the East Indies.

9. The eminent Dutch historian Robert Fruin suggested that Grotius had acted as advocate in the proceedings before the Prize Court. 'An Unpublished Work of Hugo Grotius's', *Bibliotheca Visseriana* 5 (1925), p. 1. Later scholars have found the evidence for this insufficient and unconvincing, leaving the exact reasons for the writing of *De Jure Praedae* unclear. See

e.g. W. J. M. van Eysinga, 'Mare Liberum et De Jure Praedae', in *Sparsa Collecta: een aantal der verspreide geschriften* (Leiden: Sijthoff, 1958), p. 324; and C. G. Roelofsen, 'Grotius and the International Politics of the Seventeenth Century', p. 104, n. 41. *Mare Liberum* proved to be a chapter from *De Jure Praedae*.

10. Quentin Skinner, *The Foundations of Modern Political Thought*, 2 vols (Cambridge: Cambridge University Press, 1978), esp. vol. 1, pp. x–xv; Skinner, 'Meaning and Understanding in the History of Ideas', *History and Theory* 8 (1969), p. 3; Pocock, 'The History of Political Thought: A Methodological Enquiry', in Peter Laslett and W. G. Runciman (eds), *Politics, Philosophy and Society*, 2nd series (Oxford: Blackwell, 1962), p. 183.

11. 'Political Theory, History, and Myth: A Salute to John Gunnell' (1980), repr. in John S. Nelson (ed.), *Tradition, Interpretation, and Science: Political Theory in the American Academy* (Albany, NY: SUNY Press, 1986), pp. 21–42, p. 29 and p. 27. Pocock was here endorsing the argument in chapter 3 of John Gunnell, *Political Theory: Tradition and Interpretation* (Cambridge, MA: Winthrop, 1979).

12. Pocock, 'Political Theory, History, and Myth', p. 39.

13. Transposing Pocock's remark about Machiavelli. 'Machiavelli in the Liberal Cosmos', *Political Theory* 13 (1985), p. 559.

14. Much important scholarly work on Grotius is not discussed because it does not relate directly to the lines of argument pursued in this chapter. Above all, nothing is said about recent scholarly editions of various of Grotius's works and correspondence, the most notable of which for present purposes is the invaluable reprint (Aalen: Scientia Verlag, 1993) of the 1939 *editio maior* of *JBP* (B. J. A. De Kanter-Van Hettinga Tromp), a variorum edition based (in accordance with Van Vollenhoven's views of Grotius's thought) on the 1631 edition. The 1993 edition includes (pp. 919–1074) an important set of additional notes, prepared by R. Feenstra and C. E. Persenaire, concerning in particular verification of several categories of sources used by Grotius and their connection to the text.

15. *Grotius et la doctrine de la guerre juste* (Geneva: PUF, 1983).

16. Standard accounts of international law have gradually internalised enough history to abandon descriptions of Grotius as the 'father of international law'. See e.g. Maurice Bourquin, 'Grotius est-il le père du droit des gens?', in *Grandes figures et grandes oeuvres juridiques* (Geneva: Georg, 1948); Wilhelm Grewe, 'Grotius – Vater des Völkerrechts?', *Der Staat* 23 (1984), p. 176. Cf. Karl-Heinz Ziegler, 'Hugo Grotius als "Vater des Völkerrechts"', in Peter Selmer and Ingo von Münch (eds), *Gedächtnisschrift für Wolfgang Martens* (Berlin: Walter de Gruyter, 1987), pp. 851–0. However, the view that *JBP* is a preeminent work of international law retains wide currency. Lauterpacht expressed the totemic view of generations of international lawyers that the most important theme of *JBP* was the subjection of the totality of international relations to the rule of law. 'The Grotian Tradition in International Law', p. 19.

17. Roelofsen, 'Grotius and the International Politics of the Seventeenth Century', focuses particularly on the political context and its relationship to Grotius's ideas. A useful recent biographical outline is Henk Nellen, *Hugo*

*de Groot (1583–1645): De loopbarn van een geleerd staatsman* (Weesp: Uitgeverij Heureka, 1985). Roelofsen has advocated 'a reappraisal of Bull's "Grotian system" ... by an analysis of the workings of the European system in the first half of the seventeenth century as perceived by Grotius'. 'Grotius and the "Grotian Heritage" in International Law and International Relations: The Quatercentenary and its Aftermath (circa 1980–1990)', *Grotiana* (New Series) 11 (1990), p. 19. Bull had in fact moved some way in this direction, with a full but unpublished lecture series on the Peace of Westphalia and unpublished work on the Thirty Years War.

18. *Philosophy and Government 1572–1651* (Cambridge: Cambridge University Press, 1993); Tuck, 'The "Modern" Theory of Natural Law', in Anthony Pagden (ed.), *The Languages of Political Theory in Early Modern Europe* (Cambridge: Cambridge University Press, 1987), p. 99; Tuck, *Hobbes* (Oxford: Oxford University Press, 1989). Tuck, *Natural Rights Theories: Their Origin and Development* (Cambridge: Cambridge University Press, 1979) attributes to Grotius a significant place in the development of such theories.

19. The question how to treat the 'Grotian heritage' was a theme of numerous internationally minded authors in conjunction with the 1925 and 1983 anniversaries. See e.g. Cornelis Van Vollenhoven, 'Grotius and Geneva', *Bibliotheca Visseriana* 6 (1926), p. 1; P. H. Kooijmans, 'How to Handle the Grotian Heritage: Grotius and Van Vollenhoven', *Netherlands International Law Review* 30 (1983), p. 81. One of several recurrent patterns of use of the Grotian heritage is illustrated by C. D. Ehlermann's analogy between the evolution of EC policy after 1970 and the evolution of Grotius's own views on freedom of fishing. 'Grotius and the European Community's Common Fisheries Policy', in T. M. C. Asser Instituut (ed.), *International Law and the Grotian Heritage* (The Hague: T. M. C. Asser Instituut, 1985) p. 294.

20. Haggenmacher, 'On Assessing the Grotian Heritage', in *International Law and the Grotian Heritage*, pp. 150–1.

21. Falk, 'Introduction: The Grotian Quest', in Charles Edwards, *Hugo Grotius: The Miracle of Holland* (Chicago: Nelson-Hall, 1981), p. xiii; Boutros Ghali, 'A Grotian Moment', *Fordham International Law Journal* 18 (1995), p. 1609 (asserting *en passant* that Grotius is 'the father of international law').

22. Tuck indicates in passing that he believes the basic structure of modern politics was in place by 1651 (the publication of *Leviathan*), and that the 'description of modern politics we find both in the *ragion di stato* writers and in Grotius and Hobbes, with standing armies paid for out of taxation, with self-protective and potentially expansionist states, and with citizens very unsure of the moral principles they should live by, looks like an accurate description of a world still recognizable to us.' *Philosophy and Government*, p. 348. But his commitment is to placing Grotius in the close intellectual context of his time. Roelofsen cautions that 'the search for historical analogies is not always easy ... and is sometimes better omitted'. 'Grotius and the "Grotian Heritage"', p. 13. Haggenmacher's views are discussed below.

23. *JBP*, I.x.1. This is discussed further in the next section.

24. In Roelofsen's opinion, 'to Grotius' contemporaries, the idea in itself of the rule of law in international relations can hardly have come as a surprise... it is the general respect paid to legal considerations that strikes the modern

observer of early seventeenth-century state practice'. 'Grotius and the International Politics of the Seventeenth Century', pp. 123–4.

25. *JBP*, Proleg. 58. Haggenmacher points out that the Kelsey translation of 'mathematici' as 'mathematicians' is wrong. 'On Assessing the Grotian Heritage', p. 152 n. 8.

26. See Tadashi Tanaka, 'Grotius's Method: With Special Reference to Prolegomena', in Yasuaki Onuma (ed.), *A Normative Approach to War: Peace, War, and Justice in Hugo Grotius* (Oxford: Oxford University Press, 1993), pp. 11–29.

27. On Kantian approaches, see e.g. Philip Allott, *Eunomia: New Order for a New World* (Oxford: Oxford University Press, 1990); Richard Ashley, 'The Powers of Anarchy: Theory, Sovereignty, and the Domestication of Global Life', in James Der Derian (ed.), *International Theory: Critical Investigations* (New York: New York University Press, 1995), p. 94.

28. For a comparable approach, see Haggenmacher, 'On Assessing the Grotian Heritage'.

29. *Grotius et la doctrine de la guerre juste*, p. 622 and p. 616 n. 11.

30. A letter from Grotius to his brother in April 1643 comments on *De Cive*. The letter is printed in Grotius's *Epistolae quotquot reperiri potuerunt* (Amsterdam, 1687), pp. 951–2, and in vol. 14 of the definitive edition of Grotius's *Briefwisseling* (The Hague, 1993).

31. *JBP*, Proleg. 1: 'ius illud, quod inter populos plures aut populorum rectores intercedit, sive ab ipsa natura profectum, aut divinis constitutum legibus sive moribus et pacto tacito'. The reference to divine ordinances in this passage does not appear in the 1625 text, but was inserted by Grotius in the 1631 edition, a fact treated by both Tuck and Haggenmacher as evidence that such ordinances were referred to only as an afterthought in Grotius's formulation of his scheme.

32. *Grotius et la doctrine de la guerre juste*, pp. 448–57.

33. This is the sense of *JBP*, I.i.1.

34. This discussion of legal concepts follows Haggenmacher, *Grotius et la doctrine de la guerre juste*, passim; the succinct recapitulation in Haggenmacher, 'On Assessing the Grotian Heritage'; and some points made in Onuma (ed.), *A Normative Approach to War: Peace, War, and Justice in Hugo Grotius*.

35. The basic catalogue of sources is laid out in Tadashi Tanaka, 'Grotius's Concept of Law', in *A Normative Approach to War*, pp. 38–56.

36. It is true, as Ian Harris suggests ('Order and Justice in *The Anarchical Society*', *International Affairs* 69 (1993), p. 734), that Grotius's primary focus was on laws of nature and concurrent rights, and that he pointed out that *jus gentium* varied from place to place and cast doubt on the importance of general agreement going beyond the law of nature, but he does in fact use *jus gentium* as a basis for legal opinions in a large number of specific instances. There is on this point (as on several others) some difference between his system as expounded in the abstract, and his actual application of it in matters of legal doctrine.

37. Fritz Münch, 'Staat und Völkerrecht: Zur Terminologie bei Grotius', in *Staat und Völkerrechtsordnung: Festschrift für Karl Doehring* (Berlin: Springer-Verlag, 1989), p. 625.

38. *JBP*, I.iii.7.
39. Haggenmacher, *Grotius et la doctrine de la guerre juste*, pp. 539–46. On Grotius's use of such concepts as imperium, dominium civile, and dominium privatum, and the absence of the systematic modern distinction between public authority and private right, see Masaharu Yanagihara, '*Dominium* and *Imperium*', in Onuma (ed.), *A Normative Approach to War*, pp. 169–72.
40. In *Mare Liberum*, ch. 1., Grotius argues: 'Every nation is free to travel to every other nation, and to trade with it'. The reference is to 'gentes', which does not necessarily signify 'states' *in abstracto*, and in any event this assertion of equality of rights is exceptional in Grotius's writing on international matters. See generally E. D. Dickinson, *The Equality of States in International Law* (Cambridge, MA: Harvard University Press, 1920), pp. 34–67; and Haggenmacher, 'On Assessing The Grotian Heritage', p. 155.
41. See *The Anarchical Society*, pp. 28–33, a work not cited in Haggenmacher's *magnum opus*. In 'The Importance of Grotius in the Study of International Relations', Bull, preoccupied with a broader set of concerns about universality, the place of individuals and non-state groups, the role of natural law, does casually suggest (p. 74, presumably following Lauterpacht) that Grotius aimed to systematise the whole of the law of war and peace, but this passage is unrepresentative.
42. 'The Grotian Conception of International Society', p. 66.
43. Cf. the approach of Roelofsen, 'Grotius and the International Politics of the Seventeenth Century', p. 125.
44. Cf. Onuma (ed.), *A Normative Approach to War*, p. 7; and Edwin D. Dickinson, 'Changing Concepts and the Doctrine of Incorporation', *American Journal of International Law* 26 (1932), p. 239.
45. Both acknowledged some exceptions. Wight famously lamented that 'when diplomacy acquires a certain habit of co-operation, international law crawls in the mud of legal positivism'. 'Why Is There No International Theory?', in *Diplomatic Investigations*, p. 29. Bull noted that 'in the writings of late nineteenth-century positivist international lawyers the elements of a Realist outlook are sometimes strong.' 'Hans Kelsen and International Law', in Richard Tur and William Twining (eds), *Essays on Kelsen* (Oxford: Oxford University Press, 1986), p. 323.
46. On uses of *jus* in *JBP* and other works of Grotius, see Tanaka, 'Grotius's Concept of Law', pp. 32–7; and Haggenmacher, *Grotius et la doctrine de la guerre juste*, pp. 61–2 and 462–70.
47. See e.g. Knud Haakonsen, 'Hugo Grotius and the History of Political Thought', *Political Theory* 13 (1985), p. 239.
48. Tuck, *Natural Rights Theories*.
49. *JBP* II.xii.16, II.xxiv.2, III.xiii.4. This element is stressed in Onuma (ed.), *A Normative Approach to War*, e.g. pp. 48–50, 296–7, 320–3.
50. E.g. *Parallelon rerumpublicarum liber tertius* (c. 1602) (4 vols, Haarlem, 1801–3); *De republica emendanda* (c. 1598–1600) (*Grotiana*, 1984).
51. E.g. *De imperio summarum potestatum circa sacra* (publ. 1647). See generally Tuck, *Philosophy and Government*, pp. 179–90.
52. E.g. *JBP*, I.iii. Rousseau, *The Social Contract*. Tuck, *Natural Rights Theories*, pp. 77–81. Lauterpacht, 'The Grotian Tradition in International

Law', provides a lengthy exegesis of the exceptions Grotius allows to the general prohibition on civil resistance.

53. Tuck, *Philosophy and Government*.
54. On the power of this image, see Michael Donelan, 'Grotius and the Image of War', *Millennium* 12 (1983), p. 223. Haggenmacher takes only mild literary licence in suggesting that in one sense Grotius always has the controversy about *The Catharine* in view. *Grotius et la doctrine de la guerre juste*, p. 619.
55. *JP*, chap. 2, Law XII: 'Neither the state nor any citizen thereof shall seek to enforce its own right against another state or its citizen, save by judicial procedure.'
56. *JBP*, Prolegomena 25, and *JBP*, II.i.2.
57. J. B. Schneewind, 'The Misfortunes of Virtue', *Ethics* 101:1 (October 1990), pp. 42–63.
58. 'Order in International Politics', in J. D. B. Miller and R. J. Vincent (eds), *Order and Violence: Hedley Bull and International Relations* (Oxford: Oxford University Press, 1990), p. 54.
59. Lassa Oppenheim, *International Law*, vol. 1 (London: Longman, 1905), pp. 58–93. This framework was also used by Wight – see *International Theory*, p. 14.
60. *The Anarchical Society*, pp. 127–61; Hart, *The Concept of Law* (Oxford: Oxford University Press, 1961).
61. *The Anarchical Society*, p. 159.
62. Ibid., ch. 6.
63. *International Theory*, p. 238.
64. *JP*, ch. 2.
65. See e.g. Lauterpacht, 'The Grotian Tradition in International Law', pp. 24–35.
66. Proleg. 3. The quotation from the Melian dialogue ('the more powerful do all they can, the more weak endure') was added by Grotius to the 1642 edition.
67. This theme is elaborated in Onuma (ed.), *A Normative Approach to War: Peace, War, and Justice in Hugo Grotius*, passim (see esp. p. 7).
68. Skinner, *Foundations of Modern Political Thought*; Maurizio Viroli, *From Politics to Reason of State* (Cambridge: Cambridge University Press, 1991). Tuck, *Philosophy and Government 1572–1651* (Cambridge: Cambridge University Press, 1993), traces influences of, and departures from, Machiavelli, and emphasises the break between Ciceronian and Tacitist patterns of thought in the second half of the sixteenth century.
69. 'The "Modern" Theory of Natural Law', pp. 114–15.
70. Proleg. 5. Some modern writers have treated Carneades as simply speaking here for reason of state'. See e.g. G. I. A. D. Draper, 'Grotius' Place in the Development of Legal Ideas About War', in *Hugo Grotius and International Relations*, p. 200.
71. 'The "Modern" Theory of Natural Law', p. 109. In Montaigne's celebrated encapsulation: 'what truth is that, which these mountains bound, and is a lie in the world beyond?'
72. Pufendorf's major works on natural law all make extensive reference to Grotius. However, his fullest explicit discussion of Grotius appears in 'De

origine et progressu disciplinae iuris naturalis' ('The Origin and Development of the Study of Natural Law'), which was included in his *Specimen controversiarum circa jus naturale ipsi nuper motarum* (1678) and in *Eris Scandica, qua adversus libros de iure naturali et gentium obiecta diluuntur* (1686), and to which Hont and Tuck draw attention. Carew's English translation of Barbeyrac's principal relevant essay, entitled 'An Historical and Critical Account of the Science of Morality', was printed as a preface to several editions of the Kennet translation of Pufendorf, *Of the Law of Nature and Nations* – see. e.g. the 4th edition (London: J. Walthoe *et al.* 1729), which is introduced by a translation of the second iteration of Barbeyrac's essay, pp. 1–88. Pufendorf and Barbeyrac both admired many elements of Grotius's thought, including his liberation from adherence to any one school of philosophy (i.e. his eclecticism). Barbeyrac explained such defects as remained in *JBP* by the fact that Grotius had largely to pioneer the subject himself. See Barbeyrac's essay, ss. 29 and 31.

73. See Barbeyrac, op. cit. (previous note). Various sceptical arguments of Montaigne and Charron are there considered and contested (see e.g. ss. 3 and 4).

74. *JBP*, I.i.10. *De Jure Naturae et Gentium*, II.iii.13.

75. *JBP*, I.i.12.

76. *Essays*, book II, ch. 12. The translation is taken from Carew's translation of Barbeyrac's essay, s. 4.

77. *JBP*, I.ii.1: 'the first principles of nature [are] the preservation of life and limb, and the keeping or acquiring of things useful to life.' Cf. the two first precepts of the law of nature in *JP*, ch. 2.

78. *Philosophy and Government*, p. 347.

79. The argument is most fully developed in Tuck, *Philosophy and Government 1572–1651* – the assessments are made explicitly at pp. xv–xvii and 347–8. Also important is Tuck, 'The "Modern" Theory of Natural Law', in A. Pagden (ed.), *The Languages of Political Theory in Early Modern Europe* (Cambridge: Cambridge University Press, 1987), p. 99.

80. Elements of Tuck's thesis are undoubtedly controversial. Note e.g. Istvan Hont's more general comment: 'The sharp break attributed to Grotius in the history of natural law, such a prominent feature of [Adam] Smith's account both in *The Theory of Moral Sentiments* and in the lectures on jurisprudence, can be regarded as essentially an "invention" of Pufendorf'. 'The Language of Sociability and Commerce: Samuel Pufendorf and the Theoretical Foundations of the "Four-Stages Theory"', in *The Languages of Political Theory in Early Modern Europe*, p. 258.

81. *The Anarchical Society*, p. 322 n. 3.

82. 'The Grotian Conception of International Society'.

83. Ibid., esp. pp. 54–64; *The Anarchical Society*, pp. 238–40.

84. 'The Grotian conception of International Society', pp. 66–7; *The Anarchical Society*, pp. 148–9 and 156–8.

85. As Haggenmacher puts it, Grotius is 'fully aware of the importance of independent nations and their sovereigns in international life.... However, his ultimate frame of reference remains the Ciceronian *humani generis societas* inherited from Stoicism ... a society of mankind rather than of states.'

'Grotius and Gentili: A Reassessment of Thomas Holland's Inaugural Lecture', in *Hugo Grotius and International Relations*, p. 172.

86.  'The Importance of Grotius in the Study of International Relations'; 'The Grotian Conception of International Society'.

87.  See esp. *JBP*, II.xxii–II.xxv. Cf. *JBP*, III.xff (the *Temperamenta belli*) – much of *JBP* Book III is concerned with the mitigation of war and the attainment of viable and enduring peace, which can be construed as solidarist objectives but are not necessarily based strictly on enforcement of law. On the incomplete nature of Grotius's attempts to reconcile the tradition of the just war with the imperative to regulate war (*guerre juste* and *guerre régulière*), see Peter Haggenmacher, 'Mutations du concept de *guerre juste* de Grotius à Kant', in *La Guerre* (Cahiers de Philosophie politique et juridique, No. 10, Université de Caen, 1986), p. 107.

88.  *JBP*, II.xxv, which (like other aspects of *JBP*) owes a lot to Gentili, *De Jure Belli* – see esp. Book I, ch. 16.

89.  *JBP*, II.xxff. Van Vollenhoven ('Het Theorema van Grotius') made a great deal of *JBP*, II.xx.40, on the rights of kings, etc. to demand punishment 'on account of injuries which do not directly affect them but excessively violate the law of nature or of nations in regard to any persons whatsoever'. See, however, Haggenmacher, 'Sur un passage obscur de Grotius: Essai de réponse à Cornelis van Vollenhoven', *Tijdschrift voor Rechtsgeschiedenis* 51 (1983), p. 295.

90.  Ian Harris, 'Order and Justice in *The Anarchical Society*', *International Affairs* 69 (1993), p. 725.

91.  'The West and South Africa'. *Daedalus* 111 (Spring 1982), p. 255; 'The Universality of Human Rights', *Millennium* 8 (1979); 'Natural Law and International Relations', *British Journal of International Studies* 5 (1979), p. 171; 'Recapturing the Just War for Political Theory', *World Politics* 31 (1979), p. 588. The last is of particular interest as Bull in effect criticises Michael Walzer's *Just and Unjust Wars* for failure to find a Grotian *via media* between individualist and collectivist theories of obligation, or between absolutist and relativist conceptions of morality in war.

92.  Haakonsen, 'Hugo Grotius and the History of Political Thought'.

93.  See generally Bernard Williams, *Ethics and the Limits of Philosophy* (Oxford: Oxford University Press, 1985); Terry Nardin and David Mapel (eds), *Traditions of International Ethics* (Cambridge: Cambridge University Press, 1992).

94.  Tuck, *Philosophy and Government*, p. 306.

95.  Cf. A. Claire Cutler, 'The "Grotian Tradition" in International Relations', *Review of International Studies* 17 (1991), pp. 56–8. See generally Terry Nardin, *Law, Morality, and the Relations of States* (Princeton, NJ: Princeton University Press, 1983).

96.  Hont, 'The Language of Sociability and Commerce', p. 259, referring to a letter of Pufendorf to Baron Boineburg of 13 Jan. 1663, discussed in Fiametta Palladini, 'Le due letteri di Pufendorf al Barone do Boineburg: quella nota e quella "perduta"', *Nouvelles de la République des Lettres*, I (1984), p. 134.

97.  *De Jure Naturae et Gentium*, II.iii.7 (quotation) through to II.iii.12.

98. Andrew Linklater, *Beyond Realism and Marxism: Critical Theory and International Relations* (New York: St. Martin's Press, 1990), ch. 1.

99. *Morals by Agreement* (Oxford: Oxford University Press, 1986).

100. 'Western Values in International Relations', p. 128.

101. Cf Bull, *Justice and International Relations* (Hagey Lectures, University of Waterloo, 1984).

102. *The Anarchical Society*, p. 315 and p. 316. Hedley Bull and Adam Watson (eds), *The Expansion of International Society* (Oxford: Oxford University Press, 1984), was concerned in part with the historical basis and future prospects of an expanded international society.

103. See Franco Todescan, *Le radici teologiche del giusnaturalismo laico*, vol. I, *Il problema della secolarizzazione nel pensiero giuridico di Ugo Grozio* (Milan: Giuffrè, 1983), comparing Grotius's historical theory of private property to the theology of innocence, the Fall, and the attainment of grace.

104. See e.g. David Kennedy, 'Images of Religion in International Legal History', in Mark Janis (ed.), *The Influence of Religion on the Development of International Law* (Dordrecht: Martinus Nijhoff, 1991).

105. See e.g. *JBP*, II.xx.44.

106. See e.g. *JBP*, Proleg. 42, endorsing the position of the early Christians 'that there was no philosophic sect whose vision had compassed all truth, and none which had not perceived some aspect of the truth'.

107. See e.g. Tuck, *Philosophy and Government*, p. 185. For a remarkable application of Grotius's consensus-based method in his call for transcending sectarian philosophical disputes within Christianity, see *Meletius* (c. 1611) (critical edition by G. H. M. Posthumus Meyjes, Leiden, 1988).

108. In *JP* (ch. 2) Grotius had stated as the first rule: 'What God has shown to be His Will, that is law.' The law of nature is the Will of God revealed through his design. In *JBP* (I.i.10), however, he asserted that the law of nature 'is unchangeable – even in the sense that it cannot be changed by God.' Tuck, *Philosophy and Government*, pp. 172–98, attributes this change primarily to shifts in Grotius's views about the connections between God and nature brought about by his experiences in politico-theological controversies. Haggenmacher, *Grotius et la doctrine de la guerre juste*, pp. 426–523, lays greater emphasis on several centuries of intellectual antecedents for the position taken by Grotius in *JBP*. Both observe that the famous 'etiamsi daremus non esse Deum' hypothesis was helpful in opening the law of nature to rational/scientific analysis. Tuck notes also (p. 198) that there must be an independent route to knowledge for an atheist to follow, not least in order to convert. The shift away from the voluntarism of *JP* did not have a significant impact on Grotius' views as to the *content* of natural law. See also two helpful discussions by Alfred Dufour, *Le mariage dans l'école allemande du droit naturel moderne au XVIIIe siècle* (Paris: LGDJ, 1972), and 'Grotius et le droit naturel du dix-septième siècle', in *The World of Hugo Grotius* (Amsterdam: Maarssen, 1984), pp. 15–41.

109. Tanaka, 'Grotius's Concept of Law', p. 36.

110. 'Martin Wight and the Theory of International Relations', pp. 105–7.

111. *International Theory*, p. 242.

112. 'The Importance of Grotius in the Study of International Relations', p. 93.

113. Andrew Linklater, *Beyond Realism and Marxism* (New York: St. Martin's Press, 1990), esp. p. 21. Linklater argues that Bull's work, in the last few years of his life, on justice as a value standing alongside order, manifested both a commitment to community and a bridging of the gap to the concerns of revolutionist or critical theorists. To Bull this might have seemed a characteristic revolutionist position, denying the possibility of the kind of value-laden self-inquiring detachment Bull always espoused, in order to forge an alliance the better to promote engagement and change.

114. Alasdair MacIntyre, *Whose Justice? Which Rationality?* (Notre Dame, Indiana: University of Notre Dame Press, 1988), p. 326.

115. Cf. the views on international law expressed by David Kennedy, 'A New Stream of International Law Scholarship', *Wisconsin International Law Journal* 7 (1988), p. 1, esp. pp. 7–10; and the discussion of the 'heroic practice' of sovereignty and anarchy in contemporary international relations theory by Richard Ashley, 'The Powers of Anarchy: Theory, Sovereignty, and the Domestication of Global Life'.

116. *The Anarchical Society*, p. xv. That these criteria were intended as evaluative – of himself and others – in connecting theory and practice, is illustrated by the ferocity and personalisation of his criticism of Richard Falk's turn 'from analysis to advocacy – advocacy of international betterment in the tradition of the study of international relations as it was in the 1920s. The task of the academic inquirer is not to jump on bandwagons but to stand back and assess, in a disinterested way, the direction in which they are going. Any writer can join a political movement and devote his intellectual talents to supplying the rhetoric, the exaggeration, the denunciation and the slurring of issues that will help speed it on its way. It does not seem the best use for the talents of the Albert C. Milbank Professor of International Law.' 'International Law and International Order', *International Organization* 26 (1972), p. 583, p. 588.

117. Letter to his brother, April 1643, op. cit.

118. Cf., however, Friedrich Kratochwil, *Rules, Norms and Decisions: On the Conditions of Practical Reasoning in International Relations and Domestic Affairs* (Cambridge: Cambridge University Press, 1989), esp. pp. 1–20.

# 4 Kant: Theorist beyond Limits

## Howard Williams and Ken Booth

Kant's reputation in world philosophy is secure; in the study of world politics it is still being made. For decades Kant's work was marginal and marginalised in academic international relations, though he has a justifiable claim to be the first comprehensive theorist of world politics. Kant has something to say, *inter alia*, about justice, international government, domestic politics and interstate relations, war and peace – and other priority issues on the international relations agenda. He also makes a fundamental contribution to our thinking about ontology and epistemology. If for nothing else he is a key figure because he was the first political philosopher of significance to emphasise the primacy of the international in understanding politics.

## KANT AND 'KANTIANS'

The theme of this chapter is that Kant is a philosopher whose ideas transcend the conventional limits of political and international theory and whose political hopes far exceed what has been considered practically possible by the exponents and observers of statecraft. His intellectual project challenges (and some would say overthrows) mainstream theory at nearly every barricade. Despite describing Kant in this way, we think that Martin Wight did not serve Kant well, or generations of international relations students, when he annointed Kant as intellectual figurehead of what he labelled the 'Revolutionist' tradition.[1]

While Wight writes pithily and with understanding about Kant, it will come as a surprise to those who know Wight's published work only through the descriptions of others that he did not actually say much about Kant.[2] Wight had somewhat more to say about the 'Kantians' and the 'Revolutionists' – alternative names for the 'Kantian tradition' – but Kant and the Kantians/Revolutionists are not the same thing. Wight gives warnings about reifying the traditions he identifies, and about the need to distinguish Kant from what he (Wight) described as Kantian.[3] If he believed that, it was unhelpful if not downright contrary to confuse the already complex by then insisting on making Kant the eponymous head of the re-volutionist tradition. It would be difficult to reconstruct Kant's interna-tional political theorising from Wight's account of the 'Kantian tradition', whose members (according to Wight) include, at best, Woodrow Wilson, John Foster Dulles and possibly Khrushchev, and at worst, Hitler, Verwoerd and Stalin.[4] As a result of Wight's influence as teacher and writer, Kant's work sorely needs rescuing from the image of some of Wight's 'Kantians'. However, it is to Wight's credit that he was the first modern theorist of international relations to take Kant's work seriously.[5]

Wight's labelling did Kant two further disservices. First 'Revolutionist' has connotations of violence,[6] which go entirely against the spirit of Kant's own work – a point hardly mitigated by Wight's description of Kant as an 'evolutionary' rather than revolutionary Kantian within the Revolutionist tradition. Second, Wight gives Kant's name prominence, but his published work does little to promote the idea that his work should be required reading for students. Consciously or not, Wight plays the typical English trick of putting Kant at one extreme of the spectrum in order to privilege the middle – what has become known as the 'English School'. Wight was a founder. Furthermore, in keeping with the professional norms of the Cold War, Wight – probably unintentionally – effectively ruled Kant out of serious academic international relations discourse by identify-ing him as an impractical idealist. Following E. H. Carr's critique of 'utopianism' in *The 20 Years' Crisis*,[7] first published in 1939, the 'utopian'/'idealist' label had become a professional kiss of death. Under the hegemonial realist outlook in the subject in the aftermath of Nazism and during the Cold War, there was no serious space in the developing dis-cipline for the German philosopher of perpetual peace.

The first close textual analysis of Kant in the Anglo-American strong-holds of academic international relations was F. H. Hinsley's analysis of Kant's *Perpetual Peace* in his book *Power and the Pursuit of Peace* pub-lished in 1963.[8] But Hinsley's book was more admired than read. Fifteen years later, another Cambridge scholar, W. B. Gallie, took over the task of explaining the originality and uniqueness of Kant's work in a lively essay in *Philosophers of Peace and War*.[9] Kant nevertheless remained a rather marginal figure in international political theory, which itself during these decades was a sub-field of limited attraction to many students. Unexpectedly, the seeds planted by Hinsley and Gallie began to sprout in the unlikely conditions of the 'new Cold War' at the start of the 1980s. Michael Doyle wrote about the relationship between liberal democracy and peace, a major theme of Kant's.[10] This raised the profile of Kant's work. Other factors were the decline in the hegemonial position of realism, the growing attention given to the normative traditions of international relations following a 'forty-year detour',[11] and the breaking out from decades of self-referential international relations theorising. As a result, Kant's philosophy began to be nudged towards the centre of the discipline. A further stage was reached with the liberal triumphalism at the end of the 1980s, with the collapse of the Soviet Union and the 'victory' of Western democracy and capitalism. World politics in important respects seemed to be moving in a 'Kantian' direction. Kant's name could now even be sometimes found in the press;[12] he became an obligatory figure in international political theory courses, and his writing became a staple item in books of readings of classical political texts.[13] As the 200th anniversary of the first publication of *Perpetual Peace* drew close (1995), the work for which Kant is best known in international relations, his reputation among scholars in world politics was finally beginning to match the originality and importance of his contribution.


## THE FOUNDATIONS OF KNOWLEDGE

Kant's importance to international relations scholars begins with his discussion of the nature of knowledge. This is relevant to the subject of international relations as it exists in a continuous condition of methodological upheaval. There is no widespread agreement among those who study the subject as to which might be the best approach in accounting for and influencing the phenomena of world politics. We believe that Kant's philosophy is helpful in this respect.

In his *Critique of Pure Reason*, where Kant deals with fundamental epistemological problems, he distinguishes between our knowledge of things in so far as we perceive them through our senses and understanding, and our knowledge of things as they might exist independently of our faculties. Empiricists like John Locke and David Hume take the latter to be the true model of knowledge. Kant calls the first knowledge of phenomena or appearances and the second he calls knowledge of noumena or transcendent experience. The latter are things-in-themselves as they would be known by a mind entirely unaffected by the limitations of human knowing. Transcendent 'experience' is strangely, as Kant sees it, a misnomer since he believes that we cannot possibly know things as they would exist independently of our perception of them. We must postulate them without knowing them. The only kind of knowledge we can have of the objective world of appearances we are confronted by is the phenomenal kind, and is necessarily humanly limited. This is a world already structured in our perception and understanding by categories such as 'cause and effect'. The implications for international relations of Kant's epistemology concern the use international relations scholars make of empirical knowledge and the standing of normative theory in the discipline.

In Kant's mind there has always to be doubt about the independence and reality of our knowledge (and he includes here also our scientific knowledge). Scientific knowledge is not knowledge of things as they are in themselves. It is knowledge of things as we observe them. He thinks we have to curtail our use of reason in relation to the empirically observed world, because it would be wrong to assume the world is arranged entirely accordingly to the demands of our reason. We cannot expect the external world to have the finality and completeness reason demands. At an epistemological level then Kant would argue that international relations theory can explain the world only so long as it assumes that international relations are governed by the limited categories of the human understanding. Treating international relations as a phenomenon (the first kind of knowledge) leads to an explanation based upon the notion of causality. Phenomena can be comprehended only within a framework of necessary laws. We should have to assume that states' leaders and diplomats were wholly determined in their actions. We should, in other words, have to assume they have no choice other than to act in the way they do. This is one possible way of accounting for international relations but it is not an entirely satisfactory one. It would be international relations without dilemmas and choices.

Kant would argue that such a view taken on its own, although interesting and informative, would be based upon an impoverished and one-sided conception of human action. In Kant's view, we should not look at human affairs solely from a phenomenal standpoint. We should also look at them from the intellectual or noumenal point of view. Traditionally social science has privileged positive empirical studies over normative enquiry. International relations on the whole has followed this pattern of sidelining ethical issues. This is a privileging Kant would reverse. On the grounds of knowledge and impact he would place normative studies before empirical studies without denying that empirical studies have a value of their own. Paradoxically, in one sphere Kant does not think that reason has to be epistemologically hemmed in. This is in the practical, or, in Kant's words, the moral sphere. Through the use of moral concepts we are capable of ordering our experience in accord with rational principles. Rationality may enter into the intersubjective world (of which international relations is a part) through ensuring that our wills are governed by the principles of good behaviour. It is within this second normative sphere that Kant thinks that the study of international relations has its greatest prospect of success. Insights from this sphere can be combined with our factual or phenomenal knowledge. As a result, theories of international relations can be devised which try to govern, through rules, the actions of political leaders and citizens, taking into account both the empirical and moral standpoints.

The value of Kant's theory of knowledge in his general philosophy is that it not only gives scope for the application of morality to international relations, but it does not ignore the empirical sphere. For Kant, factual and historical studies can add to our understanding of the concrete world in which we try to put our principles into action.

## THE LIMITS OF POLITICAL PHILOSOPHY

Historically, political philosophy has been state-centric. It has focused on what Wight called the search for the good life within state boundaries. Beyond the state boundaries there is only the search for survival. (This distinction could be seen in the social contract theory of Kant's time.) But Kant rejects such an approach. He argues not only that the search for the good life *should* be universal (beyond one's own boundaries) but that the search for the good life *within* one's own boundaries *cannot* be attended with success unless the universal project is completed. Thus, for Kant, international theory is ultimately of greater philosophical and practical significance than traditional political science theory.

Kant looks upon the study of politics as taken on by philosophers as a very valuable exercise. In *Perpetual Peace* he argues that rulers should always listen to the voice of philosophers through encouraging public and learned debate about political issues. Political theorists, like philosophers in general, should be able to enjoy an independent existence, immune from government interference, in order to pursue their work and inform rulers about the consequences of their political policies. In particular 'the maxims of philosophers on the conditions for the possibility of public peace should be consulted by those states armed for war'.[14]

Political philosophy in Kant's time was dominated by the idea of the social contract. This influential concept, best represented in Kant's day by Rousseau's political theory, is still highly respected today, as is evident in its application to contemporary society in John Rawls's *A Theory of Justice*. John Rawls regards Kant as a formative influence in developing his own novel account of justice, noting that 'the theory that results is highly Kantian in nature'.[15] In some respects it is true to say that Kant also is a social contract theorist. He thought highly of Rousseau and was greatly influenced by his work. Kant regards political structures from the standpoint of free individuals trying to order their mutual arrangements to preserve their autonomy. Like Rousseau, Kant is interested in discovering how full citizenship is possible. But there is a marked difference in focus between Kant and other social contract theories. Kant seldom takes over an idea without adding to it his own particular twist. Social contract theories often regard their task as completed when they have demonstrated how we can live together in harmony within a state and as citizens of a state. Rousseau classically states the position: 'The problem is to find a form of association which will defend and protect with the whole common force the person and goods of each associate, and in which each, while limiting himself with all, may still obey himself alone, and remain free as before.'[16] The focus of traditional social contract theory is internal arrangements of a state. The theory attempts to show logically how the state comes into existence which is then recognised externally by other states. The contract entered into is intended to safeguard the individual's autonomy while securing the person and property. But Kant does not stop at this point in his political philosophy. He emphasises the importance of the international dimension of social contract theorising. As he argues in his essay 'Idea for a Universal History from a Cosmopolitan point of view': 'The problem of establishing a perfect civic constitution is dependent upon the problem of a lawful external relation among states and cannot be solved without a solution of the latter problem.'[17] Kant argues this because he believes that state or internal sovereignty is merely a partial or incomplete solution to the problem which leads to political organisation and law in the first place. This problem is a reflection of the sociable/asociable nature (*ungeselige/Geselligkeit*) of the human being. Kant sees each person as both requiring the attention of other individuals and not requiring their interest and attention. Each wants to do something their own way while at the same time desiring the approval of others. We need other individuals when it comes to the satisfaction of our own needs but we tend not to want them when it is their needs that are at issue.

In Kant's view the development of the modern state (morally based upon the idea of a social contract) simply shifts on to the international plane the problem of the asociable/sociability of the human species. Kant is led to ask, 'what is the use of working towards a lawful civic constitution among individuals (i.e towards the creation of a commonwealth)? The same unsociability which drives man to this causes any single commonwealth to stand in unrestricted relation to others; consequently, each of them must expect from another precisely the evil which oppressed individuals and forced them to enter into a lawful civic state.'[18] In Kant's political thinking, in contrast to the social contract tradition, the state is not regarded as an end-point that creates a uniquely viable community. In contrast, Rousseau was so committed to his statist model of the social contract that he tried to discover the appropriate size of the domestic society which would allow the model to work optimally. In Rousseau's view, the smaller the state the more effective the social contract. Kant does not follow this path; rather he sees the state (and individual states) as necessary staging-posts in a wider process of creating a functioning peaceful world society. In this world society, competition among individuals and states will not disappear but, rather, our asociability will be harnessed to enrich human culture (just as those who live in a legal condition in relation to one another in the modern state contribute through their measured conflict to our progress). Each state's desire to possess the best weapons may represent a threat to human civilisation, but each state's competitive desire to possess the best national theatre can add to the sum of human well-being.

In taking this cosmopolitan view of political philosophy Kant does not entirely abandon the concerns of the state-centred theorists of the social contract tradition. Instead, as he explains in his 'Idea for a Universal History', he sees his international perspective as the most adequate way of dealing with the malfunctioning of states internally. Kant regards the problem of the government of individuals as the most difficult of all to resolve.[19] Indeed it will be the last problem to be resolved by mankind in its upward path towards progress: 'The greatest problem for the human species, the solution of which nature drives man, is that of attaining a civil society which can administer justice universally.'[20] This will be 'a society in which freedom under external laws is associated in the highest degree with irresistible power (i.e a perfectly just civic constitution)'.[21] The essential problem is that each individual human being requires a master, but only another human individual can be that master. Thus a constitution has to be created which reins in the ruler who is also at the same time regulating (coercively, if necessary) the activities of the citizens. This requires complex constitutional arrangements which Kant indentifies with a republic. But this republic will not take shape without the good will of those living under it and the great political experience of rulers. And such a republic (or republics) cannot take shape at all unless the chaotic conditions of international relations are brought under control.[22] Thus, in tackling the key problems of politics, priority has to be given to the external sphere. A political philosophy which pushes to the margins the issues of international relations also marginalises the central difficulties of political theory. Kant's arguments here are a rebuke to centuries of state-centred political theory. Equally, as will be argued in the next section, his arguments are a rebuke to what he would consider centuries of regressive thinking about human nature.


## THE POTENTIALITIES OF HUMAN NATURE

Whether or not it is made explicit, theories of international relations rest on a view of human nature, that is, the innate propensities and behaviour of the human species. Usually, the appeal to human nature is made by realists of one kind or another to terminate a discussion: it is asserted that something is not politically possible because it goes 'against' human nature. Kant accepts no such limits. For him the potentialities of human nature are infinite, including action in international relations. Indeed, for Kant there is a necessary relationship between the achievement of the potentials of human nature and the evolution of politics on a global scale. Without the emancipation of international relations from the war system there will be no emancipation for individual humans.

Kant's political philosophy does not begin with human nature, but running through his philosophical works there is a clear view of the innate characteristics and potentialities of individuals. Kant's view of human nature is dualistic. Human individuals, he contends, exist in two realms, the intellectual realm where reason holds sway, and the animal realm where instinct dominates. This dualism corresponds with his earlier distinction between the world of appearance (phenomena) and the world of intelligence (noumena). Humans are affected by reason, but not determined by it. The more reflective we are before we act, the more possible it is to be driven by reason. The role Kant gave to reason is recognised as a central and original contribution both to philosophy and international relations.[23]

It is Kant's belief that human beings have the potential to be rational, which is the basis for all aspects of his thinking about international relations. Through the exercise of reason in the international realm he believes it will be possible for humans to fulfil the potential of their nature. The empirical world we live in ('the world of sense') is governed by the laws of nature, and these in important respects govern our behaviour. However, the world of the intellect (the 'intelligent world') is governed by the laws of reason, and it is these which allow us to realise our freedom.[24] Realising our freedom within the arena of international relations involves a project to transcend the historic concerns, constraints and crises of the international system. In fulfilling the potential of human nature, we will leave behind our animal nature dominated by instincts such as selfishness; translated into global politics, this will involve living together in perpetual peace. Through the laws of reason, therefore, we have the potential to make ourselves fully human: but we cannot achieve such self-emancipation unless the project is conceived on a global scale. *I* cannot be emancipated – fully human – until *everybody* is emancipated. Human nature is not seen by Kant as a barrier to a better world, but essential to it. With his universalist and limitless perspective, Kant thereby breaks through the boundaries of traditional political theory, with its state-centrism and emphasis on the constraints of human nature. Human nature for Kant is where the discussion begins, not where it ends.

The relationship between the intellectual and the animal sides of humans is not a stable one.[25] Humans are both determined and autonomous. It may seem that we are constrained in some or all situations, but there is always choice: 'I choose therefore I am (human)', Kant seems to be saying. Kant's account of the interplay between reason and instinct, and the potentiality for good and for evil, is basic to his thinking about the causes, conduct and potential eradicability of war – the central concerns of most students of international relations since its emergence as an academic discipline. Unlike the fatalistic views of medieval Christian theologians such as Augustine, Kant emphasises the voluntary nature of our moral failure. The corollary of this is that we can choose 'the good', and for Kant emancipation from the power of evil is the 'highest prize' that humans can win.[26] In the arena of world politics this means transcending the war system.

Kant hates war but is not a pacifist. The latter position is unrealistic in the light of the universal empirical human condition. Consequently he has to justify the reasons for engaging in war. In attempting this he emphasises the importance of choice, because he sees choice and the possibility of morality as an essentially human phenomenon. Contemporary moral philosophers such as Michael Walzer[27] echo Kant's view that each war should be seen as arising from the conscious choice of individuals. There can therefore be no purely 'accidental' or 'inadvertent' war. War is a decision, not a fatal necessity. The corollary of choosing war is the possibility of unchoosing it. If we do not unchoose war its continued prevalence in human history is therefore an example of our moral shortcomings.[28] War, which has traditionally been the key area for students of international politics, is for Kant the area where the relationship between morality and politics is supremely difficult and supremely important.

From the realist perspective, wars occur because there is nothing to stop them.[29] Kant believes there is. What will gradually stop war, he believes, is common reason. As long as human society exists in a state of 'self-incurred immaturity'[30] recourse to war is sometimes necessary. But that does not mean that it is inevitable or can be morally justifiable. Kant rejects both the Grotian argument basing the right to go to war on the right of self-preservation as well as the Christian Just War tradition. He rejects both these approaches for the same reason, namely that they accept too readily the presence of war in the human condition, and their theories legitimise warlike behaviour. Instead of accepting violent behaviour as integral to the human condition – in the manner of Grotius and Aquinas – Kant sees war as a manifestation of international relations at an immature stage. It then becomes part of the human project to develop international politics into a set of global social relations in which the usual conditions of civil society apply. In practice war can be fought, he says, but it should never be legitimised in theory. Kant bases his justification for fighting not on a right of self-defence but on the absence of any other means of enforcing right if one is attacked. In Kant's view the only conditions which make war acceptable are those which seek to make warlike methods of resolving disputes not acceptable.[31] This means that one can try to defend oneself, to show that aggression does not pay, and that one can fight if it is believed that the result will be a future prospect of continuous peace. The latter objective, unfortunately for Kant, translates into a slogan which could have been uttered by any aggressor in history.

Kant's position on war should be understood in relation to his belief that the idea of worldwide legal conditions should form the basis for our just actions now. This view stands in contrast to traditional doctrines of Just War and international law, which are aspects of the ideology of a states-system which is a war system. Such regressive doctrines for Kant perpetuate the idea of international relations as a community of fate; he believes that the potentials of human nature are such that we can create a global community of freedom.

Kant believes that human nature has the potential to liberate itself through reason, but his understanding of people leads him to be unsentimental, as in his famous lines: 'Out of timber so crooked as that from which man is made nothing entirely straight can be built.'[32] He sees the continuation of conflict as likely, for a very long period, and accepts that human nature is a fundamental cause of war, but not in the (original sin) sense argued by Christian pessimists. Kant accepts that the animal side of human nature is a basic factor in decisions to go to war (evident in his belief that power corrupts rulers). Simply, if men were not willing to fight there would not be war. This is a position which is also accepted by neo-realist theorists such as Waltz, when they argue that human nature is a necessary but not a sufficient cause of war. They then go on to argue that structural reasons (international anarchy) are the determining factor, the sufficient cause. Kant disagrees, and turns the argument on its head. For Kant human nature is a necessary cause of *peace*. The sufficient factor for Kant, as will be argued later, is a states-system comprised of states with republican constitutions operating according to his 'Definite Articles' of *Perpetual Peace*.

The shift of perspective offered by Kant, from seeing human nature as the fundamental hope for peace, instead of a determining factor for war, represents a decisive shift from mainstream international relations specialists, and it is one whose significance has not yet been properly explored. From Kant's perspective, politics, including international politics, is completely open-ended, and based (like Greek political thought) in ethics. This view did not represent a passing moment of optimism on Kant's part: that it is central to his philosophy is evident from his classic essay on freedom of thought, 'What is Enlightenment?'[33] Kant cannot be minimised by being described as a mere optimist. Indeed there is a great deal of hard-headed understanding of human behaviour evident throughout his work. What distinguishes Kant's political thought from mere optimism is hope: the hope for a better world, marked by the fulfilment of human potential. It will not come about quickly or easily, but he has confidence in reason and 'Nature's secret path'; the latter, which will be discussed later, includes the potentially constructive role of war in forcing humans to examine their interrelationships.[34] At an empirical level we might have to be forced out of our warlike ways through the destructiveness of war. The idea of 'hope against hope' – persistence against all odds – best describes his position.[35] Unlike those who have dominated international relations, Kant does not see war as a timeless phenomenon, or human nature as a fundamental bar to peace; indeed, he sees war as a culturally-constructed phenomenon and human nature as the reason why we should look forward to peace. By shifting the perspective in this way, and giving us a progressive rather than regressive perspective on human nature and international relations, Kant leaves us with a picture of world politics without limits.

## JUSTICE WITHOUT BOUNDS

As is evident from the preceding section, Kant has a great deal to say about what we would understand as justice in his political philosophy. It is a concept he strongly favours, both in the sense of respecting the established law and in the sense of respecting moral rules which set standards for civilised life; and he sees justice in global terms, encompassing a view of international right just as much as a view of individual right. The usual German term for justice is *Gerechtigkeit* and this is the term generally used when John Rawls's seminal (but less internationally oriented) *Theory of Justice* is translated into German. Kant, however, deals with the topic under the heading of *Rechtslehre* or the doctrine of right. This gives to his writings a different tenor from modern theories of justice.

*Recht* means both law and right in its legal and moral sense. Kant deals with justice systematically in the first part of his *Metaphysics of Morals*, the *Metaphysical Elements of the Doctrine of Right*. He divides the doctrine into two sections. The first section, concerned with private right, deals primarily with the theory of property and contract and the second, public right, deals with the foundations of the state and international law. These are divisions of convenience; they do not mark a fundamental break in either theme or subject matter. Thus with right or justice, as Kant sees it, there is a continuity running from our rights as private individuals to the rights of states.

That *Recht* means both law and right implies that Kant takes together the moral treatment of justice and its legal realisation. It is customary to distinguish between the moral discussion of justice, or normative right, and the legal discussion of justice or positive right. And Kant does indeed distinguish between legal justice and normative justice. He believes the two differ primarily in terms of the incentives for their fulfilment. Positive right can rely upon both the incentive which arises from our sense of duty and the incentive which arises from the possibility that we will be punished, whereas normative rights rely solely upon the incentive which arises from our sense of duty. But because both forms of right arise from (and to some extent are dependent on) our sense of duty, Kant thinks they may be dealt with under the same rubric.

Thus although Kant's doctrine of right has been at times translated into English simply under the heading of the philosophy of law we can still see the doctrine as covering the same ground as modern theories of justice such as those of John Rawls and Robert Nozick. The best clue to this is the overall title of the work from which the doctrine of right is taken, namely, *The Metaphysics of Morals*. It is useful to bear in mind that in this overall work the doctrine of right is followed by the doctrine of virtue or Kant's theory of goodness. So Kant's theory of justice forms part of his theory of the good as a whole or his ethics.

In most contemporary theories of justice, justice is first derived within a closed system (comparable with the national political system). Some theorists go on to look at the implications of the approach at a global level.

Thomas Pogge in *Realizing Rawls* notes the limitations of this two-tier approach and goes on to suggest some modifications which might allow this Rawlsian model to be used at a global level.[36] This is an interesting issue since Rawls regards himself as building his theory of justice on a Kantian basis. It is not clear that Kant proceeds in the same way as either Rawls or Pogge suggests. Kant's theory of justice, based as it is upon universal human reason, seems not to be one derived from a closed system and then applied to the world at large. The view we shall take here is that Kant's notion of justice is cosmopolitan from the beginning. By cosmopolitan we mean (as Kant himself implies) the standpoint of a gradually emerging world citizenship.

In Kant's cosmopolitan notion of justice, there is a key distinction between human beings as individuals and human beings as citizens of states. Kant would point out that the only kind of individual who can enjoy right in its fullest sense is an individual who is the citizen of a state. Such a person can set standards of justice for social life and see some of them implemented through law. So, at this stage, the Rawlsian starting-point seems justified. However, it is not the citizen who is the starting-point of Kant's political philosophy but the human individual as such. What marks out the human individual for Kant is the capacity to act according to reason. He distinguishes between rights *a priori* which fall within the sphere of natural law and positive rights which are rights as they are found and legally enforced within a given country. Both natural law and positive law derive their justification from reason alone: 'Any action is right if it can coexist with *everyone's* freedom in accordance with a *universal* law, or if in its maxim the freedom of choice of each can coexist with everyone's freedom in accordance with a universal law.'[37]

We have just emphasised in this definition of right those words which indicate the generality of Kant's concept of right. Right pertains to the human individual as a person. Right or justice applies to individuals who are capable of exercising choice: 'Right is therefore the sum of the conditions under which the choice of one can be united with the choice of another in accordance with a *universal* law of freedom.'[38] Individual right which flows from our status as persons Kant refers to as private right. Because they derive from our one innate right of freedom, rights in this sphere can also be referred to as natural rights. For these natural rights to become externally effective public right is necessary. Public right is historically founded when a nation-state comes into being under a sovereign. Thus, it may seem that we are here moving from a universal sphere where justice cannot properly be realised to a narrower national basis where justice prevails on the foundation of state power or sovereignty. But this is a move that Kant rejects:

> The sum of the laws that need to be promulgated generally in order to bring about a rightful condition is *public right*. Public right is therefore a system of laws for a people, that is, a multitude of men, or for a multitude of peoples, that, because they affect one another, need a rightful condition under a will uniting them, a constitution, so that they may enjoy what is laid down as right.

But domestic right and right in relation to other states are connected. The same state which is a commonwealth in relation to its own citizens is a power in relation to other states: 'Hence, under the general concept of a public right we are led not only to think of right of a state but a *right of nations*. Since the earth's surface is not unlimited but closed, the concepts of the right of a state and of a right of nations lead inevitably to the idea of a right for all nations or *cosmopolitan* right.'[39]

Justice is an interconnected whole. Justice exists in principle as a global system of relationships, and if that global system is threatened, either in part or whole, then the principle itself is prejudiced. Kant not only thinks that at the moral level this is the case but it is also a development that may be empirically observed. As he puts it at the end of the programmatic section of *Perpetual Peace*, 'the peoples of the earth have reached a stage of (narrower and broader) community where a violation of rights in one place is felt in all places'.[40] Kant believes that the idea of cosmopolitan right is no mere empty phrase but is something that the growth of relations among individuals and states over the earth's surface forces upon us. Although vast, the globe which we inhabit is none the less finite. As we inhabit and transform by industry and commerce the earth's surface so we are increasingly pressed into moral and lawlike relations with one another. The alternative is widening chaos and disorder.

Clearly Kant was not the first to argue for the universality of right or justice. From its inception Christian philosophy addressed humankind as a whole, believing that those who lived outside the civilised world also possessed the potential to be saved. Christianity shared this point of view with Stoic philosophy. But early Christian thinkers like Augustine gave very little attention to earthly justice in relation to divine justice. Augustine's philosophy is genuinely otherworldly, with the focus placed firmly on attaining the peace and harmony of the *City of God*. Augustine appears quite convinced that there is no universal justice to be attained in this present life, which is bedevilled by woe, but universal justice may be earned by the select few who attain the heavenly life.

The medieval Catholic philosopher Thomas Aquinas gives a more secular turn, however, to the Christian doctrine of salvation, which brings it more in the direction of Kant's universal notion of justice. According to Aquinas there are four types of law: eternal, divine, natural, and human.[41] Eternal law is the foundation of all law and is created by God's wisdom. Divine law is God's law in so far as it is revealed to us. The ten commandments given to Moses on Mount Sinai are often regarded as examples of divine law. Some would also consider that the life of Jesus gave to us by its example many rules of divine law. Human law is God's law as it is interpreted and put into practice by states and communities. Because it is fashioned by man, human law may well be subject to error and it is, therefore, necessary from time to time to correct and improve it. But the most important kind of law from the standpoint of Kant's notion of universal justice is the kind which Aquinas refers to as natural law. Natural law should govern all our relations with the rest of humankind. It is not restricted by state boundaries nor considerations of race and blood.

> The order of the precepts of the natural law corresponds to the order of our natural inclinations. For there is in man a natural and initial inclination to good which he has in common with all substances; in so far as every substance seeks its own preservation according to its own nature. Corresponding to this inclination, the natural law contains all that makes for the preservation of human life, and all that is opposed to its dissolution.[42]

Natural law applies across borders because it applies to human individuals in general.

Many of Kant's philosophical predecessors used this notion of natural right to ground their theories of international law or the law of nations. Grotius is an interesting example. Grotius partially derives the law of nations from the past and present behaviour of states and their subjects but also he draws on what he calls the dictates of 'right reason'. For instance, in concluding that it may be just for states to engage in war, he argues, 'right reason, moreover, and the nature of society, which must be studied in the second place and are of even greater importance, do not prohibit all use of force, but only that use of force which is in conflict with society, that is which attempts to take away the rights of another'.[43] However, the use to which Grotius puts the notion of 'right reason' differs markedly from Kant's deduction of universal right. Grotius's deduction of the laws of nations depends upon a notion of the authority of God which is very vividly represented in Aquinas's account of the four kinds of law. Grotius, like Aquinas, bases his assumption of the general application of his notion of international law upon the idea of a divine creator guiding the world. Kant does not allow himself this luxury. Kant rests his view of the rationality of law and its universality upon what he regards as the *conditions for action* in a world. If, for Kant, we are to behave as *human* individuals, we have to recognise certain general rules. In Kant's view, there is only a common social world in which we and states can act if we accept certain fundamental rational ideas.

PERPETUAL PEACE

The potentialities of human nature and the interconnectedness of justice converge for Kant in the prospect of perpetual peace. These ideas are breathtaking to mainstream international relations theory, the more so since Kant's project does not involve the abolition and reconstruction from scratch of the international system: his vision of peace exists in a recognisable world of states.

The essay *Perpetual Peace*, published in 1795, is Kant's best-known piece of writing to students of international relations, and, though less than 30 pages, represents his longest statement about the subject. Although the essay is related directly to his philosophical writings, it did not arise simply from theoretical speculation about the world. It was also the result of a mixture of his personal experiences, the political circumstances of the time, and the implicit debate he was carrying out with a number of major political philosophers (the shadows of Aristotle, Hobbes, Rousseau and Machiavelli fall across his words). In addition the format of his work belongs to a long tradition of mainly continental European intellectuals who wrote peace proposals; and the eighteenth century had been particularly fruitful.[44]

Kant's essay is short but multifaceted. It is in the form of a peace treaty, but it is not one which could have been devised by any group of leaders, diplomats or international lawyers who have ever got together to draw up a treaty. Although it begins simply enough, it develops into a complex and very theoretical discussion about the relationship between politics and morality. The essay's structure is more easily summarised than its arguments. *Perpetual Peace* consists of two sections, two supplements and two appendices. The first section contains six 'Preliminary Articles'. These represent the preconditions for peace (such as 'Standing Armies Shall in Time Be Totally Abolished'). These Articles in themselves do not create perpetual peace but they represent processes or agreements that need to be in place before the goal of perpetual peace can be achieved. They are the necessary but not sufficient foundations. For the latter it is necessary to look at Kant's second section, in which he elaborates his 'Definitive Articles'. These will create the politico-legal regime which will deliver perpetual peace. The three Definitive Articles are: 1, 'The Civil Constitution of Every State Shall Be Republican'; 2, 'The Law of Nations Shall Be Founded on a Federation of Free States'; and 3, 'The Law of World Citizenship Shall Be Limited to Conditions of Universal Hospitality'. The two supplements consist of the 'Guarantee' and 'Secret Article' for perpetual peace; and the two appendices discuss the opposition between morality and politics with respect to perpetual peace, and the 'harmony' between morality and politics which is established by 'public right' (essentially the belief that if an action cannot be made public it must be unjust). In a short chapter, we cannot provide a detailed critique of the essay; instead three aspects have been selected which relate to our theme of Kant as a theorist beyond limits. These are his *guarantee* of perpetual peace, the *definitive* articles and the *harmony* of morality and politics.

## (i) The Guarantee of Perpetual Peace

Kant's 'guarantee' of perpetual peace, paradoxically, is intimately related to the profound empirical difficulty of achieving perpetual peace. The guarantee, as he puts it, is 'nothing less than the great artist, nature'.[45] Through nature's 'mechanical course', there will be produced 'a harmony among men, against their will and indeed through their discord'. What Kant is arguing here has to be read against his progressive view of history discussed earlier. His belief is that in the process of filling out the spaces of the earth, in discovering the evil and irrationality of war, in learning to live and trade together, in exercising reason and conducting moral politics – in the interplay of these processes and behaviours humans will create an ethical world community regulated by law: in short, perpetual peace.[46] Even the 'principle of evil' will help the process, since it serves as a 'whetstone of virtue'.[47] Humans can measure their moral progress against those who transgress, and in Kant's opinion 'Providence is justified in the history of the world, for the moral principle in man is never extinguished while with advancing civilisation reason grows pragmatically in its capacity to realise ideas of law'.[48] Kant does not believe that such an outcome will occur either quickly or easily, but he does ultimately consider that what he variously calls 'nature', 'fate' or 'providence' will achieve 'the objective final end of the human race'.

Expressed briefly, as above, the guarantee of perpetual peace looks simple, indeed 'almost naively providential' in Gallie's opinion.[49]

Empirical support for Kant's argument is thin, restricted to a few illustrations from anthropology to show the cunning of nature.[50] Against these and other criticisms we would draw attention to his long-term perspective, his recognition that the world is not harmonious, his assumption not of inevitable or even progress but of the human capacity to learn by trial and error, his recognition that republican constitutions do not require 'angels', and his understanding of the dialectical processes (war/peace, evil/morality) out of which rational cooperation should evolve. Is history going Kant's way? Our view is that it is too soon to say, but it might be noted that against all the disorder and violence in the twentieth century, the Great War gave birth to the first experiment in global international organisation, the nuclear confrontation between the superpowers stimulated the idea of common security, the Holocaust led to the Nuremberg principles and the Universal Declaration of Human Rights, the increasing density of interaction across borders has produced a growth of international law, and the global triumph of capitalism has created a global community of fate. Whatever one might think of the state of global order and disorder as the century comes to an end, it is undeniable that there is a greater sense of interdependence – sensitivity and vulnerability – than hitherto.

Kant rejects the idea of peace in the negative sense of the mere absence of war. Perpetual peace could not be a mere armistice, but would necessitate humans living in justice and harmony with each other. For Kant, unlike many international relations theorists, there is no clash between order and justice: order can only be delivered on a permanent basis by justice. Kant's essay does not develop a political practice of peace; institutionalisation is hinted at rather than demonstrated. Nevertheless, what he hints at has been given practical form by others. Ideas such as confidence-building and territorial defence as developed in the 1980s seem to accord closely with his ideas about creating trust and replacing standing armies with voluntary militias.[51]

How can we reconcile the argument that Kant's work contains a healthy scepticism about human behaviour with his 'guarantee' of perpetual peace? The answer is that his 'guarantee' is conditional – a philosopher's equivalent of the salesperson's small print and, as Gallie has said, it is not a guarantee 'in any known sense of the term'.[52] Kant is arguing that peace is guaranteed if we choose it. We may not choose it but he would expect us to, under the conditions of complex global interdependence. The problems of living together will stimulate ethical thinking. Out of a community of fate will emerge an ethical community, and from that a world society of perpetual peace.

## (ii)   The Definitive Articles

The political work towards perpetual peace will primarily be the result of three developments: first, countries adopting republican constitutions at home (or acting in a manner which would bring about a republican consti-tution); second, the creation of a federated pacific union in their relations with each other; and third, the growth of relationships based on the princi-ple of universal hospitality. Neither separately nor independently does mainstream international relations thought believe these Definitive Articles of perpetual peace could have the effects predicted by Kant.

International relations theory had traditionally drawn a sharp dividing line between 'domestic' and 'foreign' policy, as is evident from the simple binary oppositions of 'order'/'anarchy' and 'good life'/'survival'. This approach reaches its maximum extent with the neorealist rejection of unit-level explanations of international relations.[53] In contrast, Kant empha-sises the intimate interrelationship not only between internal and external in terms of an individual country's foreign policy, but also in terms of the character of the international system. Neo-realists believe that the system is dominant: for Kant it is the units.

Like other political theorists of the eighteenth and early nineteenth cen-turies, Kant saw a close relationship between bad governments at home and aggression in external policy. *Perpetual Peace* contains a number of fulminations against avaricious leaders. The first ingredient of Kant's recipe for a better world is a republican constitution: only in such a polity will humans be sufficiently mature to implement the other aspects of a peace policy.[54] It is a polity in which the internal constitutional arrange-ments coincide with his idea of rightful freedom (accepting only those laws one freely chooses to accept). In a republican constitution each citizen gives consent to the state's action through appropriate forms of representation: so, the rulers themselves have masters. In this sense laws emanate from the will of the citizens, while governmental action takes place within the limits set by the representatives of the citizens. Such a polity, Kant believes, would be at peace with itself, by increasing the chances for self-enlightenment, and this will also lead to peace between states. Much of Kant's argument for this is based on the historically un-tenable proposition that in a republic citizens will not choose war since they will be the ones to suffer most, either in injury or taxes.

Is Kant justified in making the connection between peace and republi-can constitutions? If we translate republics into liberal democracies, then there does seem to be at least a correlation between liberal democracy and peace. However, the sample is small and the historical conditions advantageous. Furthermore, there has been no shortage of violence between liberal democracies and states with other ideological orientations. But Kant would argue that the small sample and advantageous conditions do not negate his argument; he would emphasise that the Western nations which formed a 'security community' in the last 50 years were simply exercising their will to take advantage, as they should, of the external conditions such as war-weariness, US hegemony and the Soviet threat. In this way nature and morality work together. Circumstances may conspire which allow states to translate their relations into lasting peace, in the form of a politico-legal regime – self-regulated lawful freedom. This is Kant's second Definitive Article, 'a federation of free states'.

For Kant, as for Hobbes, the state of nature was one of war. The response of Hobbes was for individuals to submit to the Leviathan of the sovereign state, which by definition turned the international arena itself into a state of nature, since the sovereign state and international anarchy are two sides of the same coin. Given Kant's cosmopolitan perspective, with common humanity as his referent, it might have been expected that his recommended global polity would be one of world government. But he rejected this. He believed that perpetual peace must be based on free, equal and independent states; he considered that a world government would not be based upon equals.[55] In addition, he believed that such global governance would be too big to be manageable. What Kant favoured was not a world government but a federation of free states. In this and in other respects Kant is more statist than his reputation would suggest.[56]

It is in the second Definitive Article that we see Kant's idea of 'positive' rather than 'negative' peace. For Kant peace is not simply something that develops; it is not the mere absence of war, as with peace through deterrence or a treaty which may turn out merely to be an armistice. Positive peace must be 'formally instituted';[57] there must be a properly constituted pacific union, equivalent to a legal civil state, in which equal and independent parties agree not to go to war with each other. Unlike a peace treaty, which terminates one war, Kant's 'pacific federation' would seek to end all wars. He believes the idea would spread across the world: 'It can be shown that this idea of *federalism*, extending gradually to encompass all states and thus leading to perpetual peace, is practicable and has objective reality.'[58] The legal dimension of this relationship is crucial, since he emphasises that law is the embodiment of right, and a measure of human progress. As is the case in other areas, Kant's institutionalisation of his idea is weak.

The thinking behind Kant's second Definitive Article seems less radical in the 1990s than it has hitherto. The salience given to the idea of what

Deutsch and his colleagues called 'security communities' – islands of stable peace made up of accretions of liberal-democratic states[59] – gives empirical support to Kant's reasoning. Kant himself does not expect the evolutionary dialectic between republicanism and the spread of the peace process to be quick or easy. What he emphasises is the importance of the guiding idea and the rocky path of history, not a new world which could be instantly inaugurated by fiat.

The third and final Definitive Article for perpetual peace is his idea of 'universal hospitality', which he equates with the law of world citizenship.[60] This is the right all men have 'by virtue of their common possession of the surface of the earth' to be treated with hospitality so long as they occupy their places peacefully. Inhospitality, he believes, is 'opposed to natural law'. Through communications and trade Kant believes that the 'human race can gradually be brought closer and closer to a constitution establishing world citizenship'. These are ringing words, but here again they are more limited than one might expect from Wight's 'Kantian' labelling, for Kant insists that 'hospitality' be interpreted as a rejection of hostility towards foreigners rather than an automatic expression of benevolence. People, he argues, have a right to visit, but cannot expect to be house guests.

Having identified the limitations on Kant's law of world citizenship, it must be underlined that the spirit of his words goes far beyond that of the communitarian and statist thinkers who have primarily shaped international relations theory. Kant – in words as relevant today as when they were written – is critical of the 'civilised and especially of the commercial states' of Europe for their ill-treatment of other parts of the world, as is evident in their assumption of superiority in exploiting the world's resources and people. While these nations 'drink injustice like water', he says 'they regard themselves as the elect in point of orthodoxy'. Despite this, Kant believes that there has been such a development of the community of humankind 'that a violation of rights in one place is felt throughout the world'; consequently 'the idea of a law of world citizenship is no high-flown or exaggerated notion'. While to many realists such words would still seem high-flown, 200 years after they were written, those with different outlooks would recognise the strength of Kant's remarks: the critique of imperialism, the need for rational organisation under conditions of interdependence, growing global sensitivity because of communications, the strengthening view that duties do not stop at one's borders and the development of global civil society as represented by organisations such as Amnesty International or Médecins sans Frontières.

In defining the three Articles just described as *Definitive*, Kant is asserting that their adoption will deliver a politico-legal regime which will be one of perpetual peace. Together these Articles embody a comprehensive theory of politics on a global scale, which he intrudes in a footnote.[61] The Definitive Articles can be so called because they give expression to 'the *civil right* of individuals within a nation', the '*international right* of states in their relationships with one another', and the '*cosmopolitan right*' of individuals and states as 'citizens of a universal state of mankind'. Here Kant is giving a lead to lawful freedom at each of the levels of analysis described by Waltz's three images of man, the state and international anarchy. Kant's three images are of the foundations of peace rather than the causes of war. Through the evolution of *ius civitatis*, *ius gentium* and *ius cosmopoliticum*, Kant believed that war would be eradicated.

### (iii)    The Harmony of Morality and Politics

The dialectic of the good and evil principles in humans runs throughout Kant's discussion of perpetual peace. This culminates in the two appendices to the essay ('On the Opposition Between Morality and Politics with Respect to Perpetual Peace' and 'Of the Harmony which the Transcendental Concept of Public Right Establishes between Morality and Politics'). The conclusions he reaches grow predictably from what has gone before, but the argument is very abstract. In brief, Kant proposes that there is no more vital interest than acting in good faith, and that the principle of publicity is the mechanism by which to encourage the convergence of politics and morality. In these final sections of his essay Kant can be seen to be engaging in a debate with Aristotle and Machiavelli about the whole tradition of *Realpolitik* and practical wisdom.

Kant begins by emphasizing the essential *theoretical* harmony of politics and morality. Taken 'objectively', he says, morality 'is in itself practical' because 'there can be no conflict of politics, as a practical doctrine of right, with ethics, as a theoretical doctrine of right'.[62] Politics – domestic and foreign – is therefore seen as the practice of morality, and morality has to be practised in politics if the goal of perpetual peace is to be achieved. This ultimate harmony of politics and morality grows out of Kant's general political philosophy, particularly his writings on the nature of theory, practice and history.[63] The practical politico-legal regime which will deliver perpetual peace can only be built on the moral foundations of a global ethical community, and the potentiality for the latter exists in the interplay between reason and nature in the unfolding of universal history.

Kant's position is firmly but not absolutely deontological: consequences are not irrelevant. For example, he describes the sentence 'Let justice prevail even if the world perish' as a 'stout principle of right' and 'true but boastful', but he qualifies this apparent endorsement of the principle by arguing that it should not be misunderstood as 'a permission to use one's own right with extreme rigour (which would conflict with ethical duty)'. Kant is saying that justice is of more value than survival, but since one should be respectful of the right of others in exercising one's own rights, such a dilemma should never arise.

Standing on opposite sides in the debate between politics and morality are those Kant calls the 'political moralist' and the 'moral politician'. The former forges morality to conform to a state's or leader's advantage, while the latter chooses political principles that are consistent with those of morality.[64] The political moralists have '*practices*' not '*practical science*'. They flatter the power which is ruling, and, by analogy with lawyers, argue that what is 'in force at any time is to them the best, but when it is amended from above, the amendment always seems best too'. Their adroitness consists of being able to fit into all circumstances, and this gives them the illusion of judging principles according to concepts of right. They make a 'great show of understanding *men*...without understanding *man*', for they 'lack the higher point of view of anthropological observation'. Kant considers this attitude 'mechanical routine' and 'chicanery'. This critique of so-called practical men and those who flatter them can be read as Kant's verdict on the analyses and relationship with power of realists in international relations.

The political moralist subordinates principles to selfish ends, a position Kant rejects. Instead, he has no doubt that we should begin with the 'formal principles of pure reason' rather than material principles. For the political moralist perpetual peace is merely wished as a material good. In contrast, for the moral politician perpetual peace is a condition issuing from the acknowledgement of duty. He argues that perpetual peace will not come through mere pragmatism but only through rational moral behaviour. Thus he believes that morality is the best politics: 'Seek ye first the kingdom of pure practical reason and its righteousness, and your end (the blessing of perpetual peace) will necessarily follow.' This is because Kant believes that ideas determine structures:

> it is the universal will...which determines the law among men, and if practice consistently follows it, this will can also, by the mechanism of nature, cause the desired result and make the concept of law effective.

Note the condition 'if' and 'can' in this sentence. Kant is offering a logical statement and long-term perspective, not an actual prediction.

Objectively he believes that there is no conflict between morality and politics, but there always appear to be such conflicts. The categorical imperative is not a 'natural' affinity for humans, but the tension between the good and evil principles is the dialectic through which progress occurs. In international relations he notes that while contemporaries may see no injustice in practice, posterity might someday take the perpetrators as a warning example. For Kant moral politics are a matter of duty, not prudence. Political maxims must be deduced from the pure concept of the duty of right, 'from the *ought* whose principle is given *a priori* by pure reason, regardless of what the physical consequences may be'. Principles are to be derived without regard for consequences but this does not mean they are to be implemented without regard to consequences. He believes that maxims derived from duty represent prudential politics, because any other sort do not work over the long term: 'Moral evil has the inescapable property of being opposed to and destructive of its own purposes, thus it gives way to the moral principle of the good, though only through a slow process.' Kant ends Appendix II with a flourish, which reveals him to be more radically deontological than was suggested earlier. He concludes by saying that the rights of humans 'must be held sacred, however much sacrifice it may cost the ruling power', and that one cannot compromise between the morally right and the expedient: 'All politics must bend its knee before the right. But by this it can hope shortly to reach the stage where it will shine with an immortal glory.'

Theory is the foundation for practice, and morality is the foundation for politics. He criticises prudence on its own, and in so doing attacks Aristotle's notion of practical wisdom. For Kant moral wisdom is what is practical. Likewise, his criticism of the practical axioms of pragmatic politicians can be read as a debate with Machiavelli. Kant argues that the great powers are not ashamed of revealing their principles (such as 'divide and rule'), except when their maxims fail, because this means that they have not succeeded in increasing their power (which they equate with political honour).

Since Kant believes that moral politics are best, he believes that certain acts are in themselves wrong. His Preliminary Article 6 discusses a number of 'dishonourable' strategies (such as assassination). His justification here is consequentialist rather than on moral grounds, arguing that certain acts will make it more difficult for belligerents to conclude a satisfactory peace once the fighting has stopped. Kant does not belong to the school of thought which believes that since war is an arena of violence, anything can be excused in the pursuit of victory: what matters for this school is the moral justification for fighting, not the manner of conducting war. Kant instead argues for honesty and consistency – fighting the friendliest war possible – with a view to the postwar situation. For the military necessity school, personified historically by General Sherman and Bomber Harris, what matters is the quality of victory: for Kant what matters is the quality of the peace.

The discussion above has suggested the tension between morality and politics, while arguing the case for moral politics. In Appendix II Kant looks explicitly towards the harmony which 'publicity' can establish between morality and politics. His whole discussion about their relationship should be read with the notion of publicity as a footnote: without publicity there can be no justice and therefore no right. For Kant rationality requires freedom of speech, and freedom of speech requires honesty. A rational foreign policy is one characterised by honesty and publicity.

CONCLUSION

We do not believe that anybody interested in world politics who studies Kant's work with an open mind can be other than impressed by the range and depth of his ideas, though for Kant himself the 'international' represented only a minute portion of his published output. Although it is possible to criticise his thinking about world politics on the basis of its overly-abstract character or simplified view of the political world, at the same time his arguments reveal a holistic perspective which justify Chris Brown's recent description of Kant as 'the greatest of all theorists of international relations'.[65] We believe that Kant deserves this accolade because, at every stage of his argument, he widens rather than narrows horizons, he opens rather than closes borders, he makes the finishing-point of other theorists his springboard, and whereas so many want to consider international relations as a relatively autonomous area of behaviour, he seeks to explain its interrelationships with all the important things in life. Kant sought to make the theory and practice of international politics an integral part of the Enlightenment project – human emancipation from 'self-incurred immaturity'. The latter can be read as a description of political realism and the world it both tried to describe and helped to create. The 200 years since Kant wrote *Perpetual Peace* have not delivered his end-point, but Kant's 'guarantee' did not come with a time-limit. Whether or not one sees elements of Kant's theoretical system taking shape in the 'triumph' of liberal democracy and the growth of a pacific union in Europe, there is no doubt that his philosophy of enlightenment is finally starting to be treated seriously by students of world politics. This is a significant change, since for Kant the project only truly begins when people dare to know.

NOTES

1.  Martin Wight, *International Theory. The Three Traditions*, ed. Gabriele Wight and Brian Porter (Leicester: Leicester University Press, 1991), passim.
2.  Ibid. The same is true of Hobbes and Grotius, the two other figureheads.
3.  Ibid., pp. 162, 259, 265, 267. For a general discussion, see Timothy Dunne, 'Mythology or methodology? Traditions in international relations', *Review of International Studies* Vol. 19 (3), July 1993, pp. 305–18. We are grateful to Timothy Dunne for pointing out to us that our remarks about Wight are truer of his published work than of his teaching. Wight lectured on Kant and included works by Kant on his international relations reading list.
4.  Wight, op. cit., p. 160.
5.  We are persuaded of this by Timothy Dunne, and wish to thank him for other points.
6.  Raymond Williams, *Keywords* (London: Fontana, 1976), p. 227.
7.  E. H. Carr, *The 20 Years' Crisis* (London: Macmillan, 1946).
8.  F. H. Hinsley, *Power and the Pursuit of Peace* (Cambridge: Cambridge University Press, 1963), pp. 62–80. Some earlier works discussed Kant, but did not have wide readership in international relations circles.
9.  W. B. Gallie, *Philosophers of Peace and War* (Cambridge: Cambridge University Press, 1978), pp. 8–36.
10. Michael Doyle, 'Kant, liberal legacies and foreign affairs', parts 1 and 2, *Philosophy and Public Affairs*, Vol. 12 (3 and 4), 1983.
11. Steve Smith, 'The Forty Years' Detour: The Resurgence of Normative Theory in International Relations', *Millennium*, Vol. 12 (3), Winter 1992, pp. 489–506.
12. Timothy Garton Ash, 'Kant in one hand, deterrence in the other', *The Independent*, 10 May 1990.
13. See, *inter alia*, Evan Luard, *Basic Texts in International Relations* (London: Macmillan, 1992).
14. Ed. L. W. Beck, *Perpetual Peace*, in *Kant Selections* (New York: Macmillan, 1988), p. 445; *Gesammelte Schriften*, VIII (Berlin, 1902), p. 368 (hereafter *GS*).
15. *A Theory of Justice* (Oxford University Press, 1978), p. viii.
16. *Social Contract* (London: Dent, 1968), p. 12.
17. Beck, p. 420; *Gesammelte Schriften*, VIII, p. 24.
18. Beck, p. 420; *G.S.*, VIII, p. 24.
19. Beck, p. 417; *G.S.*, VIII, p. 23.
20. Beck, p. 418; *G.S.*, VIII, p. 22.
21. Beck, p. 419; *G.S.*, VIII, p. 22.
22. Beck, p. 427; *G.S.*, VIII, p. 27.
23. Respectively, Michael Foucault, 'What is Enlightenment?' in Paul Rainbow (ed.), *The Foucault Reader* (New York: Pantheon, 1984), pp. 32–51 and Gallie, op. cit., pp. 14–15.
24. Beck, p. 290; *G.S.*, IV, p. 452.
25. Beck, p. 292; *G.S.*, IV, p. 455.
26. *Religion within the Limits of Reason Alone* (New York: Harper, 1960), p. 39 & p. 85.

27. Michael Walzer, *Just and Unjust Wars* (Harmondsworth: Penguin, 1980).
28. Gregor, p. 151; *G.S.*, VIII, p. 344.
29. Kenneth N. Waltz, *Man, the State and War* (New York: Columbia University Press, 1959).
30. Hans Reiss, (ed.), *Kant's Political Writings* (Cambridge: Cambridge University Press, 1989), p. 54 ('An Answer to the Question "What is Enlightenment"?').
31. Gregor, p. 153; *G.S.*, VIII, p. 347.
32. Isaiah Berlin used this phrase as the basis for the title of his book about the glories of pluralism against the pulls of fundamentalism: *The Crooked Timber of Humanity* (London: Fontana Press, 1991).
33. Reiss, op. cit., pp. 54–60.
34. K/W/HN, p. 37.
35. For what this can mean in the empirical world, see Nadezhda Mandelstam, *Hope against Hope. A Memoir* (London: Collins Harvill, 1989), trans. Max Hayward.
36. T. W. Pogge, *Realizing Rawls* (Ithaca: Cornell University Press, 1989), p. 240.
37. M. Gregor (ed. and trans.), *Metaphysics of Morals* (Cambridge: Cambridge University Press, 1991), p. 55; *G. S.*, VI, p. 230.
38. *Metaphysics of Morals*, p. 56; *G.S.*, VI, p. 230.
39. *Metaphysics of Morals*, p. 123; *G.S.*, VI, p. 311.
40. Beck, p. 440; *G.S.*, VIII, p. 360.
41. Cf. H. Williams, *International Relations in Political Theory* (Milton Keynes: Open University Press, 1992), p. 42.
42. A. P. D'Entreves (ed.), *Aquinas: Selected Political Writings* (Oxford: Blackwell, 1959), p. 123.
43. H. Williams, M. Wright & A. Evans (eds), *A Reader in International Relations and Political Theory* (Milton Keynes: Open University Press, 1993), p. 87.
44. Daniele Archibugi, 'Models of international organization in perpetual peace projects, *Review of International Studies*, Vol. 18, 1992, pp. 295–317; Hinsley, op. cit., pp. 13–61; Hidemi Suganami, *The Domestic Analogy and World Order Proposals* (Cambridge: Cambridge University Press, 1989), pp. 40–61.
45. Beck, p. 440; *G.S.*, VIII, p. 360.
46. Beck, pp. 440–5; *G.S.*, VIII, pp. 360–9.
47. Beck, p. 452; *G.S.*, VIII, p. 379.
48. Beck, p. 453; *G.S.*, VIII, p. 380.
49. Gallie, p. 32.
50. Beck, p. 441; *G.S.*, VIII, p. 361.
51. Beck, pp. 431–2; *G.S.*, VIII, p. 345.
52. Gallie, p. 10.
53. Kenneth N. Waltz, *Theory of International Politics* (Reading, MA: Addison-Wesley, 1979).
54. Beck, pp. 434–56. Ibid., p. 436.
55. Beck, p. 436; *G.S.*, VIII, pp. 353–4.
56. This is well argued in Andrew Hurrell, 'Kant and the Kantian paradigm in international relations', *Review of International Studies*, Vol. 16 (3), July 1990, pp. 183–206.

57. Reiss, p. 98.
58. Reiss, p. 104.
59. Karl Deutsch, *et al.*, *Political Community in the North Atlantic Area* (Princeton: Princeton University Press, 1957).
60. Beck, p. 439; *G.S.*, VIII, p. 358.
61. Reiss, p. 98.
62. Beck, p. 446; *G.S.*, VIII, p. 370.
63. 'On The Common Saying: This May Be True In Theory, But it Does Not Apply In Practice', Reiss, pp. 61–92.
64. Beck, p. 448; *G.S.*, VIII, p. 372.
65. Brown, p. 50.

# 5 Vitoria and the Universalist Conception of International Relations

Martin C. Ortega[*]

Who was the first 'modern' thinker of international relations? The answer, obviously, turns on what is meant by 'modern' but, in principle, two plausible candidates present themselves. The fifteenth and sixteenth centuries ushered in a new epoch in international relations, marked by the appearance of sovereign states in Europe and by the phenomenon of their colonial expansion. Niccolò Machiavelli (1469–1527) and Francisco de Vitoria (1483–1546) were the contemporary philosophers who reflected most profoundly on these two issues. Both wrote in the first half of the sixteenth century, but for very different motives. Vitoria was a theologian faced with a new reality: his country had to govern extensive territories inhabited by different peoples hitherto unknown. Inspired by a compassion originating in his Christian beliefs, Vitoria defended the American Indians against the atrocities being committed by his fellow Spaniards. To this end, he affirmed that the Indians were rational beings equal in essence to the Europeans, which made the king of Spain duty-bound to treat them as subjects. Therefore, they could neither be treated as slaves nor deprived of their property. Machiavelli was a diplomat and a soldier who lived in a society in turmoil. According to him, the best ruler was the shrewdest one, he who obtained the greatest profit for his state against other states of equal status. For this reason, it was imperative to strengthen the armed forces, inspire fear in other states and, if necessary, renege on promises.

Machiavelli is considered to be modern in the sense that he separated religion and ethics from politics.[1] In his opinion, against the background of corruption in his time, the statesman who acted in accordance with Christian morals would inevitably be weak and pusillanimous, and therefore headed for destruction. Vitoria saw matters differently, for throughout his works he demanded respect on the part of the Christian king for the precepts of the gospel. Vitoria restored the link which was established by

Aristotle and later forgotten, between ethics and politics. Yet Vitoria may be considered to be modern in two respects. On the one hand, his energy was directed towards concrete and not speculative problems, thereby avoiding the shortcomings of the last medieval scholastics. It was no longer a matter of finding abstract solutions to the question of the nature of man, as had been the case with many philosophers, but rather of focusing on specific men and nations. His works were 'inspired by practice and intended for practice'.[2] Vitoria began his writings on the Indians because he felt that the news from America demanded a moral reaction. He was also aware that he was analysing concrete conflicts for his nation. In his introduction to *De Indis* (1539), he affirmed that the doubts raised in the work were not issues for jurists alone to solve, because they were matters of conscience. Presumably, the Spanish monarchs had acted in all propriety,

> [b]ut when we hear of bloody massacres and of innocent individuals pillaged of their possessions and dominions, there are grounds for doubting the justice of what has been done.[3]

On the other hand, Vitoria is probably the first thinker to have considered the world as a geographical reality. Many territories were yet to be explored but in 1521 an expedition circumnavigated the globe for the first time and the continents and oceans began to find their place on the map of the world. This aroused Vitoria's interest in the relations between the different peoples on the earth which he considered as a whole in his concept of *totus orbis*. Vitoria's global point of view contrasts with that of the other European political thinkers of his time, who made no reference to the new discoveries. In fact, for centuries, Western thought on international relations has centred on the relations between Christian states and paid very little attention to the relations with other peoples and cultures that were being colonised. In this regard it may be affirmed that Vitoria propounded a universalist conception of international relations while other thinkers focused their concerns on the state.

HISTORICAL CONTEXT AND LIFE

To understand correctly the scope of Vitoria's works, reference will be made, first of all, to the philosophical context of his time. The atmosphere in which Vitoria lived was very different from that of the political laicism that accompanied Italian humanism.[4] However, up to the celebration of the Council of Trent (1545–63) and the abdication of Emperor Charles V (1556), Spain also discovered the Greek and Latin classics, was exposed to the influence of Erasmus and Luther, and witnessed a public debate on her rights in America.[5] This brilliant period was very different from that which saw the subsequent triumph of the Counter-Reformation, which was to spread intolerance and prepare the way for the religious wars that tormented Europe for a hundred years. Nonetheless, during the first half of the sixteenth century, there still existed a 'medieval' attitude in Spain, the result of the recent *Reconquista* of the Iberian Peninsula from the Moors. Immediately afterwards, Spain began to expand across the Mediterranean and achieved significant victories over the Ottoman Empire. However, it was not simply the zeal to spread the faith which motivated the conquest of America.[6] The main interests were commercial, since from the middle of the fourteenth century Portugal and Spain were in direct competition for access to Africa and, above all, the discovery of a new route to India. But many of the nobles and *conquistadores* who went to America were indubitably influenced by those medieval religious attitudes. Thomism, Vitoria's principal source, was far removed from these attitudes. Aquinas minimised the importance of man's irremediable fall into sin, which justified in the medieval mind the expansion of the faith through war. Aquinas had drawn on Aristotle to attack the pessimistic view of man that was dominant in the Middle Ages. It should be borne in mind that Aquinas was criticised for attributing too excessive a role to human rationality. The passages of St Thomas's works that influenced Vitoria most were those that made reference to the qualities of natural man prior to his salvation. St Thomas affirmed in this regard the consubstantial existence of a body and a rational soul in every man from which a series of virtues and human characteristics emanates. On the other hand, Vitoria also lived in a time of religious revival, which may be seen as a prelude to the Reformation. In the face of the immoralities of the papal curia, many religious orders proposed a return to the real imitation of Christ. Vitoria quoted the fathers, the scholastics and the classics but he frequently had to rely on the New Testament itself for direct support for his reasoning.

Francisco de Vitoria belonged to the Dominican order which was involved in the denunciation of the treatment given to the Indians and, although he never set foot in America, he was in direct contact with friars sent to the New World and those who returned. He trained in Paris (1509–22), where he was influenced by humanism, studied St Thomas and assisted his master, the Fleming Peter Crockaert, in editing Aquinas's *Summa theologica*. At 40 he went back to Spain and three years later, in 1526, he secured the chair of Theology at the University of Salamanca. During the academic course Vitoria concentrated on the various questions raised in the *Summa theologica*, but of more importance are his *relectiones* or special lectures, entrusted to distinguished doctors by the university on specific occasions. The *relectiones* allowed him greater freedom to deal with current and polemic issues. The few letters that have survived portray Vitoria as a very sensitive person, contemptuous of temporal honours. Suffering from ill-health from 1528 onwards, he declined Prince Philip's invitation to participate in the Council of Trent and died on 12 August 1546.

Vitoria's *relectiones* constitute his most original and well-known works. An orthodox defence of monarchy as the best form of ruling a common-wealth is shown in *De potestate civili (On civil power,* 1528). *De temper-antia (On self-restraint,* 1537) deals with the authority of the Spanish monarchs over the Indians and, particularly, the authority to demand the abandonment of certain barbarian customs such as cannibalism. *De Indis (On the American Indians,* 1539) examines three issues: (i) whether the Indians, before the arrival of the Spaniards, had true dominion, public and private; (ii) the illegitimate titles for the reduction of the Indians into the power of the Spaniards; and (iii) the legitimate titles. The problems raised in *De iure belli (On the law of war,* 1539) concern the justice of war, and the means to limit warfare, especially among the innocent. These works are made accessible in the reliable critical edition of Anthony Padgen and Jeremy Lawrence, published in 1991.[7]

## VITORIA'S IDEAS

Vitoria's greatest contribution to the debate about the Spanish conquests was to have considered the Indians as rational beings, with a right to their territories, their families and possessions. The basis for *dominium* was that man was made in God's image, and He had granted the things of the earth to all men. God and nature had not excluded the Indians from the species' essential characteristics, including the power to reason. This was evident from the existence of a certain method in their affairs:

> they have properly organized cities, proper marriages, magistrates and overlords ... laws, industries, and commerce, all of which require the use of reason. They likewise have a form ... of religion ....[8]

This characteristic conferred on them other rights and liberties that had to be respected by the Spaniards, but it also permitted the elaboration of a new Vitorian concept, the *totus orbis.*

The Stoics and the early Christians had maintained universalist ideas, but both the Greeks and the Romans had had a mainly ethnocentric vision of the world. In the Middle Ages the talk was of an *orbis christianus* in which the Pope exercised spiritual and temporal authority, with infidels, pagans and barbarians outside its boundaries. Vitoria, without apparently appealing to any author, powerfully presented a community of Christian states, autonomous in the temporal sphere, coexisting harmoniously alongside many other political communities of different confessions, yet composed of men of equal standing. Only Christians could be enlightened by divine law, but relations in the recently explored globe would be regulated by a *ius gentium* common to all mankind, and proceeding directly from man's rational nature. The *ius gentium* which should regulate the relations among all nations as well as between foreigners and the state derived, in principle, from natural law.

> But even on the occasions when it is not derived from natural law, the consent of the greater part of the world is enough to make it binding, especially when it is for the common good of all men. If, after the dawn of creation or after the refashioning of the world following the Flood, the majority of men decided ... [certain principles], then all these things certainly have the force of law, even if a minority disagree.[9]

*Ius gentium* norms were the inviolability of ambassadors, the common ownership of the seas, the enslavement of prisoners of war, the fair treatment of temporary residents, and freedom of travel.

Vitoria's belief in the natural equality of men was in stark contrast to Aristotle's theory of natural slavery, which was in vogue in the sixteenth century,[10] and to the widespread practice of slavery in Europe and the Ottoman Empire. Among the *conquistadores*, many were very much in support of the trade in American Indians. As early as the second voyage of Columbus, the relations with the natives began to worsen, when, on failing to find enough riches, the Spaniards enslaved the Indians and used them as forced labour. Columbus, unable to fulfil his promise to send gold in such quantities as to defray the cost of his undertaking, inaugurated a new and lucrative slave trade. However, the first slaves were liberated and returned to the New World in 1500. From that time, a number of conferences of experts in theology, and canon and civil law, convened by King Ferdinand and by Charles V, discussed the question. The merit of this ethical concern on the part of Spain lies in having prevented attempts to develop a new commercial route that could have displaced large numbers of American slaves to Europe. The Spaniards employed their African slaves during the conquest and also, occasionally, enslaved the Indians but only set them to labour in the newly-discovered territories, and subject to strict regulation imposed from Spain.[11] Like many theologians and jurists of his time, Vitoria accepted certain valid grounds for slavery, such as victory in a just war, but the mere backwardness of the Indians was not in itself sufficient reason to enslave them. Faced with the theories justifying natural slavery, Vitoria affirmed the equality of all men taking direct inspiration from the Gospel: 'the Spaniards are the barbarians' neighbours, as shown by the parable of the Samaritan'.[12]

Vitoria's second important contribution lies in his concern with the justice of the Spanish occupation. He challenged the legitimacy of the following justifications or titles: (i) the Emperor's ownership of the world; (ii) the Pope's authority to grant permission for conquest; (iii) the discovery of America, which 'of itself ... provides no support for possession of these lands, any more than it would if they had discovered us';[13] (iv) the barbarians' unwillingness to accept the Christian faith; (v) the sinfulness of the barbarians; (vi) freedom of choice, since fear and ignorance had played a part; and (vii) the idea of a special legacy from God, in line with Old Testament thinking. Vitoria confirmed only seven legitimate titles by which the Indians came under the tutelage of the Spaniards: (i) the right of natural communication, which allows all men to travel and trade with others; (ii) the Indians' resistance to the preaching of the gospel; (iii) the Spanish tutelage over the Indians after their conversion to Christianity against their infidel rulers; (iv) the authority of the Pope to grant the Indians a Christian ruler if the majority of them were converted; (v) the liberation of the Indians from tyranny, particularly from the customs that threatened innocent victims; (vi) the election of the Spanish monarch by the majority in an 'Indian commonwealth'; and finally, (vii) the alliance of an Indian nation with the Spaniards against another nation.

The just titles enunciated by Vitoria differ very much one from another. The sixth and the seventh typically belong to *ius gentium* and were applied to the European system of states. The fifth constituted a just cause for intervention which is once more in vogue at the end of the twentieth century. The third and the fourth titles legitimised occupation on religious grounds. But in fact this faculty was secondary from the logical point of view, because it was only relevant upon the conversion of some natives subsequent to prior action by the Spaniards on the basis of another legitimate title. The first two titles are the most important, and Vitoria was innovative in their analysis. The first was the *naturalis societatis et communicationis*, the natural society and fellowship of all men. This meant that the Spaniards had 'the right to travel and dwell in those countries, so long as they do no harm to the barbarians, and cannot be prevented by them from doing so'.[14] This included a right to deal peacefully with the Indians and to carry on trade, by importing and exporting goods from the New World. The second title is, in fact, an aspect of the first, since in their relationships with the Indians, the Spaniards could preach the Christian faith, and the natives were under an obligation to allow this. Should they be prevented from preaching, the Spaniards had a right to declare a just war but they could not do this if the Indians would not convert.

But of prime importance now is an understanding that the main legitimate title used by Vitoria was in reality the development of rationality, of peaceful coexistence among diverse peoples through dialogue. In arguing this point, Vitoria did not content himself with reference to the Christian tradition, but also resorted to classical sources. Vitoria, of course, was familiar with Aristotle's teaching on the social nature of man, but did not make use of it because his conception apparently went far beyond. Vitoria rather used a mixture of legal, sacred, pagan and literary references to build up a concept of his own. It is curious to observe that the only quotations from Ovid, Terence and Virgil throughout *De Indis* can be found in the more lively passages on *ius communicationis*. They take us closer to Montaigne's *Essais* than to scholasticism. Vitoria's concept of communication was a principle of *ius gentium* which included the freedom to travel over the world's land and sea, freedom of trade, freedom of entry and settlement for foreigners, and logically the duty of rulers to respect those rights. While Vitoria was expounding this title, he was conscious that it had been abused by his fellow Spaniards. However, as we will see, Vitoria did not show any awareness that the right of *ius communicationis* would benefit powerful states over weak ones.

In the enumeration of the titles Vitoria showed courage in distancing himself from imperialist doctrines. The Emperor was not the lord of the world, for men were free by natural law. These declarations as well as such a critical analysis of the titles could only benefit the Emperor's enemies. In the same vein, his opposition to the authority which the papacy claimed, as it did in the Middle Ages, was brave indeed. As a Dominican, Vitoria lived in monasteries characterised by strict discipline and felt scandalised by the excesses of Rome. The reformers' indignation all around Europe had reached Spain long since.[15] The Spanish friars struggled to reform the corrupt church, directly demanding justice from the Crown. Vitoria rejected the Pope's power to grant through Bulls of Donation the territories of the New World to Spaniards or others.

Related to the fourth illegitimate title and the second legitimate one, is Vitoria's last contribution: the freedom of pagans to convert to Christianity. The doctrine of religious wars was important in the medieval Church, and justified crusades to the Holy Land; it was also applied both to the Spanish *Reconquista* and the acquisition of the Canary Islands

(1404–96). With the Fourth Crusade still in living memory, Aquinas differentiated between heretics who had had the opportunity to accept the Christian faith but had rejected or distorted it, and those who had not had the chance to listen to God's word. Vitoria emphasised that the latter were free to receive the good news because they were rational men. This view was in contrast to many religious prejudices of the age. During the same period, the Ottoman empire had quickly advanced along the Danube and successfully laid siege to Vienna in 1529. Charles V took personal command of the campaigns against the Algerian and Tunisian coasts from 1530 to 1535. The 'just wars' against the Muslims were brutal and legitimised the right to make slaves. Some commentators at the time (and, of course, many *conquistadores*) had their critical faculties dulled by these wars and therefore considered the new Indians to be as infidel as the Moors.

Vitoria resolutely opposed the obligation of the inhabitants of the new territories to embrace the Christian faith, through war, threats and torture. The Spanish Muslims who had been rapidly converted had not done so with sincerity, and this was a disservice to the Christian cause. It was not expedient, on the other hand, to employ force against the Indians on account of their sins. Independently of divine law, totally unknown to them, the natives were obliged by natural law not to engage in odious acts; but here Vitoria distinguished between contraventions of the natural law that might be committed on one's own responsibility, such as fornication or usury, and the violations which demanded external intervention, like sodomy and cannibalism.[16] The distinction was based on a respect for other people's lives. When an innocent person was about to be put to death, the Spaniards were under an obligation to save him even if he did not ask for or want help, 'just as a sick person could be forced to take in medicine'.[17] The method for spreading the word was persuasion, the strength of reason, accompanied by the testimony of a worthy and diligent life and, if possible, by the working of miracles. God had imbued every man with natural reason and had not obliged any to believe what they did not understand. Consequently, the Indians were not under an obligation to believe in Christ at the first encounter, since if the Muslim religion were also preached to them they would be at a loss to establish whether it was more authentic than Christianity. The point here is that Vitoria was convinced that the power of reason would enable the Spaniards' faith to triumph over any other religion, once the Indians had been educated.[18] The result was the elaboration of a mixture of liberty and rational obligation *vis-à-vis* Christianity which was internally inconsistent.

THE CONTRADICTIONS OF AN ACADEMIC FRIAR

Vitoria's works were first published in 1557 in Lyon (and in 1565 in Salamanca), but handwritten copies enjoyed a wide circulation, and soon reached not only the Spanish monarch but also Hispanic America. No doubt Vitoria's *De Indis* caused a stir among the Spanish *intelligentsia*, as evidenced by Charles V's demands for his advice. However, sharp criticism was also directed towards Vitoria's works at the outset. Bartolomé de Las Casas (1474–1566) was one of the first critics. Las Casas was a man of action who showed an admirable devotion to the defence of the Indians through his vehement rhetoric. A colonial priest since 1507, in 1515 he returned to Spain, under the conviction that only the king could end the enormous cruelties being committed in Cuba. His journey proved quite successful and he was appointed 'protector of the Indians'. In January 1540, a year after the famous lecture *De Indis* had been delivered, Las Casas arrived again in Spain so that he too could put pressure on the monarch. In 1542 the progressive *Leyes Nuevas* were promulgated, abolishing slavery once more, even in case of rebellion, and establishing better treatment for the Indians. Charles V designated Las Casas Bishop of Chiapas and sent him with many missionaries to oversee the enforcement of the new laws. However, the strong protests of the colonists, whose acquired rights were endangered, even led to civil strife, and made the implementation of the laws impossible. Las Casas returned yet again to Spain in 1547 and became adviser to the king. With Vitoria already dead, Charles V suspended all rights of conquest while he convened in Valladolid (1550–51) perhaps the most important of all conferences to discuss the legitimacy of the subjection of the Indians. During the proceedings, Las Casas successfully rebutted the arguments of the jurist and humanist Juan Ginés de Sepúlveda, who once more defended the Indians' natural condition as slaves.[19] But inevitably, the latter's views proved more realistic.

Las Casas rejected Vitoria's legitimate titles, because only one was acceptable to him as a justification of the Spanish presence in America: the spread of the gospel without disturbing the kings and natural lords of those territories, and without prejudice to the liberties of its peoples. To the tireless activist, the Salamanca professor must have seemed lukewarm and too deferential to the established order. Since then, Vitoria's works have been severely criticised on the grounds that they constituted the theological and legal foundation for Spain's national interests.[20] In fact, Vitoria acknowledged that a withdrawal from the Indies would bring about serious consequences for the Crown. There is some evidence that Charles V had considered relinquishing the occupation of the Indies. The idea must have been in the air because Vitoria expressly opposed the possibility of leaving the New World. For this reason, he to some extent accepted his country's *faits accomplis*.

To our twentieth-century eyes, three criticisms may be levelled against him, parallel to the three contributions hitherto examined. Though Vitoria conceded that the American native societies were characterised by a certain order represented by their rulers, magistrates, lords and religion, he did not accord international status to Indian political communities. When he discussed the possibility of a voluntary association with the Spanish Crown in the sixth legitimate title, he considered ways of adopting decisions by communities he openly called 'commonwealths' (*reipublicae*), as well as the relations between the people and the 'prince'. Nonetheless, on other occasions he entertained doubts about the ability of the Indians to maintain a government of their own.[21] This contradiction reflects a certain complaisance with the recently established regime in the Indies. He seems to have imagined an Indian commonwealth whose sovereign was the king of Spain, who had to treat his new subjects correctly. In addition to eliminating the barbarian customs and preaching the Christian faith, the king

> cannot put greater burdens on them than on his Christian subjects, either by imposing heavier taxes or by depriving them of their liberties or by any other form of oppression. ... [He] is obliged to make suitable laws for their commonwealth also in temporal matters, so that their temporal goods are protected and increased, and they are not despoiled of their wealth and gold. ... (I)t is not sufficient for a prince to give the barbarians good laws; he must also set ministers over them to ensure observance of the laws.[22]

In his government of the natives, the new Christian prince had to watch solely over the welfare of the Indian republic and not direct attention to his other subjects. For these reasons, the Indians' rights to property, their natural freedom and their equality could only be guaranteed, in Vitoria's opinion, by Spanish legislation. But all this sounds unrealistic, since at the beginning of his work Vitoria expressed concern about the robbery and murder already committed by his compatriots. In the same, rather naive, vein Vitoria emphasised the unlawful aspects of war against unbelievers in *De iure belli*, but the implementation of the laws of war was left to the prince's conscience, for 'once the war has been fought and victory won, he must use his victory with moderation and Christian humility'.[23]

The *ius communicationis* in Vitoria's works is contradictory in another respect. Apparently the right of communication existed, according to *ius gentium*, not only in the New World but also among Europeans, and all men were eligible to exercise it. Vitoria included in the right the possibility of using the *res nullius* and the *res communis* in the oceans, rivers and on land. However, he did not draw a line between these natural resources and the property belonging to the Indians.[24] It is significant how frequently Vitoria used reasoning based on analogy to underscore the equality of the Indians. He stated that they were rational men in the image of God, who could also have cherished a desire to conquer us, and that making war against them was like attacking Seville, and their backwardness was comparable to that of the rural folk of Spain. Yet when he makes reference to the rights of property acknowledged by him, he fails to continue the use of analogy. The contradiction is manifest in Vitoria's works. On the one hand, he declares that the Spaniards may take the gold and pearls of the Indies, if it is not to the detriment of the natives, because such things have no real owner, like the fish in the sea. He affirms also that other Christians may be prevented from trading in the Indies since the Spanish monarchs occupied the territories first, and also because the Pope could prohibit European states from going there in order to forestall any dissensions that might impede the spreading of the gospel. On the other hand, Vitoria stressed that the Indians could own private and public property, and were the Pope or the Emperor to have jurisdiction over them, they would still remain owners of their lands, and above all he argued that the dispositions that the Spanish king was duty-bound to enact to govern the Indians should not permit the taking of their gold and riches. Vitoria maintained also that restitution had to be made for what had been taken away if there was any doubt about the legitimacy of a war which proved later to be unjust.[25] In the face of this lack of consistency, one tends to believe that, after much thought and debate with his university colleagues, Vitoria had to write with two levels of meaning. Vitoria exhibits much vigour in his thought. He could not be blamed for lack of originality; he was already exposed, on account of his writings, to ferocious criticism by the jurists, the court and even the Inquisition. But the prudent tone of his speech suggests that he clearly realised that some consequences were not acceptable for his peers. *De Indis* reflects his mature thought, and there are indications in the text which suggest that Vitoria believed in the internationalist ideals of a later epoch, but was prevented by his historical context from expressing such sentiments.

In attempting to define the causes that legitimised war against the Indians, Vitoria rejected the doctrine of a just religious war. He thus acknowledged a certain freedom of religious choice for the Indians. Nevertheless, the ultimate aim pursued by Vitoria betrayed him, and here the third contradiction appears. He pointed out that the native Indians could attain salvation by obeying natural law and living honestly, and that they could be condemned only for grave sins, but not on the grounds of unbelief. Once the word of God was known, it was the power of reason and will, not the use of force, which would convert them. However, in his absolute belief in the religious and cultural supremacy of Christianity, Vitoria left the Indians little scope to exercise this freedom of choice. Vitoria showed great idealism and did not foresee the possibility, after indoctrination, of a rejection of his faith by the natives. Having come to power by legitimate means, it was the Christian prince's duty to oblige his subjects to forsake their anti-natural customs, and he could also oblige his Indian subjects to obey divine law. Tolerance in Vitoria is not used as a noun but rather as an adjective qualifying the laws that the Christian prince had to enact to convert the new subjects. These laws need not cause any scandal, they had to be enforced with moderation, and with time they had to be capable of changing local customs and introducing the true faith in a reasonable manner.

> It would not be a tolerable law if an edict was suddenly to be published forbidding the worship ... of idols or demanding the worship of Christ on pain of death, or even on pain of exile or confiscation of goods,[26]

he stated. In his study in Salamanca, Vitoria imagined a Socratic conversion, like his academic discussions, that was very far from reality. Juan Gil recounts the anecdote of a poor Indian who, confronted with the preacher and the landholder, was asked which of the two was worse, to which he replied after pondering for some time: 'Father, both of you are worse.'[27]

## EPHEMERAL INFLUENCE

Despite contradictions, Vitoria's works emerge as an anticipation of the doctrine of the equality of all men, irrespective of their condition, and of peaceful coexistence among diverse nations in a *totus orbis*. They exercised great influence in his university, which produced a number of illustrious theologians up to the end of the seventeenth century, whose teaching had great influence in Hispanic America.[28] Domingo de Soto (1496–1560), a friend of Vitoria's, a colleague in the order and in the university, must have discussed many issues with him, because the references to the Indies in Soto's theological work *De iustitia et iure* coincide with those of the master. However, Soto distinguishes, with much more precision than Vitoria, between natural law and *ius gentium*, which prepared the way for further developments. The jurist Fernando Vázquez de Menchaca (1512–69) is another worthy disciple of Vitoria. In his *Contro-versiarum illustrium*, this Salamanca doctor, so much admired by Grotius, emphasised the equality of all men. Vázquez's political theory opposed tyranny and stressed the rule of law, for princes should respect the laws of the state and the contracts they had made. Yet his most outstanding contri-bution was his assertion of the principle of the freedom of the seas, thus denying the Spanish claim to exclusiveness in the trade with the Indies. Vázquez de Menchaca affirmed that the rules of Roman law governing the acquisition of property were not applicable in the international arena, because whereas the lands and rivers had been shared out among nations, the seas had never been distributed, thereby going beyond Vitoria.

Luis de Molina (1535–1600) and Francisco Suárez (1548–1607) were two Jesuits belonging to the next generation, who also trained in Salamanca. In their work, the necessity to resolve concrete problems lost its urgency, which has made their formal theological constructions devoid of much significance for international relations. The separation between the natural law of all men and *ius gentium* was completed, giving to the latter a content defined by tradition. Now this *ius gentium* only obliged *almost* all peoples of the world, which meant, in fact, the 'civilised' peoples. But that separation symbolised the divorce between the ideals of the Counter-Reformation and the stark reality to which these theologians were gradually closing their eyes. One of Suárez's most important contri-butions, however, was the distinction between *ius inter gentes* (the cus-tomary norms of international relations) and *ius intra gentes* or *ius gentium intra se* (the legal institutions common to civilised states).[29] Another Jesuit, José de Acosta (1539–1600) was more of an anthropolo-gist and naturalist and began making scientific observations about the inhabitants of America,[30] thus ushering in a new cycle which hastened the decline of Vitoria's influence. It is interesting to note that the theolog-ical approach at the beginning of the century, replete with quotations, was more sensitive to the Indian problem than the rationalist analysis that fol-lowed. Acosta distinguished between three classes of barbarians; the Chinese and Japanese, the Incas and the Aztecs, and others. Influenced by the doctrine of natural incapability, he maintained that the Indians had to be taught first of all to be men and later to be Christians. The language had changed, giving birth to attitudes that persisted until the nineteenth century.

Vitoria's influence may be linked to a pleasant summer breeze that gradually gives way to the stormy winds of war in Europe. It is true that the debate about the Indian in Spain influenced the laws that were about to be approved, although they granted a superior status to the colonist. The development of the theory of natural law soon lost the vigour with which Vitoria had applied it to practical issues.[31] In spite of the fact that Vitoria's *relectiones* were republished eight times in Europe in the space of a century, it seems that his work was virtually forgotten as a result of the great wars of religion. The European political thinkers of the time made no mention of it, and the practical dimension of his thought was ignored. Yet it seems unbelievable that the internationalists themselves should not have used his works coherently. Rather than look for concrete rhetorical quotations, we only need to look at the contents of historical works to prove that many fundamental topics were abandoned. The very questions that Vitoria called *ius gentium* are those that fill up treatises: diplomatic relations, law of war, treaties, the succession of sovereigns and the law of the seas. But this *ius gentium* was applied only to relations among European powers, and no one sought to extend it to relations with the non-Christian world. Where are the rights of the natives in the newly discovered and conquered territories? Where are the debates on the justice of the use of force against them, in those treatises? Where is the search for concrete norms that regulate affairs in the *totus orbis* and not only in the Christian states? Modern international law was ethnocentric, and legitimised colonialism until the twentieth century, forgetting Vitoria's preoccupations. The rediscovery of his works began at the end of the last century, at the same moment as new conceptions of international society were begining to emerge,[32] and when the unprofitable controversy over the founders of international law arose.

The causes of this neglect are not difficult to find and are very instructive. First, there is a political reason. Spain was the dominant world power in Philip II's reign (1556–98) and, even after the Peace of Westphalia, she was still in control of most of America and the Philippines. The Dutch, English and French penetrated into North America, the Antilles and South-East Asia, which was to have an adverse effect on Spanish and Portuguese interests. Second, there is also an ideological reason. Spain became the defender of Catholicism at the moment when a strong Protestant and Anglican movement was sweeping across northern Europe. Spain was not given credit for its self-criticism in the early days of the conquest of America, but rather Las Casas' vehement works were widely disseminated and the black legend began.[33] Finally, Vitoria did not write for the printing press, nor did he produce any great work on natural law or *ius gentium*. The *relectiones* which were published from the class notes of his disciples circulated more widely in America than in Europe. Only a few graduates of Salamanca taught in

Coimbra, Rome, Ingolstadt and in some other European universities. At the end of the sixteenth century, the works of Soto and Vázquez de Menchaca enjoyed a greater popularity than those of Vitoria. Also, due to a combination of these reasons, the synthetic work of Grotius became very successful in Europe. The short but demanding lectures of the Spanish theologian faded into insignificance when compared with the voluminous *De iure belli ac pacis*, translated and reprinted many times, especially in England and France, and whose purposes were very different from those of the academic friar.[34]

## VITORIA AND MACHIAVELLI: CHARITY vs. POWER; UNIVERSALISM vs. STATISM

The works of Vitoria and Las Casas, among others, have been unjustly relegated to the background in the history of ideas, as if the American adventure had been solely a Spanish experience, remote from Renaissance Europe. As a matter of fact, the circumstances which led to Vitoria's ephemeral influence, discussed above, made it difficult to discuss the very important issues related to European behaviour towards the non-European world for centuries. But for our purposes, this does not detract from Vitoria's significance. The Spanish religious thinkers were faced with a practical question of gigantic proportions. To resolve such a question they resorted to those instruments available to them. St Thomas's works were a constant source of inspiration for Vitoria. But the Salamanca professor was not a pure scholastic, if only because the historical context favoured practical reasoning rather than deductive speculation. At the beginning of the *Summa contra gentiles*, a work well-known to Vitoria, Aquinas had warned that in debates with Muslims, other infidels, and pagans, it was impossible to use arguments based on the truth of the sacred scriptures, because they did not accept that truth. Consequently, one had to resort to natural reasoning which is acceptable to all. In *De Indis*, Vitoria put this idea into practice, not only to convert the Indians to his civilisation and faith, but also to convince his compatriots, whom he knew were not often moved by theological arguments.

But Vitoria's practical approach had a clear purpose. The same profound indignation felt by the first preachers in the Indies, the condemnation of palpable injustice, was the basis of Vitoria's entire work. The real motive force behind his discourse was a humane sensitivity of Christian origin – or, as he would have described it, the virtue of charity, a theme he had studied in detail as embodying a love for one's neighbour.[35]

To support controversial assertions he resorted directly to the gospels: the Pope did not have temporal authority over the world because Christ said, 'My kingdom is not of this world';[36] the princes alleged false rights in order to occupy territories, but 'For what is a man profited ... if he shall gain the whole world, and lose himself, or be cast away?'[37] Vitoria shared the religious desire, which was widespread in Europe and Spain at the beginning of the sixteenth century, to return to the pure doctrine of Christ. Yet he also had to combine that fervour with reality. Vitoria understood that his nation was inextricably involved in the conquest of vast territories, and he thought it necessary to extend the faith and civilisation to the Indians. His peculiar way of introducing charity (or ethics) into international relations was to appeal to the king's conscience with arguments about the need to treat the Indians with greater respect. Perhaps at that time no more could have been done.

Nevertheless, Vitoria's ideas sound too idealistic, sometimes even naive. The conquest of the New World was cruel and the natives were treated brutally, as Vitoria was well aware. The witty Vázquez de Menchaca, from a different point of view, examined some years later the arguments in favour of natural slavery, and said:

> If I am to say what I feel, it seems to me the plain truth, that the doctrine of these authors is pure tyranny introduced under the guise of friendship and good advice, the more effectively to exterminate and ruin the human lineage, because to be able to exercise tyranny, sacking and violence freely, they try to justify it with fictitious names, calling it a beneficial doctrine for those who suffer maltreatment.[38]

Faced with this 'ruin of the human lineage', the academic friar did his best to limit the damage but his appeals were not immediately successful. Las Casas' untiring activity failed as well. Both had an opportunity to influence the most powerful person of their time, Charles V. Yet the following centuries confirmed that it was quite difficult to control the boundless ambition of colonialist adventurers. From this perspective, Vitoria and Las Casas simply proved impotent to change the selfish course of history.

Vitoria's contribution to the thought on relations among peoples was his realisation that the whole world was inhabited by people who were equal in essence and in their rational nature, which conferred on them rights, property and free will. Natural law, which proceeded from the common nature of all men, embodied norms applicable to all, and *ius gentium*, a derivation from natural law, permitted men to relate to each other freely and to trade. Vitoria constructed a universalist – although rather advantageous for the powerful – vision of the world which is in sharp contrast with the statist conception dominant from the beginning of the modern age. Machiavelli, the other originator of the modern study of international relations and the forerunner of the statist conception, wrote with a dual aim, particularly between 1513 and 1520: to obtain an important public post from the Medicis, and to win power and prestige for his nation. He focused on the welfare of a republic whose ruler had to strive by all means to enhance his commonwealth's position, in competition with other states. Machiavelli was an admirer of the Romans, and his ideas about the relations of the Christian states with the outside world were dominated by the benefits of establishing colonies.[39] Colonies, according to him, were cheap, and the victims could not pose any problem if they were few in number or subdued, because they would become poor and defenceless; and grave offences could be hardly redressed. On the other hand, the authors of the Renaissance typical of Christian humanism, such as Erasmus or Vives, advocated correct behaviour on the part of the princes and defended an idealist pacifism,[40] but they were not closely concerned with the problems of the Indies, and they therefore lacked the universal conscience evidenced by Vitoria. The most graphic symbol of the statist attitude was the destruction of the isthmus that linked Utopia to the continent. Thomas More spoke of religious tolerance and other customs within that state but showed some disdain for relations with other peoples.

No doubt, the rise of statism had a lot to do with the anthropocentric point of view inaugurated by the modern age, which was immediately transformed into ethnocentrism. Nonetheless, Renaissance optimism concerning man's faculties soon gave way to the palpable recognition of his cruelty and shortsightedness, denounced forcefully by Hobbes, and bitterly by Shakespeare and Cervantes. Before them, Montaigne had recommended combating man's 'inhumanity' with restraint, that is, acting in accordance with man's ordinary capabilities.[41] Evidently the ethical dimension of the foreign relations among states has not advanced much during the modern era. By the same token, the statist conception has totally dominated international relations right up to the founding of the United Nations. The ethical dimension and the universalist view are two frustrated ideas in the theory of international relations, which perhaps do not have separate existences. Nowadays, those idea are being carefully examined; but one has the impression that the original formulation of the conflict between statism and universalism contained in the writings of these two contrasting personalities of the sixteenth century, Machiavelli and Vitoria, has not changed.

VITORIA AND THE THREE TRADITIONS

The tension between those two poles still poses an interesting problem for the theorist of international relations: the relation between the statist and universalist visions, and the three traditions of the theory of international relations defined by Martin Wight. Hedley Bull[42] seeks to link the realist tradition to statism, the revolutionist tradition to universalism, and the Grotian tradition to internationalism in its widest sense. These associations, which are perhaps introduced for didactic purposes do not manifest themselves as clearly, however, in the work of Wight. I would submit that the two conceptions of statism and universalism can be added, profitably, to the scheme of the three traditions. Martin Wight explains:

> the three traditions are not like three railroad tracks. ... They are streams, with eddies and cross-currents, sometimes interlacing and never for long confined to their own river bed.[43]

Employing his metaphor, statism would be the territory that lies (occasionally) between the currents of realism and rationalism, while universalism would be the space, perhaps more arid, that is found between the currents of the rationalist and revolutionist traditions. Thinkers who navigate between realist and rationalist waters may rest on statist land, but a realist may not be in a position to reach universalism easily. Bull's internationalism would be the bridge that connects, over the rationalist current, the two *terrae firmae*.

On the other hand, it is no easy task to decide in which of the three traditions Vitoria should be included. When dealing with the theory of mankind, and with colonialism, Martin Wight includes Vitoria among the rationalists.[44] This perhaps merits a more thorough consideration. Vitoria affirmed most resolutely the equality of all humanity. If 'the Revolutionists assert [the principle of brotherhood of man] with an emphasis suggesting that they deny not only the Rationalist's cautious qualifications about it, but any qualifications at all',[45] Vitoria is, without doubt, the first revolutionist of the modern era, as he fills the vacuum between the precursors of the revolutionist tradition mentioned by Wight, Alexander the Great and the Stoic philosopher Zeno, and the philosophers of the French Revolution.[46] Vitoria, however, like all complex thinkers, possesses other characteristics. He cannot be considered simply a realist because he always understood the relations with the 'barbarians' as a moral question. Nonetheless, he defended the expansion of his civilisation and religion in Hispanic America, while maintaining a respect for human life. This would be a form of that which Wight calls 'the Rationalist version of the Realist principle that civilization has a right to expand'.[47] Yet, as we have seen, the Spanish friar could not contradict the authority of the king on certain issues, which makes him a rationalist from this point of view. Vitoria is rationalist, above all, because he realises that his state is the only one which can defend the Indians and protect the rights which he proclaims. Thus, although his starting point is universalism, and even though he dips his toes into revolutionist waters, finally he takes his first steps on the bridge that spans the rationalist current.

Whatever the label we attach to Vitoria's views, he raised squarely one of the most important problems of international relations in the modern era, that of colonialism. David Fidler has asked a question which I have repeated constantly to myself – why have other European thinkers not confronted the same problem as Vitoria, that of trying to restrain state power during the expansion of Europe? Wight avers that realism has been the dominant tradition in the course of colonial expansion.[48] As a matter of fact, faced with this problem, the rationalists inclined, rather suspiciously, in favour of realism. I wonder whether the importance of the teaching of Vitoria consists precisely in the combination of different traditions, and of his introduction of a universalist conception and an ethical vision into the rationalist frame. The integration of different points of view may still be useful, given that the inheritance of colonialism is one of the constants of contemporary international relations.

Our discipline is, nowadays, in search of its roots. International relations is concerned with so many ethical problems that, in a sense, it constitutes a branch of social or moral philosophy in its own right. Such a dynamic discipline stands in urgent need of a meatheory. The study of Vitoria teaches some concrete lessons. First of all, that misunderstanding among thinkers of diverse geographical areas, for religious, political or other reasons, impedes the advancement of ideas. If the debate initiated in Spain in the sixteenth century had continued in the rest of Europe, or in other parts of the world, many evils might have been averted. Secondly, there is a lesson that goes to the very heart of international relations: *faits accomplis*, even if they constitute a great injustice, tend to anaesthetise the mind. A great deal of courage is needed to evaluate every historical injustice. Thirdly, even the most independent and lofty theory, which finds a place in the mind of a well-intentioned ruler, will encounter great difficulty in its practical application. The reason lies in the contradictory nature of man, who sooner or later succumbs to his selfishness and loses that which he has gained in understanding.

## NOTES

* The author would like to thank David P. Fidler, Iver B. Neumann and Tunku Varadarajan for their comments and editorial help on earlier drafts of this essay. I am also grateful to Anthony Dzimah for his valuable help in the translation of the script.

1.  Quentin Skinner, *The Foundations of Modern Political Thought. The Renaissance* (Cambridge, 1978) ch. 6.
2.  Wolfgang Preiser, 'History of the Law of Nations. Ancient Times to 1648', *Encyclopedia of Public International Law*, vol. 7 (Amsterdam–New York–Oxford, 1984) p. 151.
3.  *On the American Indians*, edition quoted in note 7 below, p. 238.
4.  Quentin Skinner, 'Machiavelli's *Discorsi* and the pre-humanist origins of republican ideas', Gilsela Bock, Quentin Skinner & Maurizio Viroli (eds), *Machiavelli and Republicanism* (Cambridge, 1990), pp. 121–42.
5.  See Laureano Robles (ed.), *Filosofía iberoamericana en la época del Encuentro* (Madrid, 1992).
6.  Cf. Michael Donelan, 'Spain and the Indies', Hedley Bull and Adam Watson (eds), *The Expansion of International Society* (Oxford, 1984), pp. 75–86.
7.  Francisco de Vitoria, *Political Writings*, ed. Anthony Padgen and Jeremy Lawrence (Cambridge, 1991). In this chapter, Vitoria's *relectiones* are quoted from this edition.
8.  *On the American Indians*, p. 250.
9.  Ibid., p. 281.
10. See Francisco Castilla Urbano, *El pensamiento de Francisco de Vitoria. Filosofía política e indio americano* (Barcelona–Mexico, 1992), pp. 245–75.
11. See José Luis Cortés López, *La esclavitud negra en la España peninsular del siglo XVI* (Salamanca, 1989).
12. *On the American Indians*, p. 279.
13. Ibid., p. 265.
14. Ibid., 278.
15. Marcel Bataillon, *Érasme et l'Espagne* (Paris, 1937).
16. *On Self-Restraint*, p. 230.
17. *Lectiones in secundam secundae Summae theologicae S. Thomae Aquinatis*, vol. I (Salamanca, 1932) ed. Vicente Beltrán de Heredia, *quaestio* X, *art.* VIII § 3.
18. *Lectiones* quoted in n. 17, vol. I, *quaestio* X, *art.* VIII § 4.
19. Lewis Hanke, *All Mankind is One. A Study of the Disputation between Bartolomé de Las Casas and Juan Ginés de Sepúlveda in 1550 on the Intellectual and Religious Capacity of the American Indian* (De Kalb, Ill., 1974).
20. See, for instance, Robert A. Williams Jr, *The American Indian in Western Legal Thought* (New York–Oxford, 1990), p. 326.
21. Vitoria added an eighth legitimate title which seemed to him a bit dubious: the near inability of the Indians to constitute and administer a commonwealth 'ordered in civil and human terms' (*On the American Indians*, p. 290).
22. *On Self-Restraint*, pp. 227–8.

23. *On the Law of War*, p. 327.
24. *On the American Indians*, p. 280.
25. *On the Law of War*, p. 313.
26. *On Self-Restraint*, p. 228–9.
27. Juan Gil, 'Conquista y justicia: España y las Indias', in Fernando Vallespín (ed.), *Historia de la teoría política*, vol. 2 (Madrid, 1990) p. 442.
28. See Antonio Garcia (ed.), *La protección del indio* (Salamanca, 1989); Luciano Pereña, *La idea de justicia en la conquista de América* (Madrid, 1992); and Demetrio Ramos (ed.), *La ética en la conquista de América* (Madrid, 1984).
29. *De legibus* (1612) book II, ch. XIX §§ 8–10; ch. XX §§ 6–8. Cf. R. J. Vincent, *Human Rights and International Relations* (Cambridge, 1986), pp. 104, 151–2.
30. Anthony Pagden, *The Fall of Natural Man. The American Indian and the Origins of Comparative Ethnology* (Cambridge, 1982; reprinted with additons, 1986) ch. 7.
31. Cf. Antonio-Enrique Pérez Luño, *La polémica sobre el Nuevo Mundo* (Madrid, 1992).
32. See Lewis Hanke, *The Spanish Struggle for Justice in the Conquest of America* (Philadelphia, 1949); and James Brown Scott, *The Catholic Conception of International Law* (Washington, 1934).
33. Ricardo García Cárcel, *La leyenda negra* (Madrid, 1992).
34. G. G. Roelofsen investigates Grotius's immediate political purposes: 'Grotius and the International Politics of the 17th Century', in Hedley Bull, Benedict Kingsbury and Adam Roberts (eds), *Hugo Grotius and International Relations* (Oxford, 1990), pp. 95–131.
35. *Relectio De augmento charitatis* (1535). An original Latin version of Vitoria's 13 known *relectiones*, with Spanish translation, was published as *Obras de Francisco de Vitoria. Relecciones teológicas*, ed. Teófilo Urdánoz (Madrid, 1960).
36. *On the American Indians*, p. 256.
37. Ibid., p. 277.
38. Fernando Vázquez de Menchaca, *Controversiarum illustrium* (1559), ed. Fidel Rodríguez Alcalde (Valladolid, 1931), book I, ch. X § 12.
39. *The Prince*, III; *The Discourses*, book I, 1 & book II, 6.
40. J. A. Fernández-Santamaría, *The State, War and Peace. Spanish Political Thought in the Renaissance, 1516–1559* (Cambridge, 1977), ch. V.
41. In his essay on the cannibals, Montaigne wrote: 'Nous les pouvons donc bien appeller barbares, eu esgard aux regles de la raison, mais non pas eu esgard à nous, qui les sourpassons en toute sorte de barbarie', *Essais*, book I, ch. XXXI, ed. Jean Plattard (Paris, 1946), vol. II, p. 99.
42. *The Anarchical Society* (London, 1977), pp. 24–7.
43. *International Theory, The Three Traditions*, ed. Gabriele Wight and Brian Porter (Leicester & London, 1991), p. 260.
44. Ibid., pp. 70–1.
45. Ibid., p. 83.
46. Ibid., pp. 83–5.
47. Ibid., p. 79.
48. Ibid., pp. 52–3.

# 6 Desperately Clinging to Grotian and Kantian Sheep: Rousseau's Attempted Escape from the State of War

David P. Fidler

'Man is born free, and everywhere he is in chains.'[1] So begins the *Social Contract* (1762), Jean-Jacques Rousseau's great effort to break the chains binding mankind so as to allow human nature to recapture some of the moral potential which civilisation had stolen. Much of the power in Rousseau's political thinking comes from the cruel connection between the chains of corrupted human nature, tyranny and war. While Rousseau might have removed some links through his fierce personal independence and solitude and his theory of the social contract state, he found the chains of war the most difficult to loosen. Since *amour propre*, tyranny, and war connect in Rousseau's thinking, any hope for even a slight moral regeneration in the individual was lost if the state of war was not somehow resolved. Man may be born free; but, in Rousseau's thinking, international relations threatened that everywhere he would remain in chains.

Understanding why Rousseau's political and moral thought foundered in the turbulent waters of international relations is not easy, for his writings in this area are fragmentary, which gives the illusion that Rousseau did not consider the subject. He hints as much at the end of the *Social Contract*. But how much of his assertion that international relations 'forms a new field which is too vast for my limited vision'[2] is humility or a disingenuous frustration? Could the professed incompleteness of his thinking in this area mask a clear and disturbing vision of international politics that haunted all his efforts to regenerate some moral potential for man? Rousseau's *caveat* on his international political thinking at the end of the *Social Contract* was written in the early 1760s, rather late in his literary

120

career, but *after* he had constructed a chilling analysis of international relations. Further, his perspective on international relations remains constant from his earliest to his latest writings.[3] By the time Rousseau wrote the final version of the *Social Contract*, the field of international relations was neither 'new' nor 'too vast' for Rousseau's vision. He had come to grips with international relations prior to 1762.[4] Rousseau had been in the French diplomatic service,[5] and he was a keen observer of the international politics of his age.[6] Rousseau displayed a sense of superiority over Voltaire on the subject of foreign affairs in the *Confessions*.[7] Further, his writings, however fragmentary, show a radical and compelling approach to international relations.[8]

The humble assertion in the *Social Contract* hides a deeper problem for Rousseau: to reveal at the end of the *Social Contract* the full thrust of his already developed theory of international relations would have been to crush his great creation at its first appearance. Rousseau's theory of international relations has been interpreted as one of the most pessimistic perspectives. The development of this perspective within the context of his overall political thought, however, suggests that Rousseau himself could not accept the full horror that his analysis produced because that would mean that all mankind's chains would forever exist and that his own independent spirit and republican convictions were in fact the real illusions.

Essential to understanding Rousseau's perspective on international relations is comprehending that his thinking forms an intertwined system of thought.[9] As a result, we cannot understand Rousseau's concern about the state of war without appreciating his attitude on human nature, society and the state. To speak of Rousseau's 'theory' of international relations loses sight of the fact that he studied international relations as part of his overall attempt to explain and influence the political life of individuals and peoples. For example, after Rousseau established himself in the Hermitage in 1756, he planned three projects that demonstrate his connected system of thought. One project involved examining the formation of man's morality, which Rousseau wanted to call *The Morals of Sensibility*.[10] A second project related to the following question: 'What is the nature of the government best fitted to create the most virtuous, the most enlightened, the wisest, and, in fact, the best people, taking the word "best" in its highest sense?'[11] This question, of course, provides the subject for Rousseau's *Social Contract*. The third project was editing the writings of the Abbé de

Saint-Pierre, the first selection of which Rousseau turned to being Saint-Pierre's *Project for Perpetual Peace.*[12] But within his system of political thought, international relations, as we shall see, takes on an awesome role.

In brief, Rousseau's system of political thought propounds the following: human nature before the development of society was marked by *amour de soi*, a concern for self-preservation combined with a sense of compassion. The advent of society destroyed the idyll of the state of nature and began the corruption of human nature, transforming the peaceful *amour de soi* into the petty and vain *amour propre*. Society, however, also awakens in human nature moral sensibility – the ability to remain an autonomous being and to live in harmony with others by participating in self- and community-governance through rules he creates and obeys. The passions and violence stirred up by *amour propre* shackle the moral sensibility as insecurity of person and property alienate the individual from the community and from the sense of autonomy. The need for a state becomes paramount, and Rousseau portrays the development of civil society as a trick designed by the rich and powerful to trap the poor and weak into a condition of fear and dependence.

Tyranny within the state makes life miserable at home and exposes the citizens to new dangers abroad, as princes and leaders find war an attractive means of growing richer and more powerful. But tyranny is not the only cause of war. Rousseau also believes that the very system created by the interaction of independent states forces states, even good states, into the 'state of war'.[13] So, the state of war combines three problems: the corruption of human nature by the advent of civilisation, the unequal and oppressive conditions of citizens under tyrannous governments, and the very nature of the international system.

## 1.  THE CORRUPTION OF HUMAN NATURE

Rousseau's fame began with his early writings, in which he challenged the Enlightenment assumption that man had made moral and political progress since ancient times through science and art [14] Rousseau's thesis was that civilisation and all its trappings had corrupted human nature from its original state of ignorance and innocence. Rousseau's famous depiction of man in the state of nature was his metaphor for what he sensed was a primal goodness in human nature. In the state of nature, the 'goodness' in human nature was not 'goodness' in a moral sense, for Rousseau did not believe morality as such existed before society developed. The 'goodness', rather, was a liberty and autonomy that did not create violence, fear or want in the self or in others. This autonomy mingled peacefully with the other-regarding aspect of *amour de soi*; Rousseau believed that natural man possessed the ability to feel compassion for others – not a paternalistic pity, but a natural, untainted emotion that provided an unspoken and unwritten bond between the free souls of the forest.

This mystical state of personal liberty and compassion, however, could not sustain the changes brought about by the development of society. Rousseau proposes that the state of nature ended when the first person enclosed some land and claimed it for his own. Perhaps the first enclosure was innocent, but such a change to the prior freedom of movement and forage forced men to come into more contact with each other. Rousseau believed this led to families and small collectivities of numerous families. Pre-political society was born, and never again would human nature be uncorrupted. Rousseau argued that society, even one without a formal government, changed the behaviour of humans. Personal autonomy was curtailed as property was enclosed, the gathering of food was organised, and the satisfaction of sexual urges ritualised. The natural sense of compassion mutated by regular contact with others into a self-centred emotion of vanity and insecurity. The happiness of the state of nature, which was the equality of nature and the equality of ignorance and independence, disappeared, to be replaced by dependence, competition and inequality.

Rousseau, however, saw an even darker side to this corruption of human nature. The coming of society did not obliterate the lingering sense humans retained that life would be better if personal autonomy could be enhanced while at the same time forging real communities between people. This feeling was the echo of *amour de soi*, and is the source, however faint and threatened, of morality in society. But the echo was also a source of frustration as human relations became regularised in patterns of unhealthy envy and conflict. Man could sense the moral but could not have it. What a far cry from the state of nature where happiness, like ripe fruit upon the tree, was within easy and abundant reach.

## 2.   THE DEVELOPMENT OF TYRANNY

Human relations had deteriorated so much in pre-political society that communities realised that some form of government was needed to guarantee personal safety and property. The rich came to understand that the safest way to preserve wealth and advantage was to control the poor. The poor believed that the best way to secure life and what little they had from the arbitrary power flowing in pre-political society was to join with the rich and institute a government that would protect all. The creation of a government also appealed to the nascent moral sense: perhaps through government autonomy could be restored and real community established.

However, Rousseau describes the formation of the state as an unequal bargain from the first moment. He writes in *Discourse on Political Economy*:

> The terms of the social compact between these two orders of people may be expressed in a few words: 'You need me because I am rich and you are poor – we will therefore come to this agreement: I will permit you to have the honour of serving me on the condition that you give me what little remains in your possession, in return for the pains I shall take to command you.'[15]

Pre-political society had already created the dependency upon which tyranny in the state would be built.

With the origins of government tainted by inequality, fear and dependence, the development of the state and of the institutions exercising central power and control accelerated the corruption of human nature and legitimised the oppression of the weak many by the fortunate few.[16] In *The State of War*, Rousseau surveyed the domestic political conditions in Europe and saw 'unfortunate nations groaning under yokes of iron, the human race crushed by a handful of oppressors, a starving crowd overwhelmed with pain and hunger, whose blood and tears the rich drink in peace, and everywhere the strong armed against the weak with the formidable power of the law'.[17] This macabre view becomes even darker when we understand the frustrated moral urges society and community awaken in human nature. In a situation of tyranny, where the rulers' interests diverge from the needs and cares of the ruled, achieving moral autonomy as a citizen and as an individual becomes impossible. Yet for many, the moral sensibility continues to yearn in vain; and the subject assumes the position of an innocent Tantalus, perpetually close to nourishment forever denied.

## 3.  THE STATE OF WAR

Rousseau's international thinking builds upon his analysis of the corruption of human nature and the development of tyranny but also adds a third chain through his perspective on the structure and dynamics of the international system. Given the interlocking aspects of Rousseau's thinking, international relations does not separate from the fortunes of human nature and the political conditions within states. Rousseau's systemic view of international relations thus not only partakes of the consequences of the spoilage of human nature and the growth of tyrannous government but also explores phenomena that exacerbate such consequences. One is left with the sense that the chain in most need of breaking is the state of war. Rousseau believed this and struggled desperately to escape the conclusions of his perspective on international relations.

Rousseau might be seen as a 'first image'[18] theorist: the advent of civilisation degrades human nature, which produces the conditions for tyranny, which generates interstate conflict. Note, however, that for Rousseau *corrupted* human nature plays a role in war; Rousseau focuses on a process rather than a condition. The processes of informal communal interaction in pre-political society and later formal contacts in society warped human nature from its original constitution. International relations form yet another set of interactions that reinforce the warping and perhaps encourage warping anew.

As noted earlier, *amour propre* creates within human nature vanity, insecurity and dependence. The nature of international relations sharpens these vices because the uncertainty and danger projected by a system of near-anarchy encourages individuals to seek self-image, security and satisfaction of needs within their immediate communities. In *Discourse on Political Economy*, Rousseau observes that an individual's sympathy and association for others weakens the further from his immediate community such feelings extend.[19] Such could not have been the case in Rousseau's state of nature because humans wandered free from passions of association and dependence. The corruption of human nature by the advent of civilisation created the conditions for fear of and prejudice against 'foreigners'. In this respect, Rousseau contends that international relations connects with the most basic passions of human nature in society. Men are not, as Hobbes argued, sheltered from the forces alive in the international system. International relations, as a result, 'nationalises' human nature.[20] This process further tortures man's remaining moral sensibility because, paradoxically, individuals draw closer together through alienation from other communities. The moral horizon is limited and confined. Perhaps here is the key to Rousseau's curious use of nationalism in his solution to the state of war examined in the next section.

The effect international relations has on *amour propre* flows into the dynamics of tyrannous governments. As mentioned above, the uncertainty generated in international relations forces citizens to depend emotionally and politically on their leaders. The unequal social contract formed as men first entered into political society is the mirror-image of the process that continues after states are formed and international relations begin. The dangers inherent in the anarchical environment of international relations demand a power structure within a state that can provide the people with security. Those with power and position within the state become the diplomatists and statespersons. One difference from the formation of the original social contract is that the dependence upon the powerful created by international relations lacks any echo from *amour de soi*. The formation of government appealed to the moral sensibility developed in the transition from natural equality and autonomy to social dependence. Rousseau, however, believed that the development of society limited the moral sensibility so that it had no real effect beyond the boundaries of a particular community. Diplomacy, as a result, lacked any potential to contribute to the moral regeneration of mankind. It was an endeavour based on expediency and naked fear.

Diplomacy also could not be isolated from the dynamics of domestic politics; and the inequality between rich and poor fed into the nature of diplomacy. Diplomacy, in other words, was a tool of tyranny. Princes used international relations to increase power at home and to satisfy ambition abroad.[21] In Rousseau's eyes, the illegitimate basis for the ruler's power domestically provided the worst foundation upon which to act internationally because absolute power increased at home, further alienating classes of society, and only the narrow, vain interests of the powerful were objects of diplomatic and military activity, which threatened the security of the entire people. War was one of the consequences of a diplomacy built upon the unequal social contract.[22]

From this analysis, it might appear that Rousseau is a 'second image' writer as tyranny produces conflict and war.[23] But again we must be careful not to label Rousseau. He believed that absolute governments did promote war and violence in the pursuit of security or advantage. The answer to the 'second image' cause of war, of course, is to change the nature of the states in the international system. Although Rousseau had a theory for constructing a just and moral state, his analysis of international relations made a 'second image' solution impossible. Rousseau also had a systemic (or 'third image') aspect to his international thinking.[24] As early as *Discourse on Political Economy*, Rousseau argued that the very structure of the international system rendered security and peace fragile.[25] Thus, even the well-constructed state that promised some moral regeneration and autonomy for its citizens would be trapped in the dynamics of competition and dependence fostered by international relations. These dynamics, in the end, threaten to unravel the whole political and moral effort to regenerate autonomy and moral sensibility in society. Rousseau has constructed his political theory in a manner that requires the resolution of the state of war before moral or political reforms within a society can have anything other than a precarious existence.

Rousseau addressed normatively the corruption of human nature, the development of tyranny, and the state of war in his political thinking. The state of war, however, proved the most difficult chain as Rousseau struggled to find an answer strong enough to snap its constricting links. Rousseau's entire project was imperilled; and he faced two alternatives, either to declare that he could not break the remaining chain, which would have been an admission that he could not remove any chains from mankind, or to pretend that he had not considered the question, and leave open the possibility of a solution to the state of war. Rousseau, in a sense, did both, which illustrates the deep trouble international relations caused in his thinking.

Since human nature itself was not originally corrupt, the problem in regenerating moral autonomy under Rousseau's perspective was society and the impact that it had on human passions. Society, and the individual's relationship to it, had to be reformed before human nature could regain even a glimmer of its original freedom. Such a reformation would have to include the nature of government itself, for moral autonomy after the fall could only come through participatory governance. Republicanism, in turn, had to be supported by a particular type of economic society that would produce the material goods to allow the people to be self-sufficient.

The *Social Contract*, of course, was Rousseau's great effort to break the chains of corrupted human nature and tyranny. The underlying principle of Rousseau's republicanism in the *Social Contract* is that some moral autonomy can be regained by allowing people to rule themselves. Such direct democracy gives each citizen the right to decide the rules of social behaviour. Such a right substitutes for the full freedom of the state of nature. Republicanism, further, develops that moral sensibility towards others stimulated by society but frustrated by the alienation caused by the unequal social contract struck between the rich and the poor. With all citizens determining the rules of the society, equality accompanies the new freedom republicanism gives to each individual. Such equality blunts the dependence and vanity created by *amour propre* thus strengthening the ancient echo of *amour de soi*.

Rousseau, however, realised that producing new forms of freedom and equality through republicanism required certain political and economic conditions. It is in these conditions that one sees how Rousseau's perspective on international relations influenced his analysis of human nature and the state. Rousseau believed that the conditions of individual equality and freedom could only be achieved through a small state.[26] The republican emphasis on direct democracy, of course, highlights the appropriateness of a small community. In Rousseau's mind also is his belief that equal and free associations of people can only transpire in a contained or limited context. Rousseau saw in large states and empires the imprint of conquest and subjugation, which he thought could never be the foundations of legitimate political power. Rousseau observed the Seven Years' War (1756–63), and he realised '[m]ore than most people … that the Seven Years War was a new kind of war', not about dynastic succession 'but a struggle for colonial territory overseas.'[27] In December 1759, Rousseau explained to fellow Genevans Favre and De Tournes that the Seven Years' War was a war of empire-building overseas and that the English were out to 'build up a great empire, destroy the Spanish fleet and dominate the commerce of the southern seas'.[28] At the end of this war, England had gained an empire in Canada, the Caribbean and India. Such imperial ambition and success contributed to Rousseau's refusal to see England as a 'mirror of liberty', which was a popular view among many French Enlightenment figures.[29] The first version of the *Social Contract* contains a fierce attack on colonialism as Rousseau believed conquest 'could never produce a civil state, but merely a modified state of war'.[30]

In essence, Rousseau argued that the dynamics of international relations poisoned the potential of many communities to form proper politics. As Rousseau argues in the first version of the *Social Contract*, the state of war had already rendered some people incapable of republican government through the ravages of war and subjugation.[31] Rousseau, in a sense, writes off great chunks of Europe as despoiled by the state of war. This was not a conclusion that Rousseau came to easily, nor can it be interpreted as an empty generalisation. During 1762, for example, Rousseau believed that Frederick the Great, within whose territory Rousseau was then in exile, '[o]nce peace was made … with his military and political glory at its height, … would win glory of another kind by reviving his dominions, by restoring their agriculture and commerce, by creating a new soil and populating it anew, by maintaining peace among all his neighbors, and making himself the arbiter of Europe where once he had been its terror.'[32] When Rousseau perceived that Frederick was not seeking 'glory of another kind', he 'ventured to write to him on the subject … in order to bring to his ears the sacred voice of truth which so few kings are born to hear'.[33] The spectacle of Rousseau placing hopes for a new Europe upon a despot at the very time the republicanism of the *Social Contract* was flowing through his mind indicates the depth of his desire to find a way out of the state of war. Rousseau's analysis of international relations and perhaps his disappointment with Frederick the Great led him to believe that, for some peoples, there was no hope of breaking the international political chain weighing down man's moral autonomy and political potential.

Geographical limits, however, are not the only conditions Rousseau thought necessary to establish equality and freedom in the social contract state. A specific type of economic system would also be required. Rousseau favoured an agricultural economy as most conducive to the development of freedom and equality.[34] Rousseau believed that agriculture promoted equality between citizens as it did not foster dependence and inequality of wealth as did commerce and industry. Agriculture also brought people closer to a relationship with nature that was lost in the development of civilisation. Rousseau drew power and inspiration from the rustic lifestyle he adopted after leaving Paris in 1756,[35] and he believed that close contact with the forces of nature ennobled the spirit by nurturing virtue.[36]

International relations also plays a major role in Rousseau's insistence on an agricultural economy. Just as commerce and industry created dependence and inequality among individuals and classes within society, Rousseau believed that trade between nations similarly fostered dependence, inequality, and thus conflict between states.[37] Rousseau emphasised agriculture because such an economy would provide a nation with autonomy. He also believed that an agriculturally based economy would not produce the type of wealth and affluence that would make other states fearful or whet the appetite of rapacious princes. It would be neither profitable nor manly to conquer a people so poor and dull.

Economic autarky further contributes to the final element in Rousseau's restoration of moral potential through republicanism – patriotism. Rousseau believed that a civic religion – love of country – was needed to solidify the republican process and to assure the success of an autarkic agricultural economy.[38] We observed earlier that Rousseau maintained that the corruption of human nature by the advent of society limited man's moral horizon. Moral sensibilities weakened beyond the boundaries of an individual's immediate community. Rousseau did not believe in the possibility of a universal or cosmopolitan morality, and he attacks cosmopolitan values and those professing to be cosmopolitan.[39] Here Rousseau does not attempt to undo the damage done by the coming of society; rather he attempts to use this moral limitation in his attempt to bring equality, freedom and happiness back to human nature and society. In Rousseau's view, love of country was meant to reinforce direct democracy and a self-sufficient economy by elevating participation in the political life and dedication to the fertility of the land to almost religious stature. Political stability and material prosperity would be the parents and progeny of patriotic virtue.

At the international level, Rousseau's patriotism was designed to achieve two objectives. First, Rousseau understood that the corruption of human nature and the machinations of tyranny combined to generate a fear of and hostility toward foreign states and peoples. Rousseau hoped to make nationalism a positive rather than a negative force by strengthening the political, economic, and moral bonds between citizens within the state and reducing the need and ambition for contact with foreigners.[40] A patriotic nation would be a content and confident nation without hatred for foreigners or the need or pretence to become entangled in the affairs of other states.

Second, Rousseau wanted his patriotism to be a deterrent in the international system. A people dedicated to their independence and equality would prove a savage foe on the battlefield.[41] Such a people would be fighting not on the whim of a dynastical tyrant but for the preservation of a way of life dear to their hearts.

Such, in brief, was Rousseau's attempt to break the chains of corrupted human nature and tyranny. We note, however, that while Rousseau attempts to alter the structure and dynamics and politics within the state, he makes no similar attempt at the international level. In fact, at many points Rousseau has factored into his social contract theory the dangers and uncertainties of international relations. The impression conveyed by this is that the chain representing the state of war cannot be broken. Rousseau, in fact, came to this conclusion and formulated a response to the problem of international relations that attempted to remove the social contract state from the entire structure and process of international politics. Rousseau himself, however, indicated how unrealistic his solution was as he formulated a further policy for the social contract state. In doing so, Rousseau admitted that the debilitating forces of international relations could not be avoided but could at most only be held at bay.

In this section, we will look at Rousseau's responses to the state of war by comparing them to the responses found in the Hobbesian (realist), Grotian (rationalist), and Kantian (revolutionist) traditions of international relations thinking.

Rousseau is most frequently associated with the realist tradition of international relations theory because his structural analysis of international relations revealed a condition of anarchy, conflict and war between states. Rousseau's thinking, however, does not rest comfortably within the realist tradition.

The most obvious problem in arguing that Rousseau is a realist is that his normative thought was unrealistic. If, in Martin Wight's words, realism 'concentrates on the actual, what is, rather than the ideal, or what ought to be; on facts rather than obligations',[42] Rousseau's strategy of isolating small social contract states from other states is the type of utopian thinking antithetical to the realist tradition. Realist foreign policy teaches that there is no escape from anarchy, conflict and war. Rousseau resisted embracing such a conclusion.

Rousseau is also at cross-purposes with the realist tradition on the point of international society. In its various forms, realism finds either no place for conceptions of international society, or sees a crude and minimal society between great powers or between states. Rousseau, however, seems bothered that a deep and sophisticated international society exists. In the *Abstract of Saint-Pierre's Project of Perpetual Peace*, Rousseau describes a European international society with interests and values that transcended borders.[43] Rousseau did not think, however, that this was positive because international society contributed to tension, conflict and violence in the international system. Rousseau's focus on the nation and its retreat from international relations demonstrates his desire to put an end to international society. Rousseau turns what Grotians and Kantians view as positive and desirable into a source of evil.

The key to understanding Rousseau's view on international society is found in his theory of the development of society itself. For Rousseau, the coming of society was regressive rather than progressive. Society functions on the dynamics generated by inequality and oppression. Thus, those commanding civil societies collectively create international society. Rousseau likened the reign of terror within the state to the culture of power, militarism and war that pervaded the ruling classes of the European states. It was this culture that Rousseau tried to persuade Frederick the Great to abandon for 'glory of another kind'. His contempt for cosmopolitanism also stems from this analysis.

Rousseau's conception of society also plays an important role in another difference between his perspective and the realist tradition: his moral passion. Realists tend to view morality as a byproduct of the structuring of power. The permanence of anarchy between states prevents a morality between states or a transnational morality from coming into existence. Rousseau's thinking differs in three ways. First, his morality stems not from the structure of the domestic society but from the echoes of *amour de soi*: individual autonomy and freedom. Second, the process of ordering power within society does not create morality but debases moral potential through the aggravation of *amour propre*. Third, morality at the international level is impossible not because of anarchy but because the corruption of human nature by the development of society has limited the moral potential of man. Thus, Rousseau's moral passion focuses on the nation and the state. Rousseau's nationalism is the redemptive force for mankind's moral potential. If the nation is the source of moral regeneration, it must be preserved from external corruptive forces. Isolation is a moral imperative. Rousseau is not the detached realist; he is the anguished moralist desperately seeking a way to redeem some small fragment of human morality.

The moralism driving Rousseau's thinking on international relations might suggest an affinity with the Grotian and Kantian traditions. Any affinity does not occur in Rousseau's descriptive analysis. The Grotian tradition is made up of 'those who concentrate on, and believe in the value of, the element of international intercourse in a condition predominantly of international anarchy'.[44] Rousseau believed that diplomacy, international law and international trade exacerbated the problems created by the anarchical structure of international relations. Instead of being marks of rational thought, Rousseau saw such international intercourse as characteristics and catalysts of baser passions.

The Kantian tradition is concerned with 'the multiplicity of sovereign states form[ing] a moral and cultural whole'.[45] The normative project of the Kantian tradition is to solidify or even create an international and transnational community. As we have seen, Rousseau poured scorn upon notions of cosmopolitanism. He sought to terminate the social contract state's international and transnational links.

Although Rousseau's positions conflict with the Grotian and Kantian traditions at many points, his thinking contains some ideas associated with those traditions. Recall that Rousseau's political thinking is so connected that if the chain of war remains unbroken his political and moral hopes would be dashed. Rousseau sensed that his strategy of isolation was inadequate to ensure the survival of his hopes. Rousseau realised that isolated, small social contract states always faced the threat of aggression because of the nature of the international system. Although a state may extract itself from international society, it cannot escape the international system. To overcome this dilemma, Rousseau suggested that small social contract states form defensive confederations to deter aggression.[46] In essence, Rousseau advises that diplomacy and treaties would be a rational course of action for social contract states. Here is a weak echo of Grotian thinking, because Rousseau's confederative strategy arises from his belief in the value of at least limited international intercourse between social contract states. The confederative strategy is not realist because Rousseau advises that such alliances be entered into only among social contract states, so the strategy does not represent balance-of-power politics. The basis for the strategy is not purely self-interest but a philosophical likemindedness. Republicanism acts as Rousseau's 'natural law' to which reason responds in forming the social contract state and the alliance of social contract states. This strategy reflects Rousseau's estimation that social contract states could keep their relations rational and void of the power machinations pervading international relations generally.[47] As Cranston explains Rousseau's view, '[o]nly in a republic ... could true liberty be achieved; and only republics could be expected to live side by side in orderly tranquillity.'[48]

The confederative strategy for social contract states raises another question. Is there something in the likemindedness of social contract states that would allow them to keep their relations rational rather than manipulative? Was Rousseau's attempt to bring these philosophically similar states into an alliance an admission of the possibility, however limited, of a non-violent *society* of certain states? What distinguishes Rousseau's confederation from balance-of-power politics is the political nature of the regimes in question. Republican homogeneity could work because all the states involved would be committed to principles of non-intervention and non-aggression. Presumably, limited diplomatic contacts and treaties would not produce the type of conflict such intercourse generated between non-social contract states because the republican nature of the social contract states would blunt the damaging effects of 'the evil practice of "comparing oneself in order to know oneself"'.[49] Social contract states would share common values (deterrence of aggression and non-intervention) and common institutions (treaties) and thus form a peculiar type of international society.[50] Rousseau's confederative strategy moves, however incompletely, towards the Kantian tradition in postulating the possibility of a limited family of states and nations.[51]

My conjectures about Rousseau's confederative strategy are supported somewhat by Kant's close study of Rousseau. Kant understood Rousseau's point that the state of war threatened individual moral potential and domestic political stability. Kant's plan for perpetual peace projects Rousseau's confederative strategy for republican states on to a universal canvas.[52] Kant, however, does not write off great chunks of Europe as morally wasted by the ceaseless torment of tyranny and war. Instead, Kant makes war the author of peace through a historical process by which states grope towards republican government and a confederative international arrangement.[53] The ultimate difference, then, is not political but moral. Rousseau believed war had destroyed the moral potential of much of mankind. Kant believed that war had yet to awaken the full moral potential of most of mankind.

Regardless whether the confederative strategy hints at Grotian and Kantian elements, it is vulnerable to Rousseau's own systemic analysis of international relations. If a good state can engage in an unjust war, as Rousseau asserts in *Discourse on Political Economy*,[54] then the limited relations between social contract states might develop the tragic dynamics of traditional diplomacy under the tremendous pressures created by an anarchical system of sovereign states. Rousseau's effort to keep a flicker of hope alive may in the end be engulfed by the darkness of his own perspective.

Analysing Rousseau's thought against the Hobbesian, Grotian and Kantian traditions perhaps produces more confusion than clarity. The image of Rousseau as a realist ignores his desperate attempt to provide an escape from the state of war. In this attempt we find traces of rationalism and revolutionism. The 'permanent dialogue' between Kant and Rousseau may be conducted on more common ground than is generally appreciated.[55] Extreme readings of Rousseau and Kant make the dialogue stark and harsh. More tempered interpretations point to a common path upon which both thinkers tread. Wight noted the presence of a middle road between the realist descent into anarchy and the revolutionist flight towards universalism.[56] Perhaps our interpretation of the dialogue between Rousseau and Kant should recognise that Rousseau took tentative steps upon this middle road, whose hesitant footprints Kant followed on a more ambitious walk. These common steps remain obscured because Rousseau's brooding perspective overshadows the tentative and limited nature of his effort and because the robust energy of Kant's thinking encourages radical hopes. As Wight notes, famous thinkers can be found at times upon this middle road but at other moments dashing off in another direction. If Kant 'shows a disquieting tendency to dart away ... towards the crags and precipices' of revolutionism, then Rousseau exhibits a penchant for retreating in moral agony 'downwards towards the marshes and swamps of realism'.[57]

Despite the originality and complexity of Rousseau's perspective on international relations, some do not find his perspective relevant to the contemporary study of international relations. T. J. Hochstrasser, for example, writes that 'the case for Rousseau's relevance to the contemporary study of international relations seems ... to remain unproven. At most he seems to tell a familiar cautionary tale of how "the very intercourse of nations breeds conflict; that it is not possible to end such intercourse, that the only remedies are fragile mitigating devices"'.[58] Such dismissals of Rousseau's thinking fail to appreciate the tormented mixture of his political analysis and moral hopes, in which contemporary studies of international relations can find power and pathos.[59]

The collapse of communism and the Soviet empire has stimulated thinking in practical and theoretical areas about the dynamics of the 'new world order'. Rousseau is relevant to this dialogue because his analysis of international relations pierces many of the complacent assumptions and unfounded hopes of scholars and politicians who fail to appreciate, as Rousseau did, the forces of the competition dynamic in international and domestic politics. The end of the Cold War has not altered the basic structure of international relations but has rather accelerated the competition dynamic as new states emerge and old ones readjust to transformed power distributions. The 'new world order' has so far been heralded by war, ethnic violence, the rapid decay of civil and political systems, and worsening trade relations between the major economic powers. As Rousseau argued, there is no respite from the competition engendered among nations by the structure of international relations.

Even those concepts in which Rousseau placed moral import – patriotism and isolation – find expression in the current international environment, but not in the forms Rousseau embraced. Patriotism in the form of aggressive nationalism has emerged from the vacuum left by the collapse of the Soviet Union. The upheavals caused by this collapse have also contributed to the re-emergence of isolationist sentiments in some states, characterised by anti-foreigner passions and an awakening to the magnitude of domestic threats to prosperity and order. Rousseau wanted patriotism to be a channel for the individual to regain autonomy through direct participation in the life of the nation, and he hoped that isolation would give this channel opportunity to redeem some of humanity's lost morality. The nationalism of today aims at power and bears all the marks of the competition dynamic, and contemporary isolationism reflects fear rather than moral purpose.

Rousseau's attempted escape from the state of war tells far more than a 'familiar cautionary tale'. His perspective contains a search for a conception of humanity haunted by, among other things, international relations. Rousseau's perspective gives moral meaning to the analysis of international relations, connecting it with deeper questions about the human condition. The 'new world order' was welcomed by many for its promise to transform international relations from an obstacle to a catalyst for improving the human condition. The disappointment that no 'new world order' has evolved now disturbs and perhaps in some drowns those earlier hopes. The disappointment that has developed because of the failure of a new world order to form also serves as a way to illustrate Rousseau's relevance as a thinker on international relations. He refused to admit that the chain of war could not be broken at least for some peoples because his moral sensibility could not abandon hope. The lesson from Rousseau's desperate attempt to avoid utter despair is that a moral imperative keeps alive the search for a solution to the state of war. The belief in such a moral imperative is traditionally associated with Kant, whose universalistic ambition made the imperative bold and clear. Rousseau's perspective obscures his moral imperative. Through his structural analysis of international relations and his theory of the corruption of human nature and the development of tyranny, Rousseau found himself within a Cyclops' cave of his own making from which he felt compelled to find an escape. Even Rousseau, the purportedly deepest and most pessimistic realist, would not groan and be silent, waiting to be eaten. Rousseau's efforts to escape make him less a realist than a tragic moralist defeated by his own appreciation of the difficulty of moral regeneration in the face of the state of war. Rousseau's appreciation and his defeat remain in tension in all those who observe international reality with any semblance of moral regret.

## NOTES

1. Jean-Jacques Rousseau, *Social Contract*, bk I, ch. I in Ernest Barker (ed.), *Social Contract: Essays by Locke, Hume, and Rousseau* (Oxford: Oxford University Press, 1960), p. 169.
2. *Social Contract*, bk IV, ch. IX, p. 307.
3. For a detailed analysis of the development and consistency of Rousseau's thinking on international relations during his literary career, see 'Introduction' in Stanley Hoffmann and David P. Fidler (eds), *Rousseau on International Relations* (Oxford: Clarendon Press, 1991), pp. xi–xxxvii. See also Grace G. Roosevelt, *Reading Rousseau in the Nuclear Age* (Philadelphia: Temple University Press, 1990).
4. Of Rousseau's writings that are important to his perspective on international relations, he had written *Discourse on Political Economy* (1755), *The State of War* (c. 1755–56), *Fragments on War* (c. 1755–56), *Abstract and Judgment of Saint-Pierre's Project for Perpetual Peace* (1756), and *First Version of the Social Contract* (1761) prior to 1762.
5. Rousseau served as secretary to the French ambassador to Venice, the Comte de Montaigu, from September 1743 to about September 1744. In the

*Confessions*, Rousseau reports that he undertook his duties with 'an honesty, a zeal, and a courage which deserved a better reward from [Montaigu] than in the end I obtained.' Jean-Jacques Rousseau, *Confessions*, J. M. Cohen (trans.) (Harmondsworth: Penguin, 1953), p. 283. Cranston confirms that 'the main work of the Embassy was done by Rousseau himself'. Maurice Cranston, *Jean-Jacques: The Early Life and Works of Jean-Jacques Rousseau 1712–1754* (Harmondsworth: Penguin, 1983), p. 173. Rousseau at first was very much drawn to a career in diplomacy as he devoted his spare time 'to studying the profession I was entering, in which, after my successful start, I reckoned later to gain more lucrative employment', *Confessions*, p. 287. Rousseau admits that, had Montaigu 'possessed any common sense,' '[m]y journey to Venice would have launched me into public life', ibid., p. 385. Although Rousseau did not become a career diplomat, he remained, despite his mistreatment by Montaigu, attracted by the craft of diplomacy. In 1761, the Duc de Choiseul, the French Foreign Secretary, offered Rousseau a job should he wish to return to the diplomatic corps. Rousseau's lingering interest in diplomacy appears in his response to this offer: 'I am not at all certain whether, if my health had permitted my considering it, I should not have made a fool of myself again despite all my resolutions' ibid., p. 511.

6.    See, for example, Rousseau's observations on the Seven Years' War explained later in this chapter.

7.    Voltaire's response to Rousseau's *Letter to M. d'Alembert* contained a jab that Rousseau should have paid more attention to foreign affairs. Cranston notes that Voltaire 'observed that it was a pity that Rousseau did not write against the tragedy that was then engulfing the theatre of Europe – the Seven Years War as it was afterwards known – rather than against the idea of a theatre of comedy in Geneva', Maurice Cranston, *The Noble Savage: Jean-Jacques Rousseau 1754–1762* (Harmondsworth: Penguin, 1991), p. 148. Voltaire also criticized Rousseau for taking a chimerical position in the *Abstract* (see M. Perkins, 'Voltaire's Concept of International Order,' *Studies in Voltaire and the Eighteenth Century*, 36 (1965), p. 110). Voltaire, however, did not know that Rousseau's real opinion, found in the unpublished *Judgment*, did not accord with Saint-Pierre's. In the *Confessions*, Rousseau writes that if the *Judgment* 'ever appears the world will see what amusement I must have derived from Voltaire's witticisms and his complacency on this subject', *Confessions*, p. 507.

8.    'Incomplete as his own treatment of relations among states was, the frequency and intensity of his references indicate the depth of his concern', Stanley Hoffmann, 'Rousseau on War and Peace,' in ibid., *Janus and Minerva: Essays in the Theory and Practice of International Politics* (Boulder, CO: Westview, 1987), p. 25.

9.    'Rousseau himself stressed that his thinking formed a "system", that his ideas on different aspects of political life were interrelated', 'Introduction' in *Rousseau on International Relations*, p. xiii.

10.   See *Confessions*, p. 381.

11.   Ibid., p. 377.

12.   Ibid., pp. 379, 394.

13.   See *The State of War* in *Rousseau on International Relations*, pp. 33–47.

14. See *Discourse on the Moral Effects of the Arts and Sciences* in G. D. H. Cole (ed.), *The Social Contract and Discourses* (New York: Dutton, 1955), pp. 143–74 and *Discourse on the Origin of Inequality*, Maurice Cranston (trans.) (Harmondsworth: Penguin, 1984).

15. *Discourse on Political Economy* in *Rousseau on International Relations*, p. 30.

16. Oddly enough, Rousseau's stint as a diplomat in Venice gave him his first taste of the institutional inequality that later formed such a large part of his political theory. Rousseau fell out with Ambassador Montaigu and went to Paris to redress the wrongs he felt he had suffered at the hands of Montaigu. His efforts were in vain. In the *Confessions*, Rousseau writes: 'The justice and fruitlessness of my complaints left a seed of indignation in my heart against our absurd civil institutions, whereby the real welfare of the public and true justice are always sacrificed to some kind of apparent order, which is in reality detrimental to all order, and which merely gives the sanction of public authority to the oppression of the weak and the iniquity of the strong', *Confessions*, p. 306.

17. *The State of War* in *Rousseau on International Relations*, pp. 42–3.

18. See Kenneth N. Waltz, *Man, the State and War* (New York: Columbia University Press, 1959), pp. 16–41.

19. *Discourse on Political Economy* in *Rousseau on International Relations*, p. 2.

20. In *Émile*, Rousseau writes that '[e]very patriot is harsh to foreigners', *Émile*, Allan Bloom (trans.) (New York: Basic Books, 1979), bk I, p. 39.

21. *Judgment of Saint-Pierre's Project of Perpetual Peace* in *Rousseau on International Relations*, p. 90.

22. Cranston reports an interesting exchange between Rousseau and the official censor concerning the *Abstract of Saint-Pierre's Project for Perpetual Peace*. The censor suggested adding the phrase 'without forgetting the virtues of princes'. Rousseau would not accept this; and, given his view of the manipulation and oppression of the people by princes, his refusal comes as no surprise. See Cranston, *The Noble Savage*, p. 259. The passage in question was published as follows: 'whatever may be the truth as to the virtues of princes, let us confine ourselves to their interests', *Abstract of Saint-Pierre's Project of Perpetual Peace* in *Rousseau on International Relations*, p. 77.

23. See Waltz, *Man, the State and War*, pp. 80–123.

24. Ibid., pp. 159–86.

25. *Discourse on Political Economy* in *Rousseau on International Relations*, p. 4.

26. See the *First Version of the 'Social Contract'* in *Rousseau on International Relations*, pp. 101–38.

27. Cranston, *The Noble Savage*, p. 273.

28. Ibid., p. 207.

29. Ibid., pp. 273–4.

30. *First Version of the 'Social Contract'* in *Rousseau on International Relations*, p. 117. The same sentiment is found in the final version of the *Social Contract*. See *Social Contract*, bk I, ch. IV, p. 178.

31. *First Version of the 'Social Contract'* in *Rousseau on International Relations*, pp. 121–2.

32. *Confessions*, p. 554.
33. Ibid.
34. 'Commerce produces wealth, but agriculture ensures freedom', *Constitutional Project for Corsica* in *Rousseau on International Relations*, p. 145. See also 'Introduction' in *Rousseau on International Relations*, pp. xxxv–xxxvi.
35. *Confessions*, p. 375.
36. In response to Diderot's cutting remark about Rousseau's rustic, solitary lifestyle that 'only the wicked man is alone', Rousseau wrote: 'It is in the country that one loves to love and serve humanity; in the cities all one learns is to despise it', *Confessions*, p. 427.
37. 'With any movement of trade and commerce, it is impossible to prevent destructive vices from creeping into a nation', *Constitutional Project for Corsica* in *Rousseau on International Relations*, p. 157.
38. 'Introduction', in *Rousseau on International Relations*, p. xxxi.
39. Rousseau writes in *Confessions* that '[c]orruption at present is everywhere the same; virtue and morality have ceased to exist in Europe', *Confessions*, p. 504. See also *Considerations on the Government of Poland* in *Rousseau on International Relations*, pp. 168–9.
40. Rousseau understood the double-edged power of patriotism. In the *Confessions*, Rousseau admits to a penetrating love of France even after he had condemned all that France stood for. He writes that his love of France 'gained so deep a root in my heart ... that when afterwards, in Paris, I was playing the anti-despot and proud Republican, I unwillingly felt a secret partiality for that same nation which I adjudged servile, and even for their government which I set out to condemn', *Confessions*, p. 177.
41. See Rousseau's comparison of the qualities of Christian soldiers with those of 'proud peoples consumed by a burning love of glory and homeland', in the *First Version of the 'Social Contract'* in *Rousseau on International Relations*, pp. 133–4.
42. Martin Wight, *International Theory: The Three Traditions*, Gabriele Wight and Brian Porter (eds) (Leicester: Leicester University Press, 1991), p. 17.
43. *Abstract of Saint-Pierre's Project of Perpetual Peace* in *Rousseau on International Relations*, pp. 53–9.
44. Wight, *International Theory: The Three Traditions*, p. 13.
45. Ibid., p. 7.
46. 'Introduction' in *Rousseau on International Relations*, pp. lxiii–lxiv. J. L. Windenberger claims that Rousseau's manuscript on confederations was lost. See J. L. Windenberger, *La République confédérative des petits états: essai sur le système de politique étrangère de J. J. Rousseau* (Paris: Alfonse Picard et Fils, 1900), ch. 2. On Rousseau's confederations, see C. E. Vaughan (ed.), *Political Writings of J.-J. Rousseau*, I (Cambridge: Cambridge University Press, 1915), pp. 95–102.
47. In *Considerations on the Government of Poland*, Rousseau suggests an alliance that deviates from the confederative strategy he recommends for social contract states. He advises the Poles to make one exception to his general rule of not making treaties, and the exception was to be made with the Sultan of Turkey. Rousseau's reason for this has a realist slant: he believes that the Poles can counterbalance the power and menace of Russia by gaining the support of the Sultan, with whom the Russians were then at

war. Rousseau makes it clear, however, that such balance-of-power politics is not advisable except in 'this unique circumstance'. His general advice remains constant: 'do not waste your energies in vain negotiations; do not bankrupt yourselves on ambassadors and ministers to foreign courts; and do not account alliances and treaties as things of any moment'. See *Considerations on the Government of Poland* in *Rousseau on International Relations*, pp. 192–3.

48.    Cranston, *The Noble Savage*, pp. 273–4.

49.    'Introduction' in *Rousseau on International Relations*, p. lxv.

50.    Rousseau's condemnation of economic intercourse between states suggests that the peculiar international society existing between social contract states would lack a commercial and material aspect. Rousseau, however, might not have vehemently objected to trade relations between social contract states once the confederative alliance had operated benignly for a period of time. Evidence for this assertion can be found in *Considerations on the Government of Poland* where Rousseau discusses the Polish alliance with the Sultan of Turkey. Rousseau calls the Turkish alliance the 'one exception' to his general prohibition against intercourse with other states, but he also excepts 'perhaps a few trade treaties later on'. See *Considerations on the Government of Poland* in *Rousseau on International Relations*, p. 192. Whether Rousseau believed that the strategic defensive alliances between social contract states could later be supplemented by trade treaties is, however, merely conjecture. Whatever trade Rousseau foresaw developing within the social contract alliance would surely be minimal, well below any level that might actually produce interdependence. Even with *de minimis* trade, the international society between social contract states would not be characterised by a shared value in the process of commerce.

51.    Burke's Commonwealth of Europe is also a limited family of states and nations as Burke does not extend this family to include, for example, India. Rousseau's limited family is more restrictive because he bases participation not on membership in an ancient transnational cultural–historical community but on ideological similitude. See, generally, Jennifer M. Welsh, 'Edmund Burke and the Commonwealth of Europe: The Cultural Bases of International Order', Chapter 8 in this collection.

52.    'Kant was the funnel through which the intoxicating alcohol of Rousseau was poured into the veins of international society', Wight, *International Theory: The Three Traditions*, p. 263.

53.    On Kant's international relations thinking, see Carl J. Friedrich, *Inevitable Peace* (Cambridge, MA: Harvard University Press, 1948), Pierre Hassner, 'Les Concepts de guerre et de paix chez Kant,' *Revue française de science politique*, 11 (1961), 642–70; Kenneth N. Waltz, 'Kant, Liberalism, and War,' *American Political Science Review*, 56 (1962), pp. 331–40; Francis H. Hinsley, 'Kant', in ibid., *Power and the Pursuit of Peace: Theory and Practice in the History of Relations between States* (Cambridge: Cambridge University Press, 1967), pp. 62–80; Andrew Hurrell, 'Kant and the Kantian Paradigm in International Relations', *Review of International Studies* 16 (1990), pp. 183–205; and Howard Williams and Ken Booth, 'Kant: Theorist Beyond Limits', Chapter 4 in this collection.

54.    *Discourse on Political Economy* in *Rousseau on International Relations*, p. 4.

55.  'Whoever studies contemporary international relations cannot but hear, behind the clash of interests and ideologies, a kind of permanent dialogue between Rousseau and Kant', 'Introduction' in *Rousseau on International Relations*, p. lxx.

56.  Wight, *International Theory: The Three Traditions*, p. 15.

57.  Ibid., pp. 15, 14.

58.  T. J. Hochstrasser, 'Review of *Rousseau on International Relations*', *Cambridge Law Journal* (1992), p. 163.

59.  'Today the history of relations among states may be moving toward an important turning point.... At this crucial juncture Rousseau's analysis of the competing claims of freedom and security, his eloquent reminders of what is gained and what is lost by entering a social contract, and his compelling portraits of both the humanitarian and the patriot provide a fruitful starting point for the political and educational choices that lie ahead', Roosevelt, *Reading Rousseau in the Nuclear Age*, p. 180.

# 7 Adam Smith and the Liberal Tradition in International Relations[1]

Andrew Wyatt Walter

## INTRODUCTION

The name of Adam Smith is most commonly associated with the notion of a natural 'harmony of interests' between individuals in the market, whereby the 'invisible hand' of competition turns self-regarding behaviour into aggregate social benefits. Joseph Cropsey echoes this view in suggesting that 'Smith is of interest for his share in the deflection of political philosophy towards economics and for his famous elaboration of the principles of free enterprise liberal capitalism.'[2] Smith is often seen as standing in a long line of British political philosophers stretching back to Hobbes and Locke and on to Bentham to culminate in John Stuart Mill, his principal contribution to the liberal tradition being his role as the great spokesman of *laissez-faire* and the minimalist state.[3]

This common view of Smith is mirrored in international relations literature, with Smith usually being portrayed as one of the founding fathers of 'economic liberalism' in political economy and of the 'liberal internationalism' that E. H. Carr was to attack sharply in the 1930s for its utopianism. Carr saw Smith as the spokesman 'of a wishful vision of universal free trade' or *laissez-faire*, believing that the 'individual could be relied on, without external control, to promote the interests of the community for the very reason that those interests were identical with his own.'[4] In similar fashion, Kenneth Waltz held Smith to have 'laid the formal foundations of English liberalism', with its emphasis on individual initiative regulated by competition rather than an interventionist state, and its belief in progress and the irrationality of war.[5] Martin Wight appears to have placed Smith (along with the *laissez-faire* doctrine) in his 'Revolutionist' tradition, firmly setting him apart from Realism.[6]

A variant of this view in the international relations literature is that Smith represents the bridge between the liberal internationalist tradition

142

identified by Carr and the liberal tradition in international political economy. Robert Gilpin argues that 'from Adam Smith to [liberalism's] contemporary proponents, liberal thinkers have shared a coherent set of assumptions and beliefs about the nature of human beings, society, and economic activities'.[7] A key element in this tradition is the idea that economic linkages between peoples are a uniting, pacifying force in international affairs, and that the realm of economics operates according to its own powerful logic. Smith's apparent belief in the possibility of progress at the international level locates him firmly in the idealist or utopian tradition of liberal international relations theory for most commentators, often represented by the term 'commercial liberalism'.[8]

This conventional view of Smith derives its force from the picture of Smith as the great ideological opponent of the mercantilists. He is widely held to have rejected the key tenets of mercantilist thought: the obsession with national power, the strong association between power and national economic wealth, and the emphasis upon war that the mercantilists share with realist thinkers on international affairs. While Smith himself is not always explicit on such matters, the conventional view holds the implications of his ideas to be clear. For James Shotwell, 'The political doctrine of international peace is a parallel to the economic doctrine of Adam Smith, for it rests similarly upon a recognition of common and reciprocal material interests, which extend beyond national frontiers.'[9] Michael Howard similarly places Smith broadly in this liberal anti-war tradition, based on the view that 'Providence had linked mankind by a chain of reciprocal needs which made impossible, *a priori*, any clash of economic interests', leading to Thomas Paine's declaration little more than a year after Smith's death that free trade 'would extirpate the system of war'.[10]

Though there are variations, the conventional view is that Smith is firmly situated within the liberal internationalist tradition in international relations of the late eighteenth century to the early twentieth century, and clearly at odds with the realist and mercantilist traditions. In addition, since Smith's thought is seen as prefiguring that of later liberals and radicals, its value for international relations scholarship has been seen as limited on the presumption that these later authors, from Paine to Shotwell, were more explicit than Smith himself.

This essay argues that this conventional view of Smith is mistaken, owing more to a tendency to read back nineteenth-century ideas into Smith than to a close analysis of Smith's own works, his purposes, and his intellectual milieu.[11] Two main questions will be asked here. First, to what extent can Smith be associated with the harmony-of-interest idea in social theory, which achieved its fullest fruition in the nineteenth century?

Second, and more specifically, to what extent did he hold to the view that 'irrational politics' would gradually be displaced by the rising primacy of commerce in human affairs, leading to more rational, peaceful and productive relations between states? I wish to argue that Smith firmly rejected the idea of a natural harmony of interests in his most important book, *The Wealth of Nations* (1776), and that on international matters, Smith is often closer to the realist and mercantilist traditions in international relations than to liberal internationalism.[12] In addition, Smith is especially worth reading for students of international relations and political economy for his sophisticated analysis of the sources of international conflict, and the bridge he offers between realist and liberal analyses of the relationship between wealth and power in international relations. More generally, however, Smith's thought leads us to reject the necessary association between liberalism and utopianism that is implied in the criticisms of Waltz, Carr, Gilpin and Howard.

The essay has the following structure. First, Smith's concept of natural underlying order in the social world will be examined, and its relation to the harmony-of-interests doctrine discussed. Second, Smith's understanding of the relationship between the rise of commerce and of 'liberty' in human affairs will be considered, and the extent to which this might spill over into progress in international relations. Third, his apparent pessimism regarding the reform of international relations and its institutions is outlined. The conclusion discusses the grounds for and consequences of Smith's divergence from idealist liberalism, while also noting elements of convergence with the liberal tradition in international relations more broadly defined.

## THE NATURAL ORDER: A HARMONY OF INTERESTS?

### The System of Natural Liberty

Smith's central concern, like that of many eighteenth-century thinkers and those of the Scottish Enlightenment in particular, was how to reconcile the acquisitive and materialistic pursuits of people in commercial society with the concerns of the civic republican and Christian traditions relating to the virtue of the good citizen.[13] Bernard Mandeville's solution in his *Fable of the Bees or Private Vices, Publick Benefits* (1714) was that men's vices could not be eliminated but could work to the public benefit if channeled through the appropriate institutions. While Smith felt a need to reject the cynicism of Mandeville, he made good use of this idea in *The Wealth*

*of Nations*, particularly in his notion that private interests were the genera-
tor of economic and social progress. In *The Theory of Moral Sentiments*
(1759), Smith had given more attention to the way in which social institutions might channel men's passions towards virtue. Yet it is his portrayal
of the public benefits which flow from the pursuit of economic interest
which is best known and most often quoted:

> As every individual, therefore, endeavours as much as he can both to
> employ his capital in the support of domestick industry, and so to direct
> that industry that its produce may be of the greatest value; every indi-
> vidual necessarily labours to render the annual revenue of the society as
> great as he can. He generally, indeed, neither intends to promote the
> publick interest, nor knows how much he is promoting it. By preferring
> the support of domestic to that of foreign industry, he intends only his
> own security; and by directing that industry in such a manner as its
> produce may be of the greatest value, he intends only his own gain, and
> he is in this, as in many other cases, led by an invisible hand to promote
> an end which was no part of his intention.[14]

Smith is closest to Mandeville when he goes on to argue that:

> Nor is it always the worse for the society that it was no part of it. By
> pursuing his own interest he frequently promotes that of the society
> more effectually than when he really intends to promote it. I have never
> known much good done by those who affected to trade for the publick
> good. It is an affectation, indeed, not very common among merchants,
> and very few words need to be employed in dissuading them from it.[15]

According to Smith, there is an underlying natural order built upon the
unintended consequences of self-interested behaviour, discoverable
through the application of scientific methods to human affairs. This natural
order will operate most effectively through a system of 'natural liberty', a
programme of economic liberalisation which was required due to the
myriad of regulations and proscriptions by which governments had fet-
tered commerce. As Viner has pointed out, Smith's radical programme
involved the promotion of free choice of occupation, free trade in land,
free internal trade and free trade in foreign commerce (the latter of which
is commonly associated with the 'mercantile' system).[16] It proposed the
abolition of laws relating to settlement and apprenticeships, laws of entail
and primogeniture, local customs taxes, and the plethora of duties, bounties, prohibitions and trading monopolies associated with foreign commerce in Smith's time. In these areas, there was a close correspondence
between private and public interest, and in contrast to the discussion of

the role of human sympathy and benevolence in *The Theory of Moral Sentiments*, it was safe in this case to rely upon greed:

> It is not from the benevolence of the butcher, the brewer, or the baker, that we expect our dinner, but from their regard to their own interest. We address ourselves, not to their humanity but to their self-love, and never talk to them of our own necessities but of their advantages. Nobody but a beggar chuses to depend chiefly upon the benevolence of his fellow-citizens.[17]

However, self-interest had to be kept within the confines of justice,[18] and the ironic suggestion that the public is better off with overtly self-interested behaviour than with superficial public-minded virtue is not the only theme of *The Wealth of Nations*, let alone *The Theory of Moral Sentiments*. Anyone who could believe, as did Gunnar Myrdal, that Smith was 'blind to social conflict' and adhered to a naive harmony-of-interests doctrine, need only casually peruse *The Wealth of Nations* to obtain a sense of Smith's concern over how easily powerful private interests, particularly those of merchants and manufacturers, might subvert the public interest through their influence in the political process.[19] It was these 'merchants and manufacturers ... [who] seem to have been the original inventors of those restraints upon the importation of foreign goods, which secure to them the monopoly of the home-market'.[20] In general, 'People of the same trade seldom meet together, even for merriment and diversion, but the conversation ends in a conspiracy against the publick, or in some contrivance to raise prices.'[21] As one of many examples of this, Smith noted that 'Whenever the legislature attempts to regulate the differences between masters and their workmen, its counsellors are always the masters.'[22]

The fundamental flaw in the natural order derives from man's nature, which in Smith's view is far from the *homo economicus* of later, more formal economic theorising. As Nathan Rosenberg has pointed out, Smith's natural man is slothful, given to indolence and dissipation, particularly once wealth has been acquired. The effect of high profits, Smith suggests, is to threaten the very process of capital accumulation, since it 'seems every where to destroy that parsimony which in other circumstances is natural to the character of the merchant. When profits are high, the sober virtue seems to be superflous, and expensive luxury to suit better the affluence of his situation.'[23] Hence, *laissez-faire* is a misleading description of Smith's prescriptions, since what is necessary is not complete freedom from constraint and the prevention of collusion between agents, but on the contrary, institutional mechanisms which bring people to act in socially beneficial ways.

There were various institutional solutions to these flaws in the natural order. Central to Smith's ideal institutional structure was the institution of the market itself which, by balancing the interests of merchants, manufacturers, masters and apprentices, could produce public opulence. The mercantile system had benefited those who enjoyed monopolies at the expense of society at large, and was therefore highly undesirable. Extending the market would take greater advantage both of the possibilities of the division of labour and of man's natural propensity to exchange, the two motors of economic growth which had been constrained under the mercantile system.[24] But a market solution was not appropriate or sufficient in all cases, and the market itself had to be supported by other appropriate institutions. Smith briefly outlines in Book IV what could be seen as a 'minimalist' role for government:

> According to the system of natural liberty, the sovereign has only three duties to attend to; three duties of great importance, indeed, but plain and intelligible to common understandings: first, the duty of protecting the society from the violence and invasion of other independent societies; secondly, the duty of protecting, as far as possible, every member of the society from the injustice or oppression of every other member of it, or the duty of establishing an exact administration of justice; and thirdly, the duty of erecting and maintaining certain publick works and certain publick institutions, which it can never be for the interest of any individual, or small number of individuals, to erect and maintain.[25]

Yet in order to judge how 'minimalist' Smith's conception is, we must remember his rhetorical purpose; after all, the rhetorical dilemma of just how much to emphasise flaws in the natural order, and how to assess the potential for 'market (and government) failure' has plagued economists ever since Smith.[26] As Viner argued, it did not suit Smith's rhetorical purpose overly to emphasise the positive roles of government, given his strong sense of the misapplication of government authority in his day.[27] His scepticism concerning the ability of government, especially British government, to intervene judiciously and effectively was deep. 'It is the highest impertinence and presumption, therefore, in kings and ministers, to pretend to watch over the oeconomy of private people...[when] they are themselves always, and without any exception, the greatest spendthrifts in the society.'[28] Even this was more a matter of experience than dogma, since Smith actually approved of the mercantile projects of small, 'aristocratic' governments such as those of Venice and Amsterdam, whom he noted for their 'orderly, vigilant, and parsimonious administration', in contrast to Britain's 'slothful and negligent' government.[29]

It is clear from Smith's scattered remarks throughout his works that he envisaged a significant role for government which went well beyond nineteenth-century *laissez-faire* dogma. First, Smith did not dispute the claim of what came to be known as the 'mercantilist' writers that national defence was a primary condition of national wealth, and that wealth in turn laid the foundation of an adequate system of defence.[30] The pre-eminence of Britain as a trading and investing nation made both her navy and her merchant marine crucial to her national security, as recognised by the mercantile system in the Navigation Act of 1660, which 'endeavours to give the sailors and shipping of Great Britain the monopoly of the trade of their own country' through various prohibitions and burdens upon foreign shipping.[31] For Smith, as is well-known:

> The act of navigation is not favourable to foreign commerce, or to the growth of that opulence which can arise from it. ... As defence, however, is of much more importance than opulence, the act of navigation is, perhaps, the wisest of all the commercial regulations of England.[32]

As for 'the administration of justice', Smith's failure to write his planned third major work on jurisprudence has left us only with the short outlines in his *Lectures on Jurisprudence* (based upon the reports of two students in the 1760s) and in Book V of *The Wealth of Nations*. This function of government appears potentially all-encompassing at first sight, the duty of the sovereign being said to be 'that of protecting, as far as possible, every member of the society from the injustice or oppression of every other member of it'.[33] Yet this amounts in large measure to the need for a system of positive law to enumerate rules of justice providing for the security of the property of individuals and the enforcement of contracts, without which accumulation is impossible.[34] In a broader sense, however, Smith framed his criticisms of restrictive legislation which entrenched privilege and inequality on the basis of their *injustice* as well as their inefficiency, and justifies his system of natural liberty as leading to 'that universal opulence which extends itself to the lowest ranks of the people'.[35]

The third function, of providing 'certain publick works' in addition to defence and justice, includes institutions for the facilitation of commerce and for public education. The former category includes 'good roads, bridges, navigable canals, [and] harbours', and the latter local schools for the education of the lower orders of society, though Smith held whenever possible to the 'user pays' principle.

Finally, there were various pragmatic exceptions to the system of natural liberty. Smith accepted the argument that free trade should not be introduced so rapidly as to incur unacceptable costs of adjustment, for reasons of 'humanity' (and, presumably, good politics).[36] He also outlines more than a hint of an 'infant industry exception' to free trade in his defence in some cases of 'temporary monopolies', which later critics such as Alexander Hamilton and Friedrich List were to emphasise as the appropriate path towards industrialisation for countries which followed Britain.[37] He even recommends legislation fixing an upper limit to the rate of interest, lest a high market rate encourage 'prodigals and projectors, who alone would be willing to give this high interest' (for which he was criticised by Bentham).[38] Of course, all these examples of market failure did not negate the fact that the system of natural liberty was in general the best practical guide to policy, especially because government was often incompetent and more often subject to special interest pressures. Some things, such as the secret conspiracies of merchants, were impossible to prevent in a tolerably free society, but the government certainly ought not to encourage them.[39] Quite in contrast to the conventional view of Smith as an idealist, in fact he was very sober as to the prospects for his proposed system of natural liberty:

> To expect, indeed, that the freedom of trade should ever be entirely restored in Great Britain, is as absurd as to expect that an Oceana or Utopia should ever be established in it. Not only the prejudices of the publick, but what is much more unconquerable, the private interests of many individuals, irresistibly oppose it. ... This monopoly [of manufacturers] has so much increased the number of some particulars tribes of them, that, like an overgrown standing army, they have become formidable to the government, and upon many occasions intimidate the legislature.[40]

## International Anarchy as a Flaw in the Natural Order

If there is little prospect of an approximate harmony of private and public interest in practice, and only in theory with appropriate institutions to balance and channel people's actions, what does this imply about the international realm? Although Smith rarely addresses the issue head-on, this essay argues that there is implicit in much of his argument the idea that there are irreconcilable conflicts of interest between states, which produce a security dilemma for individual states, and that this constitutes another fundamental flaw in the natural order. The oft-quoted sentence from *The Wealth of Nations*, that 'defence is of much more importance than opulence', is not the 'trivial exception' to the system of natural liberty that it is so often seen to be.[41] Rather, it is firmly grounded upon what could be seen as a fundamentally realist view of international relations.

This is reasonably clear from Smith's discussion of defence as a core state function, and his various 'national security' exceptions to the system of natural liberty. There is a crucial strategic industry exception to free trade, 'when some particular sort of industry is necessary for the defence of the country', as with the manufacture of gunpowder and sail-cloth.[42] Smith certainly holds that the mercantile system prompted excessive and irrational enmity between states and accepts that 'the act of navigation... may have proceeded from national animosity'. But he goes on to argue that such 'animosity at that particular time aimed at the very same object which the most deliberate wisdom would have recommended, the diminution of the naval power of Holland, the only naval power which could endanger the security of England'.[43]

In other words, although Smith holds mercantile policies with their zero-sum view of international relations to have been pursued in the partial interests of 'rapacious merchants and manufacturers', he makes a clear distinction between such partial interests on the one hand and national interests on the other. The latter dictate prudence and caution on the part of the statesman but often demand essentially similar policies to the mercantile system. Accordingly, war could not be merely a product of ignorance or the folly of statesmen, as it was for Bentham and other nineteenth-century radicals, but more fundamentally a product of international anarchy. Sensible policy was to maximise wealth as a means to national defence, making exceptions to the free-trade principle where necessary for national security purposes:

> The riches, and so far as power depends upon riches, the power of every country, must always be in proportion to the value of its annual produce, the fund from which all taxes must ultimately be paid. *But the great object of the political œconomy of every country, is to encrease the riches and power of that country.*[44]

In this, Smith was in agreement with the mercantilists. The core mercantilist premise, as Viner argued, was that 'wealth and power are each proper ultimate ends of national policy' and that 'there is long-run harmony between these ends, although in particular circumstances it may be necessary for a time to make economic sacrifices in the interest of military security and therefore also of long-run prosperity'.[45] Smith not only agreed with this doctrine, but actually went further than many mercantilists in suggesting that 'defence is more important than opulence', a view implicit in the italicised quotation above. In contrast to many later liberal writers, Smith did not lose sight of the complex relationship between wealth and power in international relations.

Indeed, this understanding of the complexity of the issue prevented Smith from elaborating any hard and fast rules on statecraft in this area. A good example is his treatment of the navigation acts. After explicitly stating how enlightened this legislation was as an exception to the free-trade principle, he appears to have second thoughts when he recommends the gradual end to monopoly restrictions on the colonial trade later in Book IV.[46] In this repetitive section, Smith seems to suggest that in encouraging an 'overgrown' trade with the colonies to the detriment of trade with Europe, the acts reduced British wealth and thereby reduced British naval power and national security. Consistent with this is his argument that Britain's historic naval supremacy over the Dutch and French may have owed nothing to the acts. This is somewhat at odds with his earlier view, and shows how Smith was capable of switching position to suit a particular rhetorical purpose.[47] He even adds a new argument which is interesting in the present context. The navigation acts may not only have reduced British power by limiting its opulence, but also because of a strategic consideration:

> The monopoly of the colony trade... by forcing towards it a much greater proportion of the capital of Great Britain than would naturally have gone to it, seems to have broken altogether that natural balance which would otherwise have taken place among all different branches of British industry.... Her commerce, instead of running in a great number of small channels, has been taught to run principally in one great channel. But the whole system of her industry and commerce has thereby been rendered less secure. ... The expectation of a rupture with the colonies, accordingly, has struck the people of Great Britain with more terror than they ever felt for a Spanish armada, or a French invasion.... Some moderate and gradual relaxation of the laws which give to Great Britain the exclusive trade to the colonies, till it is rendered in a great measure free, seems to be the only expedient which can, in all future time, deliver her from this danger. ...[48]

Characteristically, Smith suggests that it was best left 'to the wisdom of future statesmen and legislators' as to how and to what extent all restraints upon colonial trade, including the navigation acts, ought to be removed.[49] States had to balance issues of power and wealth with issues of strategic dependence upon particular markets, and practical statesmen rather than philosophers were the best judge on such matters. Where Smith truly departed from the mercantilists, then, was in the realm of *means* rather than ends, arguing that his system of natural liberty for the most part constituted a much superior means of maximising national wealth and power.

It was for this reason that Smith criticised the rather extreme mercantilist view of the likes of Colbert and Josiah Child that international commerce was 'perpetual combat' or war by economic means.[50] By the maxims of mercantilism, Smith held, 'nations have been taught that their interest consisted in beggaring all their neighbours. Each nation has been made to look with an invidious eye upon the prosperity of all the nations with which it trades, and to consider their gains as its own loss.' The wealth of neighbours ought to be a matter for 'national emulation, not of national prejudice or envy.... In such improvements each nation ought, not only to endeavour itself to excel, but from the love of mankind, to promote, instead of obstructing the excellence of its neighbours'.[51]

Against the line of argument taken in this chapter, it might be suggested that the last quotation shows that Smith did hold a harmony-of-interests doctrine in international relations. Indeed, in the previous passage from *The Wealth of Nations*, Smith says that under the mercantile system, 'Commerce, which ought naturally to be, among nations, as among individuals, a bond of union and friendship, has become the most fertile source of discord and animosity.'[52] But this objection is not sustainable, as Smith goes on to argue that the mutual interests of nations are limited. There is a fundamental contradiction in the natural order, since the accumulation of national wealth is both politically threatening and economically advantageous to other states:

> The wealth of a neighbouring nation, however, *though dangerous in war and politicks*, is certainly advantageous in trade. In a state of hostility it may enable our enemies to maintain fleets and armies superior to our own; but in a state of peace and commerce it must likewise enable them to exchange with us to a greater value.[53]

The contradiction between national economic and political interests is particularly acute for neighbouring countries. Britain and France could gain much from removing the mercantile restrictions on their economic intercourse:

> But the very same circumstances which would have rendered an open and free commerce between the two countries so advantageous to both, have occasioned the principal obstructions to that commerce. *Being neighbours, they are necessarily enemies, and the wealth and power of each becomes, upon that account, more formidable to the other*; and what would increase the advantage of national friendship, serves only to inflame the violence of national animosity.... Mercantile jealousy is excited, and both inflames, and is itself inflamed, by the violence of national animosity.[54]

Mercantile doctrine and vested interests are not, then, the cause of national animosity, though they tended to fan it to new heights of intensity. Geographical propinquity and wealth itself create conflict between states, since wealth provides the means to wage war and because 'a wealthy nation, is of all nations the most likely to be attacked'.[55] There is little trace of the nineteenth- and twentieth-century liberal argument that war is an irrational and wealth-destroying enterprise. The 'love of mankind' could hardly constitute a major constraint upon international conflict, since the possibilities of sympathy and actions of benevolence were confined to individuals' families above all, to their closest neighbours and, at most, the state itself.[56] As a result, envy and prejudice tend to reign in international relations, and there is an inherent tension between man and citizen. Notice how Smith reconciles private interest with public national interest in the (single) invisible-hand passage in *The Wealth of Nations*, where 'every individual...*by preferring the support of domestic to that of foreign industry...*[is] led by an invisible hand to promote an end which was no part of his intention'.[57] The love of one's country might help reconcile the interests of citizens and state, but it creates conflict at the international level between states.

## COMMERCE, PROGRESS AND WAR

### Commerce and Social Conflict

The preceding analysis suggests that Smith can hardly have believed that even if mercantilist policies were to be abandoned and trade flourished, conflict between states would disappear, since mistaken economic doctrine was not the problem. Nevertheless, since Smith does hold to the view that expanding commerce brings with it progress of sorts in human affairs, it is worthwhile to consider whether he believed commerce might increase the prospects for international peace. This means to international harmony took two interconnected routes in utopian thought in the eighteenth and nineteenth centuries. First, in the notion that reform of the international realm could be achieved through domestic political reform, largely by constraining the irrational passions of the rulers of humankind. Second, in the idea that commerce could reveal a true harmony of interests between nations, which even unrepresentative governments might not ignore. Did Smith hold to either of these propositions?

For Smith, the rise of commercial society brings with it considerable social benefits, including the gradual introduction of 'order and good government, and with them, the liberty and security of individuals, among the inhabitants of the country, who had before lived almost in a continual state of war with their neighbours, and of servile dependency upon their superiors'.[58] Characteristically, Smith allows a key role for the unintended consequences of individual and class behaviour in producing such benefits. The rise of the towns and of manufactures led the feudal lords in their vanity to promote the commercialisation of agriculture and of the tenant–landlord relationship. 'For a pair of diamond buckles perhaps,…for the gratification of the most childish, the meanest and the most sordid of all vanities, they gradually bartered their whole power and authority.'[59]

The benefits of this miscalculation (or, in Hirschman's terms, the triumph of passion over rational self-interest) were considerable, since it allowed for the development of less demeaning and more interdependent social relationships between people of different ranks of society, and since 'the great proprietors were no longer capable of interrupting the regular execution of justice, or of disturbing the peace of the country'.[60] Thus Smith hoped to explain how commercialisation of society could allow a greater scope for liberty and justice, in the sense of security of property as well as greater social interdependence, a common theme among liberal thinkers.[61]

Did this greater domestic social stability afforded by the commercialisation process spill over into more peaceful international relations? After all, Smith had written that 'Commerce…ought naturally to be, among nations, as among individuals, a bond of union and friendship'.[62] Does this not suggest a similar view to that of Montesquieu, who held that 'the natural effect of commerce is to lead to peace', or of his friend Melon, who believed that the 'spirit of conquest and the spirit of commerce are mutually exclusive in a nation'?[63]

It is very doubtful that Smith ever subscribed to such a view. There is little sense of the restraining role of representative government in his writings, as in those of other eighteenth-century writers such as Kant and Paine. Indeed, he noted how the British government 'in time of war has constantly acted with all the thoughtless extravagance that democracies are apt to fall into'.[64] Smith's realism on this score is in marked contrast to that of later liberal writers such as the Mills, Dunham, Cobden, Bright and Angell. For Smith, as for J. K. Galbraith more recently, wars amuse rather than disgust the modern citizen, and 'this amusement compensates the small difference between the taxes which they pay on account of the war, and those which they had been accustomed to pay in time of peace. They are commonly dissatisfied with the return of peace, which puts an end to their amusement, and to a thousand visionary hopes of conquest and national glory, from a longer continuance of the war'.[65] Neither democracy nor commerce might ensure peace. As citizens have passions as well as economic interests, Smith (like Galbraith) might have seen the argument of Michael Doyle, that liberal democracies have a low propensity to war, as resting upon an excessively narrow view of human nature.[66]

Smith's attitude to the colonies also brings out his complex view of human nature and the emphasis upon man's non-pecuniary passions. He saw the relationship between European states and their colonies as economically inefficient and unprofitable, but doubted that this in itself would be sufficient to bring these states to surrender their colonies voluntarily.

> No nation ever voluntarily gave up the dominion of any province, how troublesome soever it might be to govern it, and how small soever the revenue which it afforded might be in proportion to the expense which it occasioned. Such sacrifices, though they might frequently be agreeable to the interest, are always mortifying to the pride of every nation, and what is perhaps of still greater consequence, they are always contrary to the private interest of the governing part of it.[67]

Nevertheless, he made some powerful economic arguments in favour of voluntary British decolonisation. The existing system, he argued, was the worst of both worlds, since the resentful Americans refused to pay taxes while the British had to defend their interests there. The very last sentence of *The Wealth of Nations* is a powerful plea for the British to give up the failed project of empire which might have made Cobden or Bright proud:

> If any of the provinces of the British empire cannot be made to contribute towards the support of the whole empire, it is surely time that Great Britain should free herself from the expense of defending those provinces in time of war, and of supporting any part of their civil or military establishments in time of peace, and endeavour to accommodate her future views and designs to the real mediocrity of her circumstances.[68]

Yet Smith is more conservative on the issue than his radical successors. He was fascinated with the subject of the American rebellion around the time of the publication of *The Wealth of Nations*, and in a private memorandum of February 1778 to Alexander Wedderburn (Solicitor-General in Lord North's government) he worried about the loss of domestic and international prestige that a voluntary withdrawal might entail for the government. At the same time, he offers a *Realpolitik* solution which would have horrified nineteenth-century liberals: by restoring 'Canada to France and the two Floridas to Spain, we should render our [independent] colonies the natural enemy of these two monarchies and consequently the natural allies of Great Britain'.[69] In his public writings on the subject in *The Wealth of Nations*, however, Smith preferred to put faith in the post-decolonisation revival of a 'natural affection of the colonies to the mother country'.[70]

Understanding that there was little chance of a voluntary British withdrawal from America, Smith proposed as an alternative a full political and economic union between Britain and America. The 'natural aristocracy' of every nation was motivated primarily by considerations of their own self-importance, power and prestige. A union could allow the British to retain their sense of self-importance, while 'a new method of acquiring importance, a new and more dazzling object of ambition would be presented to the leading men of each colony'.[71] If it were to be objected that such attitudes were the preserve of a doomed aristocracy, it need only be countered that Smith simply did not think in such terms. Smith did not, of course, identify 'liberty' with democracy, and for him absolutism was not incompatible with a flourishing commercial society.[72]

In contrast to Montesquieu, and the liberal internationalists of a later time, then, for Smith the passions of men could not be overcome by mere economic interest. What accounts for this 'realism'? Fundamentally, it is because Smith, unlike these other writers, sees people as motivated by a more complex and powerful set of passions than simply economic self-interest. It posed no difficulty for him to envisage people acting 'irrationally' from the point of view of their economic interest. And if this is true for individuals, it is even more true for nations, whose behaviour is so often dominated by the passion of national sentiment. For Montesquieu, however, human character was more simple: 'it is fortunate for men to be in a situation in which, though their passions may prompt them to be wicked, they have nevertheless an [economic] interest in not being so'.[73] This was the basis of his belief that the growth of commerce might constrain the tendency to war. For Smith, even if the irrational mercantilist pursuit of national economic advantage could be prevented from further disrupting international relations, this would hardly be sufficient to envisage the elimination of conflict in human affairs. For example, even excessively burdensome taxes might not be sufficient to reduce public support for war. 'When a nation is already over burdened with taxes, nothing but the necessities of a new war, nothing but either the animosity of national vengeance, or the anxiety for national security, can induce the people to submit, with tolerable patience, to a new tax.'[74]

Finally, it should be emphasised that despite this emphasis upon human passions, Smith's account of the causes of war is not, to employ Kenneth Waltz's categories, an entirely 'first image' explanation.[75] As our discussion of the flaws in the international order that Smith observed has shown, the existence of international anarchy creates a security dilemma for every state: 'Independent and neighbouring nations, having no common superior to decide their disputes, all live in continual dread and suspicion of one another.'[76] Yet it is the passions of citizens which work to exacerbate this potential for conflict between states, as 'the mean principle of national prejudice is often founded upon the noble one of the love of our country'.[77] This accounts for his scepticism as to the likelihood that democracy would eliminate war, since international anarchy is the permissive cause of conflict and war, and the passions of individuals the driving force.

## Commerce, Finance and Corruption

As is clear from the above observations, when Smith refers to the way in which commerce renders the feudal landlords 'no longer capable of interrupting the regular execution of justice, or of disturbing the peace of the country',[78] he is speaking of domestic peace rather than international, the domestic scene being the whole focus of Book III of *The Wealth of Nations*. In Book V, chapter 3, he takes up the subject of the constraints that commercialisation places upon the sovereign (as opposed to feudal lords). Here, Smith discusses how the process of commercialisation has some corrupting effects, and accordingly may not restrain national passions. The sovereign's 'frivolous passions' are all too likely to lead him to indulge himself 'with all the costly trinkets which compose the splendid, but insignificant pageantry of a court' and in so doing to 'spend upon those pleasures so great a part of his revenue as to debilitate very much the defensive power of the state'. Yet because of the institutionalisation of the system of public debt in a commercial society, the government 'is very apt to repose itself upon this ability and willingness of its subjects to lend it their money on extra-ordinary occasions…and therefore dispenses itself from the duty of saving'. It is the very ease of financing such extraordinary expenditures which prevents the financial constraint upon profligate sovereigns (or for that matter profligate democracies) from biting, even if it 'will in the long-run probably ruin, all the great nations of Europe'.[79]

True to form, Smith proposes a reform of institutional mechanisms to overcome such problems. He suggests that all wars should be financed only by taxes, so that 'The foresight of the heavy and unavoidable burdens of war would hinder the people from wantonly calling for it when there was no real or solid interest to fight for.' Wars might then 'be more speedily concluded, and less wantonly undertaken'.[80] Here, however, his penchant for reform gets the better of him, since it rests on the view he had earlier dismissed that economic interest properly channelled might constrain the appetite to war. In any case, with such an efficient system of public finance as Britain had developed by the late eighteenth century, this reform was not politically realistic. Nor could Smith seriously have believed it would be very effective in curbing war, on the basis of his own arguments. It must be suspected that Smith's intense distaste for public indebtedness allowed his rhetoric, not for the first time, to run beyond his core beliefs on this matter. Indeed, Smith the pessimist shines through when he goes on to despair 'of making such progress towards that liberation [of the publick revenue] in time of peace, as to prevent or to compensate the further accumulation of the publick debt in the next war'.[81]

Moreover, far from hoping that commerce would eradicate the motivation to war by undermining the political position of the aristocracy, Smith feared that it might rather make civilised nations weak and vulnerable. As noted earlier, Smith feared that the attainment of wealth was corrupting of civic republican values, and he extends this theme in his discussion of the decline of the 'martial spirit' of society. The basis of this corruption was the very source of economic progress itself, the division of labour:

> In the progress of the division of labour, the employment of the far greater part of those who live by labour, that is, of the great body of the people, comes to be confined to a few very simple operations.... The man whose whole life is spent in performing a few simple operations has no occasion to exert his understanding, or to exercise his invention.... He naturally loses, therefore, the habit of such exertion, and generally becomes as stupid and ignorant as it is possible for a human creature to become. The torpor of his mind renders him, not only incapable of relishing or bearing a part in any rational conversation, but of conceiving any generous, noble, or tender sentiment, and consequently of forming any just judgment concerning many even of the ordinary duties of private life. Of the great and extensive interests of his country, he is altogether incapable of judging; and unless very particular pains have been taken to render him otherwise, he is equally incapable of defending his country in war.... His dexterity at his own particular trade seems, in this manner, to be acquired at the expense of his intellectual, social, and martial virtues. But in every improved and civilized society this is the state into which the labouring poor, that is, the great body of the people, must necessarily fall, unless government takes some pains to prevent it.[82]

History had shown that the great civilisations of Greece and Rome collapsed because commerce made them vulnerable to attack by highly militarised barbarian nations (and remember that wealth invited attack).[83] The wealthy European nations of Smith's time were vulnerable in a similar way. Although the invention of firearms had shifted the balance of power away from barbarian nations in favour of wealthier commercial nations, which was 'certainly favourable both to the permanency and to the extension of civilisation', this only enhanced the importance of wealth for purposes of national security.[84] Wealthy nations, because of their vulnerability, needed professional standing armies because of 'the natural superiority which the militia of a barbarous, has over that of a civilised nation'.[85] But Smith was not content to leave it at this. The need for the state to inculcate martial virtues among even its lowliest citizens receives substantial treatment both in his *Lectures* and in *The Wealth of Nations*. Such virtues might be instilled through citizens' militias, supplementing a standing professional army.[86]

Therefore, while Smith agreed with the liberal view that economic progress could promote the spread of more gentle and pacifistic sentiments among the body politic, for him this was something to be lamented (due to international anarchy and the inconsistent march of progress) and hopefully reversed by appropriate reforms. In view of his stress on the role of national animosity and of envy of wealthy nations, his real fear seemed to be that Britain might become lazy and neglect its defence while other nations (even wealthy ones) would be only too pleased to see Britain diminished. While it is surely a fundamentally realist proposition that the only secure way to preserve civilisation and liberty is to prepare for war, a position Smith adopts without faltering, he does not elaborate on this possible contradiction in his argument. As such, he falters between realism and liberalism. One might only add that in the case of barbarous countries, he seemed to place more hope in a Hobbesian solution than in commercialisation: 'As it is only by means of a well-regulated standing army that a civilised country can be defended; so it is only by means of it, that a barbarous country can be suddenly and tolerably civilised'.[87]

## INTERNATIONAL POLITICS AND INSTITUTIONAL REFORM

Given Smith's scattered yet sophisticated remarks on war and international affairs, is it not surprising that he does not address himself directly to questions of international relations, as other eighteenth-century writers such as Kant and Rousseau had done? It might not be too unfair to pose such a question, since Smith took a characteristically broad eighteenth-century view of his chair in moral philosophy. It is of particular interest for scholars of international relations because of Smith's emphasis upon the role of social institutions in shaping and channelling human interests and action. As Rosenberg suggested, Smith's argument in this regard 'applies to the whole spectrum of social contrivances and is not restricted to economic affairs'.[88] In considering in such detail the institutional process of channelling and balancing the interests across the whole spectrum of human affairs at the domestic level, Smith gave relatively minimal attention to how this might be done at the international level. Having rejected the notion that our deliverance from war might follow from democratisation and commercialisation at the domestic level, why did he not go further?

Smith follows his institutional instincts to some extent in briefly referring in *The Theory of Moral Sentiments* to the way in which statesmen, by pursuing national interests through alliances, may indirectly preserve the independence of states and the peace through the operation of the balance of power.[89] Yet further than this he does not go, despite the fact that the ground had been covered by thinkers with whom Smith was very familiar, such as Grotius, Pufendorf, Montesquieu, Hume and the mercantilists. His scepticism concerning the equilibrating role of the balance of power seems to prevent him from making a possible analogy with the invisible hand of domestic economic self-interest.

Another factor which one might expect to have brought Smith to deliberate on international matters more fully was the absence of moral relativism in his thought. This is implicit in the device of the 'impartial spectator' of *The Theory of Moral Sentiments*, the objective basis by which people might distinguish virtuous from base behaviour. However, as we have seen, Smith states practical limits to this device, and the tension between man and citizen which appears so clearly in *The Wealth of Nations* is also apparent in his moral philosophy. In *The Theory of Moral Sentiments*, Smith recognises how our 'love of nation' places geographical limits on our sympathy for and love of humankind. We envy and fear the wealth and power of neighbouring nations, and while we usually bear no ill-will to distant nations, 'It very rarely happens, however, that ...[this] can be exerted with much effect'.[90] This is not simply a resigned acceptance of the obstinacy of the base sentiments of man, but more a recognition of their complexity, since love of country is one of the main drivers of human progress. Smith is disdainful of the detached view of the philosopher who, contemplating the totality of God's creation, takes a universalist moral standpoint and thereby risks neglecting 'the care of his own happiness, of that of his family, his friends, his country'.[91] In his *Lectures*, Smith brings these contradictions to the fore:

The real cause why the whole nation is thought a reasonable object of resentment is that we do not feel for those at a distance as we do for those near us. We have been injured by France, our resentment rises against the whole nation instead of the government, and they, thro' a blind indiscriminating faculty natural to mankind, become objects of an unreasonable resentment. This is however quite contrary to the rules of justice observed with regard to our own subjects.[92]

Because of the depth of national passions, international politics is even more prone than domestic politics to the domination of partial interests, making it much more difficult in international affairs to obtain the position of an impartial spectator.[93]

Nevertheless, Smith condemned the 'savage injustice' of European policies against the colonial peoples.[94] International law, which is only discussed briefly in *The Theory of Moral Sentiments* and in one account of his *Lectures*, is dismissed as a fairly weak rod with which to constrain the passions and interests of powerful nations. 'From the smallest interest, upon the slightest provocation, we see those same rules every day, either evaded or directly violated without shame or remorse.'[95] Smith repeats this point in the *Lectures*, arguing that 'This must necessarily be the case, for where there is no supreme legislative power nor judge to settle differences, we may always expect uncertainty and irregularity.'[96] Even the laws of war are constantly violated, and are 'laid down with very little regard to the plainest and most obvious rules of justice'.[97] Like most realists, Smith by implication places limited faith in the institutions of international society to constrain state behaviour and to promote international justice. Furthermore, he argues in explicitly realist language that it is only through increased power that weaker nations might eventually come to prevent such injustice and instil mutual respect:

Hereafter, perhaps, the natives of those countries may grow stronger, or those of Europe may grow weaker, and the inhabitants of all the different quarters of the world may arrive at that equality of courage and force which, by inspiring mutual fear, *can alone overawe the injustice of independent nations into some sort of respect for the rights of one another*. But nothing seems more likely to establish this equality of force than that mutual communication of knowledge and of all sorts of improvements which an extensive commerce from all countries to all countries naturally, or rather necessarily, carries along with it.[98]

This passage is also revealing because it suggests that the real contribution that commerce might make to peace and justice between nations is by reducing the inequality of wealth and power that characterises relations between states over the long term. In other words, it is the balance of power (a term which Smith does not employ here and to which he only briefly alludes in his other works)[99] through which greater mutual respect between nations might emerge, rather than through international law or 'love of mankind'. While Smith could hardly, therefore, have agreed with Bright and later liberals that commerce would eventually outmode national borders and the balance of power,[100] nor did he place much faith in other institutions of international society to ensure international peace and justice. He devotes some attention in the *Lectures* to the way in which growing commerce between nations in modern times exacerbates rather than reduces conflict, necessitating the exchange of permanent ambassadors between states. Yet his assessment of the potential contribution of this particular institution is characteristically cautious.[101]

Smith therefore fails to consider the possibility of institutional reform at the international level, though clear flaws exist in the international order. There is a pessimism reminiscent of Rousseau in his suggestion that 'The violence and injustice of the rulers of mankind is an ancient evil, for which, I am afraid, the nature of human affairs can scarce admit of a remedy.'[102] In contrast to Bentham and later liberals, he is sceptical that international law can maintain the basic principles of natural justice in the face of inequality of power between states. For Smith, power politics ruled in international affairs, and he was therefore far from the view, common to both liberal utopians and Marxists, that economic forces would ultimately triumph over politics.

Perhaps the main reason for this gap in Smith's oeuvre is his view of the very limited role for the application of Kantian pure reason in international affairs. Whereas he saw a role for the 'legislator' acting according to general principles in the domestic realm, he tended to leave the international realm to the pragmatic political skills of the 'crafty statesman or politician'. Consider, for example, his interesting departure from what was to become the policy dogma of free-trade unilateralism in Britain in the later nineteenth century:

> The case in which it may sometimes be a matter of deliberation how far it is proper to continue the free importation of certain foreign goods, is, when some foreign nation restrains by high duties or prohibitions the importation of some of our manufactures into their country. Revenge in this case naturally dictates retaliation, and that we should impose the like duties and prohibitions upon the importation of some or all of their manufactures into ours. Nations, accordingly seldom fail to retaliate in

this manner.... There may be good policy in retaliations of this kind, when there is a probability that they will procure the repeal of the high duties or prohibitions complained of.... *To judge whether such retaliations are likely to produce such an effect, does not, perhaps, belong so much to the science of a legislator, whose deliberations ought to be governed by general principles which are always the same, as to the skill of that insidious and crafty animal, vulgarly called a statesman or politician, whose councils are directed by the momentary fluctuations of affairs.*[103]

This passage is particularly revealing because Smith's general view is that ethics and political economy were 'sciences' in which the consistent application of Newtonian method was appropriate.[104] Here and elsewhere in his writings, he explicitly excludes the international realm from 'the science of the legislator' and the application of Newtonian method, arguing pragmatically that we had best rely upon the prudence of the statesman. In other words, Smith does not employ the analogy of so many theorists of international relations, that the scientific method used in the study of human nature might equally be applied to states in the international realm, and in this he departs company with many realists and liberals alike. The international realm for Smith is unpredictable and dangerous, and general principles for foreign policy other than prudence and vigilance are difficult to formulate. In addition to Rousseau, then, another parallel is with Martin Wight, who was sceptical about the very possibility of elaborating any general international theory, on the basis of his sharp distinction between the domestic and the international spheres of life.[105] Smith is similarly reluctant to envisage large roles for morality and for theory in international affairs. In the end, it is perhaps this which deflects Smith from a thorough analysis of international relations.

CONCLUSION

There is a considerable danger in interpreting Adam Smith's views on international relations, since he rarely addresses directly the issues normally associated with the subject. In addition, there is Viner's comment that 'Traces of every conceivable sort of doctrine are to be found in that most catholic book, and an economist must have peculiar theories indeed who cannot quote from *The Wealth of Nations* to support his special purposes.'[106] However, this point can be exaggerated, and what is reasonably clear is the considerable divergence between Smith's thinking about inter-

national relations and the thought of contemporary and later liberal internationalists with whom he is commonly associated. As we have seen, for
Smith there is no natural harmony of interests between nations. Nor is the
tendency to international conflict for him necessarily ameliorated by the
rise of responsible government and of commerce; indeed, Smith suggests
that in important respects the rise of commerce can exacerbate conflict.
Finally, Smith is sceptical concerning the possibility of reforming the
institutions of international society to lessen conflict, preferring instead to
focus upon the requirements of an adequate system of national defence,
and relying ultimately upon the balance of power to instil mutual respect
between states. As Winch and others have shown, while it is possible and
indeed tempting to project back nineteenth-century images into Smith's
works, to do so does considerable injustice to his particular and complex
form of political scepticism.

   This essay has attempted to show that this is also true for Smith's
thought concerning international relations. It is also interesting that in this
area, there is no significant disjuncture between *The Wealth of Nations* and
*The Theory of Moral Sentiments*; Smith's realism pervades his discussion
of international relations in all his major works.[107] This, it should be noted,
is also true for his correspondence, which reveals the same pragmatism and
irony so evident in *The Wealth of Nations*. Smith's letters reveal that he
was intensely interested in the affairs of his day, but with the important
exception of his letters on the conflict in America, they are disappointingly
devoid of significant additional reflections on international affairs.

   What distinguishes Smith's 'realism' as something more than a pessimism derived from the existence of international anarchy is his complex
view of human nature. The notion that people are prone to self-indulgence
and misperception of their own interests, but are in the end social beings
with a passion for the approbation of others and with some capacity for
sympathy and benevolent imagination is crucial. Such sympathies con-
spicuously fail to extend beyond national borders, and not even extensive
international commerce (let alone democracy) promises to deliver human
society from the flaws due to international anarchy. While Smith is concerned to establish the benefits to civilisation and opulence of liberty and
predictability in the domestic realm, he was relatively unconcerned with
the problem of constraining the exercise of arbitrary power in international
affairs, which for Michael Smith is the defining characteristic of the liberal
perspective in international relations.[108]

   It might even be said that there is a hint of complacency in his view of
war as an ever-present reality which required the citizens to be educated in
the republican martial virtues, and on a number of occasions he implies

that the bad policy of the mercantilists was at least as destructive of human advancement and prosperity as war. Perhaps if he had lived through the Napoleonic wars, as many of his more outraged successors did, he might have shifted his emphasis somewhat. This complacency may also have been due in part to Smith's 'national perspective'; he was above all preaching to *British* legislators to reform their practices and institutions in *The Wealth of Nations*, and Britain was the dominant economic and political power, relatively immune to the disorders of the European continent. However, he can hardly be accused of excessive partiality in his works, which are marked rather by their humanism and the acuteness of perception of human frailty, and thus it might be more accurate to hold to the comparison with Rousseau's despair about progress in international relations.

On the question of Smith's responsibility for the impoverishment of the political in the 'political economy' of the nineteenth century and beyond, the conclusion must be an ambiguous one, though there is little question in this author's mind that Smith was more sinned against than sinning in this regard. Smith undoubtedly gave an unparalleled boost to the subject of economics (as it eventually came to be known) in providing a powerful metaphor of a self-ordering system which captured the imagination of those that came after, above all the more analytical mind of David Ricardo. This metaphor came in nineteenth-century Britain to underpin the doctrines of free trade and the minimalist state, its power deriving in part from the coincidence with British national interest which Smith himself did much to elucidate. There are also certainly occasions on which Smith characterises economic forces as verging on the all-powerful. In his critique of Quesnay's 'exact regimen of perfect liberty and perfect justice', Smith chides him for failing

> to have considered that in the political body, the natural effort which every man is continually making to better his own condition, is a principle of preservation capable of preventing and correcting, in many respects, the bad effects of a political oeconomy...[which] though it no doubt retards more or less, is not always capable of stopping altogether the natural progress of a nation towards wealth and prosperity, and still less of making it go backwards. If a nation could not prosper without the enjoyment of perfect liberty and perfect justice, there is not in the world a nation which could ever have prospered. In the political body, however, the wisdom of nature has fortunately made ample provision for remedying many of the bad effects of the folly and injustice of man; in the same manner as it has done in the natural body, for remedying those of his sloth and intemperance.[109]

However, this faith in the resourcefulness of individuals and markets who are pitted against the folly of governments does not bring Smith even close to the idealism of many later liberals and radicals. For writers such as Bentham, the Mills, Cobden and Angell, the progressive *Zeitgeist* of history was individual self-interest, but one which was so powerful as to overcome the passions of people and to displace politics almost entirely.[110] Since economic bonds between people were displacing other kinds of social bonds, nationalism ceased to be important and the balance of power mere folly or (in Cobden's words) 'a chimera'. From the nineteenth-century perspective, a corollary of this was that as industry gradually displaced agriculture and territory as the basis of national power, war became the most irrational of human endeavours. Finally, the displacement of the feudal elites as part of the process of the commercial revolution would gradually bring governments to act in the interests of the common people.

Yet Smith's consistent refusal to presume that human motivation could be reduced to mere economic self-interest prevents him from succumbing to the political naivety which has often plagued liberal thought, particularly liberal economic thought, since he wrote. He might well have found some agreement with the more reactionary Thomas Carlyle who criticised in 1843 'that brutish god-forgetting Profit-and-Loss Philosophy' with its tendency to reduce all social bonds between people to mere 'cash-nexus'.[111] George Stigler, a noted Chicago economist, criticises Smith for failing to apply the assumption of self-interested behaviour to the political realm: 'Do men calculate in money with logic and purpose, but calculate in votes with confusion and romance?' Stigler goes on to answer the question: 'no clear distinction can be drawn between commercial and political undertakings: the procuring of favourable legislation *is* a commercial undertaking.'[112]

This criticism is unfair, since self-interest (as well as passion) plays an important role in Smith's analysis of politics. Furthermore, it was precisely Smith's point *not* to reduce political, or for that matter economic, behaviour to the textbook *homo economicus* of later generations, and the contemporary vogue for 'economic theories of politics' would have been alien to him.[113] The analytical 'clarification' of Smith's model, which occupied economists for a century or more after the publication of *The Wealth of Nations*, lost the sense of history, of rhetoric and irony, and above all of the complexity of human nature that is present in Smith's thinking. In the process, the perspective associated so often with Smith's name, liberal internationalism, also lost that which is useful in Smith's thought for contemporary scholars of international relations and political economy. For the importance of Smith's thinking, particularly that about political economy, is that a central role for the economic in human affairs need not marginalise the importance of institutions nor trivialise the political.

This brings us to conclude on the question of Smith's relation to the liberal tradition in international relations, since there are many contemporary liberal theorists who would share his realism on a number of matters.[114] There can be no doubt that Smith is an important figure in the liberal tradition conceived broadly, if not of the idealist pre-1914 part of that tradition with which he is often associated. With many liberals, Smith shares a belief in the powerful effects of economic progress through the market, the way in which human reason can be applied to the issue of institutional reform, and the need to constrain overbearing government and powerful interest groups.

Yet his belief in progress at the international level is tenuous to say the least, and his scepticism regarding the likely success of his suggested reforms is deep. His emphasis on the fundamental insecurity of states due to structural factors and human nature suggests that he could be seen as a bridge between economic liberalism and the realist and mercantilist traditions of thought in our subject. Alternatively, and more satisfyingly, we ought to accept that traditions of thought in international relations are neither watertight nor mutually exclusive. The richness of Smith's thought on such issues ought to be interpreted as an indication of the richness of the liberal tradition itself (and, more specifically, of 'commercial liberalism'). Smith is refreshing above all because his thought demonstrates that a theory of 'natural liberty' could systematically avoid the utopianism on international affairs which critics such as Carr and Waltz have argued was part and parcel of the liberal tradition and its central weakness.

## NOTES

1. I would like to thank Ian Clark, Iver Neumann, Adam Roberts, Tim Dunne, Byron Auguste, Holly Wyatt-Walter and Mark Zacher for helpful comments on an earlier draft of this essay.
2. Joseph Cropsey, 'Adam Smith and Political Philosophy', in Andrew S. Skinner and Thomas Wilson (eds), *Essays on Adam Smith* (Oxford, 1975), p. 132.
3. See also E. H. Carr, *The Twenty Years Crisis 1919–1939* (London, 1946), pp. 43–5.
4. Ibid., p. 43.
5. Kenneth N. Waltz, *Man, the State and War: A Theoretical Analysis* (New York, 1959), pp. 86, 90. It ought to be noted, however, that Waltz does view

Smith's comments on international relations as 'uniformly more perspicacious than those of most liberals of the period.' (Ibid., p. 96, note 33).

6.  Martin Wight, *International Theory: The Three Traditions*, ed. Gabriele Wight and Brian Porter (Leicester and London, 1991), p. 263. See also p. 115.

7.  Robert Gilpin, *The Political Economy of International Relations* (Princeton, 1987), p. 27.

8.  For a discussion, see Mark W. Zacher and Richard A. Matthew, 'Liberal International Theory: Common Threads, Divergent Strands', in Charles W. Kegley (ed.), *Controversies in International Relations Theory: Realism and the Neoliberal Challenge* (New York, 1995).

9.  James Shotwell, *War as an Instrument of National Policy* (New York, 1921), quoted in Waltz, *Man, the State and War*, p. 98.

10.  Michael Howard, *War and the Liberal Conscience* (Oxford, 1981), pp. 25, 29.

11.  Michael J. Shapiro, *Reading 'Adam Smith': Desire, History and Value* (London, 1993), also departs from the conventional view in claiming Smith as 'a quintessential critical theorist', a different line of enquiry to that taken in this essay.

12.  The full title of Smith's work is *An Inquiry into the Nature and Causes of the Wealth of Nations* [1776], ed. R. H. Campbell and A. S. Skinner (Oxford, 1976). Citations from this and other of Smith's works will use the now standard format associated with the Glasgow bicentennial edition of Adam Smith's works and correspondence (published by Oxford University Press), including the following abbreviations:

    *WN*  *The Wealth of Nations* [1776], ed. Campbell and Skinner (1976).

    *TMS*  *The Theory of Moral Sentiments* [1759], ed. A. L. Macfie and D. D. Raphael (1976).

    *LJ*  *Lectures on Jurisprudence* [Reports of 1762–3 and 1766], ed. R. L. Meek, D. D. Raphael and P. G. Stein (1978).

    *Corr.*  *Correspondence of Adam Smith*, ed. E. C. Mossner and I. S. Ross (2nd edn, 1987).

13.  See Jerry Z. Muller, *Adam Smith in his Time and Ours: Designing the Decent Society* (New York, 1993), ch. 3, and more generally, Istvan Hont and Michael Ignatieff (eds), *Wealth and Virtue: The Shaping of Political Economy in the Scottish Enlightenment* (Cambridge, 1983).

14.  *WN*, IV.ii.9.

15.  Ibid.

16.  Jacob Viner, 'Adam Smith and Laissez Faire', *Journal of Political Economy*, 35, April 1927, pp. 198–232, reprinted in Viner, *The Long View and the Short: Studies in Economic Theory and Policy* (Glencoe, 1958), p. 227.

17  *WN*, I.ii.2.

18.  *WN*, IV.ix.51. For a discussion of the role of benevolence and sympathy in the moral order of *TMS*, see Viner, 'Smith and Laissez Faire', and Thomas Wilson, 'Sympathy and Self-Interest', in Thomas Wilson and Andrew S. Skinner (eds), *The Market and the State: Essays in Honour of Adam Smith* (Oxford, 1976).

19.  Gunnar Myrdal, *The Political Element in the Development of Economic Theory* (London, 1953), p. 107.

20. *WN*, IV.ii.21.
21. *WN*, I.x.c.27.
22. *WN*, I.x.c.61. For similar concerns, see *TMS*, VII.iv.36.
23. *WN*, IV.vii.c.61. See Rosenberg, 'Institutional Aspects', p. 558, and also Viner, 'Smith and Laissez Faire', pp. 228ff.
24. *WN*, I.iii.
25. *WN*, IV.ix.51.
26. For an assessment of the role of rhetoric in economics and the social sciences in general, see Donald N. McCloskey, *The Rhetoric of Economics* (Madison, 1986).
27. Viner, 'Smith and Laissez Faire', pp. 231–5.
28. *WN*, II.iii.36.
29. *WN*, V.ii.a.4.
30. For a similar argument, see Jacob Viner, 'Power versus Plenty as Objectives in Foreign Policy in the Seventeenth and Eighteenth Centuries', in Viner, *Long View*, and Edward Meale Earle, 'Adam Smith, Alexander Hamilton, Friedrich List: The Economic Foundations of Military Power', in Earle (ed.), *Makers of Modern Strategy: Military Thought from Machiavelli to Hitler* (Princeton, 1971).
31. *WN*, IV.ii.24ff.
32. *WN*, IV.ii.30.
33. *WN*, V.i.b.1.
34. *TMS*, VII.iv.36; *WN*, V.i.b.2–3, 12, and V.iii.7.
35. *WN*, I.i.10, and editors' introduction, p. 37.
36. *WN*, IV.ii.40–4.
37. *WN*, IV.vii.c.95, V.i.e.30. See also Gilpin, *Political Economy*, pp. 180–3.
38. *WN*, II.iv.15.
39. *WN*, I.x.c.27.
40. *WN*, IV.ii.43.
41. See Carr, *Twenty Years' Crisis*, p. 45.
42. *WN*, IV.ii.24. See also *WN*, IV.v.a.36, where Smith also recommends for national security reasons bounties upon the exportation of British sail-cloth and gunpowder.
43. *WN*, IV.ii.29.
44. *WN*, II.v.31, italics added.
45. Viner, 'Power versus Plenty', p. 286.
46. *WN*, IV.vii.c.22–64.
47. Note the potential contradiction with his earlier views on the acts: compare *WN*, IV.vii.c.23 with IV.ii.29. It is also notable that this potential contradiction was pounced upon by Governor Thomas Pownell, MP, in his letter to Smith of 25 September 1776. [*Corr.*, Appendix A, pp. 357–8.]
48. *WN*, IV.vii.c.43–4. See also *Corr.*, letter 262.
49. *WN*, IV.vii.c.44.
50. Albert O. Hirschman, *The Passions and the Interests: Political Arguments for Capitalism before Its Triumph* (Princeton, 1977), p. 79.
51. *WN*, IV.iii.c.9, and *TMS*, VI.ii.2.3.
52. *WN*, IV.iii.c.9.
53. *WN*, IV.iii.c.11, italics added.
54. *WN*, IV.iii.c.13, italics added.

55. *WN*, V.i.a.15.
56. *TMS*, VI.ii.2–3.
57. *WN*, IV.ii.9, italics added.
58. *WN*, III.iv.4. As Smith notes, this was a theme on which Hume also had much to say (and indeed the Scottish Enlightenment as a whole). Smith in his writings identified four stages of socio-economic development: the stages of hunters, of shepherds, of agriculture and of commerce.
59. *WN*, III.iv.10. See also *WN*, III.iv.17.
60. *WN*, III.iv.15.
61. See Zacher and Matthew, 'Liberal International Theory'.
62. *WN*, IV.iii.c.9.
63. Both quoted in Hirschman, *Passions and Interests*, p. 80. Hirschman's book is a fascinating account of the origins of the idea of the civilising effects of commerce, but I depart from his view that in *WN*, there is no place for non-economic drives to human behaviour (ibid., pp. 107–13). On the contrary, it is precisely this role for non-economic passions which leads Smith to depart so fundamentally from much eighteenth- and nineteenth-century radical thought on social conflict.
64. *WN*, V.ii.a.4.
65. *WN*, V.iii.37. For an equally cynical and remarkably similar view of the relationship between democracy and war, see John Kenneth Galbraith, *The Culture of Contentment* (London, 1993), ch. 9.
66. See Michael W. Doyle, 'Kant, Liberal Legacies, and Foreign Affairs', *Philosophy and Public Affairs*, 12 (3&4), Summer and Fall 1983 (parts 1 and 2).
67. *WN*, IV.vii.c.66.
68. *WN*, V.iii.92.
69. *Corr.*, Appendix B: 'Smith's Thoughts on the State of the Contest with America, February 1778', pp. 382–3.
70. *WN*, IV.vii.c.66.
71. *WN*, IV.vii.c.74, 75. Smith's proposal entailed full equality of representation and taxation, freedom of trade, and even a provision for the future removal of the seat of the Empire to that part 'which contributed most to the general defence and support of the whole'. (See *WN*, IV.vii.ci.75–9.)
72. For Smith's scepticism regarding the relationship between commerce and representative government, see Duncan Forbes, 'Sceptical Whiggism, Commerce, and Liberty', in Skinner and Wilson, *Essays on Adam Smith*. Forbes also indicates how Smith's emphasis upon man's baser instincts led him to scepticism that economic progress would bring about the demise of slavery, which Smith held to be economically inefficient as well as immoral (Ibid., pp. 199–200).
73. Montesquieu, *De l'esprit des lois* [1748], XXI, 20, quoted in Hirschman, *Passions and Interests*, p. 73.
74. *WN*, V.iii.40.
75. Waltz, *Man, the State, and War*.
76. *TMS*, VI.ii.2.3.
77. Ibid.
78. *WN*, III.iv.15.
79. *WN*, V.iii.3, 8, 10. Smith shared with Burke, Hume and others of his time a grave concern about the corrupting influence of increasing public indebted-

ness. See J. G. A. Pocock, 'The Political Economy of Burke's Analysis of
the French Revolution', *Historical Journal*, 25(2), June 1982, pp. 331–49.
For the classic account of the 'financial revolution' of the seventeenth
century which enhanced the war-making capabilities of the British state, see
P. G. M. Dickson, *The Financial Revolution in England: A Study in the
Development of Public Credit, 1688–1756* (London, 1967).

80. *WN*, V.iii.50.
81. *WN*, V.iii.67.
82. *WN*,V.i.f.50.
83. *WN*, V.i.a.36, and V.i.f.59.
84. *WN*, V.i.a.43–4.
85. *WN*, V.i.a.39.
86. See the discussion in Winch, *Adam Smith's Politics*, pp. 105–12.
87. *WN*, V.i.a.40. In his Lectures, Smith is more Lockean in the case of Britain
    (*LJ(A)*, iv.178), though his general position is that a standing army loyal to
    King and country is the best guarantor of domestic liberty (*LJ(A)*, iv.179,
    and *WN*, V.i.a.41).
88. Rosenberg, 'Institutional Aspects', p. 560.
89. *TMS*, VI.ii.2.4.
90. *TMS*, VI.ii.2.6. See also *TMS*, III.3.4.
91. *TMS*, VI.ii.3.6.
92. *LJ(B)*, 344–5.
93. See Knud Haakonssen, *The Science of a Legislator: The Natural
    Jurisprudence of David Hume and Adam Smith* (Cambridge, 1981),
    pp. 133–4, and *TMS*, III.3.42.
94. *WN*, IV.i.32, and IV.vii.c.80,100.
95. *TMS*, VI.ii.2.3.
96. (*LJ(B)*), 339. Smith's discussion is largely confined to the laws of war and
    diplomatic immunity (based on reciprocity). See *LJ(B)*, 339–58, and *TMS*,
    III.iii.43, VI.ii.2.2–5, and VII.iv.37.
97. *TMS*, III.3.42.
98. *WN*, IV.vii.c.80 (italics added).
99. *LJ(B)*, 355–6, and *TMS*, VI.ii.2.6.
100. See Howard, *War and the Liberal Conscience*, pp. 42–4.
101. *LJ(B)*, 353–8.
102. *WN*, IV.iii.c.9.
103. *WN*, IV.ii.38–9 (italics added).
104. See *WN*, editors' introduction, pp. 1–4.
105. Martin Wight, 'Why Is There No International Theory?' in Herbert
     Butterfield and Martin Wight (eds), *Diplomatic Investigations* (London,
     1967).
106. Viner, 'Smith and Laissez Faire', p. 221.
107. For a discussion of the long-debated 'Adam Smith problem' concerning the
     supposed inconsistency of *WN* and *TMS*, see editors' introduction, *TMS*,
     pp. 20–5.
108. Michael Joseph Smith, 'Liberalism and International Reform', in Terry
     Nardin and David R. Mapel (eds), *Traditions of International Ethics*
     (Cambridge, 1992), p. 202.
109. *WN*, IV.ix.28.

110. For an account of the apoliticism of much liberal thought, see Sheldon S. Wolin, *Politics and Vision: Continuity and Innovation in Western Political Thought* (London, 1961), pp. 299ff.

111. Quoted by Albert O. Hirschman, 'Interests', in *The New Palgrave: The World of Economics*, ed. John Eatwell, Murray Milgate and Peter Newman (London, 1991), p. 355.

112. George J. Stigler, 'Smith's Travels on the Ship of State', in Skinner and Wilson, *Essays on Adam Smith*, pp. 237–8. See the more extended critique of Stigler in Winch, *Adam Smith's Politics*, pp. 165–72.

113. In *TMS*, VII.iii.I, Smith firmly rejects the idea that moral theory could be based entirely upon individual 'self-love'.

114. See Zacher and Matthew, 'Liberal International Theory', pp. 120ff.

# 8  Edmund Burke and the Commonwealth of Europe: The Cultural Bases of International Order

Jennifer M. Welsh

John Vincent was the first to note the neglect of Edmund Burke's mind by scholars of international relations, compared with the considerable attention that has been heaped on his ideas by biographers, historians, literary theorists, and political philosophers.[1] I will not try to replicate his overview of Burke's international theory. Instead, I propose to deal more specifically with two aspects of Burke's thought which most interested Vincent in his own scholarly work: the question of intervention[2] and the role of culture in world politics.[3] In the writings and speeches of Burke, these two areas of international relations theory can be examined most usefully through his unique conception of European international society, which he refers to as the 'Commonwealth of Europe'. Accordingly, this chapter will first outline the features of this Commonwealth of Europe, and its substantive cultural underpinnings. It will then move on to discuss Burke's theory of intervention, which emerges directly from the French Revolutionary challenge to that Commonwealth. It will conclude with some thoughts about Burke's relationship to Wight's three traditions, and the relevance of his ideas on culture and international order to the present theory and practice of international relations.

## BURKE'S THEORY OF EUROPEAN INTERNATIONAL SOCIETY

### The Commonwealth of Europe

According to Martin Wight, international theory can be described as a 'tradition of speculation about the relations between states ... the twin of speculation about the state to which the name "political theory" is appropriated'.[4] Adopting this definition, Burke's theory would seem to deal directly with many of the perennial issues of international relations: diplomacy, empire, trade, the balance of power, or war. In fact, Wight remarked that the 'only political philosopher who has turned wholly from political theory to international theory is Burke'.[5] Moreover, the number of references to Burke in Wight's lectures suggests that he considered Burke a torch-bearer of his Rationalist position.[6]

In a Rationalist fashion, Burke observes the existence of a European international society, sustained by institutions such as the balance of power and regulated by that 'great ligament of mankind', international law.[7] While this 'vast commonwealth'[8] is marked by a degree of autonomy and decentralisation, Burke believes any diversity of interests is possible only because of an underlying sense of community among European states and a collective commitment to maintaining order. As Vincent aptly put it: 'The system worked within a society; pluralism worked because of a deeper solidarity.'[9]

But what is the real nature of this deeper solidarity? In Burke's theory, it is not just a Rationalist order among states which is part of the 'immutable nature' of things. There is also a particular social and cultural order which drives across sovereign frontiers. Though he acknowledges the importance of 'national character'[10] and is intensely patriotic about Britain, he is also concerned with preserving the long-standing traditions of a larger European civilisation.

Burke goes as far as to portray Europe as 'virtually one great state', with some 'diversity of provincial customs and local establishments'.[11] He accentuates the presence throughout Europe of the Christian religion,[12] monarchical principle of government, Roman law heritage, and Gothic custom. There may be local variations on these themes, he states, but '[at] bottom, these are all the same'.[13] In addition, Burke describes the members of this Commonwealth as united by free trade and economic interdependence. For him, as for many of his Enlightenment contemporaries, the economic ties between European states are praised for binding states together in a community of interests.[14] In contrast to Rousseau, who shuns interdependence for its contagious potential,[15] Burke believes the members of European international society can be strengthened by participation in a larger collective.

But although this congruence of political, legal and economic factors is critical to Burke's conception of European international society, he follows Montesquieu in placing greater emphasis on the cultural mores or 'manners' shared by the peoples of the Commonwealth of Europe. This 'antient system of opinion and sentiment' accounts for Europe's preponderance and distinguishes it from the outside world.[16] Such manners, which grew out of the feudal traditions of nobility and chivalry, 'softened, blended, and harmonized the colours of the whole', providing a deeper foundation for all other laws and institutions. 'The law touches us but here and there, and now and then', Burke writes, but manners 'are what vex or soothe, corrupt or purify, exalt or debase, barbarize or refine us'.[17] A crucial part of this common set of manners is the similar structure of education which exists for Europeans.[18] As a result 'no citizen of Europe could be altogether an exile in any part of it.... When a man travelled or resided for health, pleasure, business or necessity, from his country, he never felt himself quite abroad.'[19] For Burke, Europe refers to a way of life, rather than a territorial or legal construct.

In Burke's Commonwealth of Europe, the strongest link among members is the bond of 'sympathy', born of familiarity. Though there is no treaty or compact uniting bearers of the Christian–Roman–Germanic tradition, there is a deep affection arising from their historical experience of co-existence. This emphasis on habit and sentiment is crucial to understanding Burke's 'non-Rationalist' approach to international order. It is captured in the following excerpt from the *Letters on a Regicide Peace*, one that Vincent himself was fond of quoting:

> In the intercourse between nations, we are apt to rely too much on the instrumental part.... Men are not tied to one another by papers and seals. They are led to associate by resemblances, by conformities, by sympathies. It is with nations as with individuals. Nothing is so strong a tie of amity between nation and nation as correspondence in laws, customs, manners, and habits of life. They have more than the force of treaties in themselves. They are obligations written in the heart.... The secret, unseen, but irrefragable bond of habitual intercourse, holds them together, even when their perverse and litigious nature sets them to equivocate, scuffle, and fight about the terms of their written obligations.[20]

True to form, Burke trumps formal or institutional considerations with more intangible factors. While his theory of international order invokes all of the Rationalist instruments for maintaining stability among European states, of greater significance is their underlying cultural similitude.

In presupposing this common culture for his international society, Burke should not lumped with 'second image'[21] theorists of international order, who assert that world peace between states can be achieved by creating doctrinal uniformity (usually a form of democracy or republicanism) within them.[22] Burke's interpretation of uniformity is much more conservative, focused on stability rather than perfection. Because he sees a basic 'infirmity'[23] in human nature he denies that one particular ideology is necessarily the messiah of world peace. For him war 'cannot be wholly avoided' and may be 'the sole means of justice among nations'.[24]

Burke therefore admits that the political, social and cultural solidarity among European states will not do away with all conflict. Nonetheless, he is confident that their 'conformity and analogy ... has a strong tendency to facilitate accommodation, and to produce a generous oblivion of the rancour of their quarrels'. With this similitude, 'peace is more of peace, and war is less of war'.[25] If rivalries do arise, Europeans will play them out in the 'spirit of gentlemen'.

## Homogeneity and International Legitimacy

In theoretical terms, the key to Burke's vision of European international society lies in his conservative approach to the question of 'international legitimacy', defined by Wight as the consensus on the 'rightful member-ship of the family of nations, how sovereignty may be transferred, and how state succession is to be regulated...'.[26] More specifically, Burke's conception of international legitimacy is a substantive rather than a proced-ural one. It is premised not only on agreement about 'the permissible aims and methods of foreign policy',[27] but also on a more basic agreement or 'homogeneity'[28] concerning the domestic composition of states. It is there-fore an *intra*-national conception of legitimacy, with an eye to the 'princi-ples that prevail ... *within* a majority of the states that form international society, as well as in the relations *between* them'.[29]

Although Burke permits some diversity within the Commonwealth of Europe, 'rightful membership' in his family requires conformity with the standards of European civilisation. Furthermore, this homogeneity has a crucial 'reinforcing effect' on the maintenance of order among and within the members of the Commonwealth. The political and social orders of European states are integrally linked and rely on each other for survival: '[I] consider the conservation in England of the antient order of things, as necessary to preserve order every where else, and ... the general conserva-tion of order in other countries, as reciprocally necessary to preserve the same state of things in those Islands.'[30] In Burke's theory, a homogeneous and stable international society depends upon preservation of a domestic status quo.

Burke's 'legitimist' view of international order distinguishes him from pluralist eighteenth-century philosophers like Vattel, who conceive of Europe first in terms of its separation into sovereign states, and only secondly as a voluntary association of those states into an international society. This emphasis on division, as opposed to unity, was reflected in the development of a positive international law to codify inter-state relations and to achieve an external order among sovereign units. Burke often appeals to these 'writers on the public law of Europe'[31] when depicting his vision of international society. In reality, however, he more closely approximates medieval philosophers,[32] or later peace theorists such as William Penn and the Abbé de Saint Pierre. In particular, Burke's theory shares their desire to guarantee dynastic rulers not merely an external or territorial *status quo*, but also a political and social status quo *within* their frontiers.[33]

To sum up, while Burke explicitly draws on the works of his pluralist contemporaries, his conservative notion of the European Commonwealth is a unique one, which combines elements of pluralism and solidarism, and which frequently looks back to the Middle Ages.[34] He conceives the problem of international order as involving both external and internal elements – both substantive and procedural solutions.

In this sense, Burke's conservative international theory does contain Revolutionalist overtones. As Wight argues, although the dynastic principle of legitimacy Burke espouses was rooted in custom rather than doctrine, at times it exhibited a tendency to develop into an ideology of 'international dynasticism'.[35] As we shall see below, Burke's substantive version of international legitimacy, with its strong commitment to preserve homogemeity in Europe, can have serious ramifications for the traditional rules and procedures which regulate state relations, particularly in the face of a revolutionary challenge in any part of the Commonwealth.

## THE COMMONWEALTH OF EUROPE AND THE FRENCH REVOLUTION

### The Nature of the Revolutionary Threat

In Burke's lifetime, the greatest threat to the solidarity and stability of the Commonwealth of Europe came in the wake of the French Revolution. Under William Pitt's leadership, the British government assumed a Realist posture in response to the events of 1789, clearly distinguished between the internal and external behaviour of France, and maintained a position of neutrality until vital national interests were challenged by a physical act of aggression.[36] Burke, by contrast, perceives the Revolutionaries as undermining the very foundations of order in Europe through their challenge to established religion, property and dynastic legitimacy. More significantly, he charges them with having inaugurated a complete 'revolution in sentiments, manners, and moral opinions'.[37] This 'savage' Jacobin assault on the values of chivalry and honour strikes the greatest blow to 'the glory of Europe'.[38] It is therefore the social and cultural dimensions of the Revolution in France which concern Burke most: 'What he dreaded most was the destruction of the whole order of civil life; not only that we should lose king, lords, and commons, but our property, our wives, every thing that was dear and sacred.'[39]

For Burke, the Revolutionary threat is not a physical one, premised on military might, but an ideological one, based on subversive and contagious principles. Furthermore, unlike previous bids for hegemony from the French state, the present danger is transnational, emanating from a less tangible, but more potent, revolutionary dogma. The real novelty of this 'armed doctrine'[40] of the Revolution is its ability to reach the very minds of human beings – whatever state they happen to inhabit.[41] As a corollary, individuals 'become more attached to the country of their principles, than to the country of their birth.'[42] In Burke's mind, the Revolution has blurred the traditional lines of international politics. In the war between popular and dynastic legitimacy, citizens no longer desire victory for their own state, but for the particular brand of legitimacy to which they adhere.[43]

Burke insists that such a monumental defiance of property, religion, monarchy and manners can never be contained in its own country of origin. Part of the revolutionary essence, he maintains, is an 'example effect' that necessarily affects all members of the Commonwealth. The subversive doctrine of the Revolution 'violates the right upon which not only the community of France, but those on which all communities are founded'.[44] Consequently, while shots have not yet been fired, France 'by the very condition of its existence' and 'by its essential constitution, is in a state of hostility with us, and with all civilized people'.[45]

This characterisation of the French Revolutionary threat leads Burke to advocate extraordinary means – or Holy War – to counteract the plague which has fallen upon the Commonwealth of Europe. 'This evil in the heart of Europe must be extirpated from that center', he warns, 'or no part of the circumference can be free from the mischief which radiates from it ...'[46] His remedy is a joint military intervention on the part of Christian sovereigns, in conjunction with the French émigrés, to restore the dignity, property, honour, virtue and religion of Europe.[47] Moreover, he instructs European statesmen not to treat this counter-revolutionary campaign as a 'common political war with an old recognized member of the commonwealth of Christian Europe'.[48] To meet the unique social and transnational challenge of the Revolution, Burke proposes a 'moral war' of an entirely new kind, where the traditional language of diplomacy and the 'mode of civilized war'[49] cannot be practised. His understanding of international order, which rests upon a substantive conception of international legitimacy, justifies such a suspension of the 'usual relations of peace and amity'.[50]

## Burke's Theory of Intervention

Burke's reflections on the French Revolution are also interesting for the way in which they justify a policy of intervention. In this way, his interventionism can be seen not only in the context of the British foreign policy debate of his time, but also as part of his more comprehensive theory of international order. Interspersed in his writings and speeches are three main arguments to rationalise intervention in the affairs of the French state: the pretext of preventive war, derived from his understanding of the relationship between intervention and the balance of power; the right of intervention in civil conflict, which stems from his reading of eighteenth-century international law; and the right of vicinage, extrapolated from the Roman civil-law notions of Vicinity and Neighbourhood.

### *Preventive War and the Balance of Power*

Burke's promotion of intervention against Revolutionary France can be interpreted as an extension of his particular views on the balance of power. Indeed, war and intervention were considered by many eighteenth-century theorists and politicians to be a legitimate means of safeguarding and revising the balance, despite prevailing norms concerning state sovereignty and non-interference.[51] This hierarchical relationship between the balance of power and the principle of nonintervention reflected the conviction that a balance among the major European powers was something which ought actively to be sought, as opposed to a phenomenon which was spontaneously generated.[52] Burke himself adopts this Rationalist rather than Realist approach to the balance of power, describing the existing equilibrium in Europe as the result of prudent collective management and the 'unremitting attention' of sovereigns to potentially disturbing developments.[53] He also alleges that cases of intervention on behalf of the balance of power 'fill half the pages of history', referring in particular to the 'several Treaties of Guarantee to the Protestant Succession'.[54]

More importantly, Burke asserts that prudent balance-of-power politics may require intervention to combat not just *de facto* aggression, but also an 'imminent threat' of attack. Drawing on the works of Vattel,[55] he concludes that established international law allows for such preventive war in cases of hostile intention. He then extends Vattel's sanctioning of preventive intervention to encompass political and social as well as military threats. In his interpretation, the violation of state rights need not come in the form of 'formidable forces', but may also exist in the form of 'pernicious maxims' – i.e. a challenge to existing conceptions of international legitimacy.[56]

### Intervention in Civil Conflict

Burke's treatment of civil conflict and intervention also draws on the writings of eminent international jurists and their provisions for aiding the just side in a civil war.[57] Extrapolating from Vattel, however, Burke argues that the law of nations on civil conflict allows 'abundant liberty for a neighbour to support *any* of the parties according to his choice'.[58] In other words, he does not limit the 'just side' to the forces of rebellion,[59] but extends the right of intervention to the benefit of the *ancien régime*. While to 'interfere in such dissension requires great prudence and circumspection', he states, 'an abstract principle of public law, forbidding such interference, is not supported ... by the Authorities on the Subject' nor by the practice 'of any civilized nation in the world'.[60]

This endeavour to demonstrate the legality of intervention in France within the terms of the existing law of nations stems from Burke's conservative respect for precedent and 'established wisdom'. Nonetheless, he also moves beyond conventional interpretations when arguing his case against the Revolution. He conceives intervention by the European powers against the Jacobin regime not as a war against the French *state*, but as a crusade against a revolutionary *faction* which has ripped apart the Commonwealth of Europe. Consequently, he reasons that this intervention is not *foreign* as such, but rather part of a larger, European civil war.[61] Once more, he turns to historical precedent to argue that supporters of the *ancien régime* should be characterised not as external invaders, but as friends coming to the aid of a neighbouring Prince: 'Foreign Powers have hitherto chosen to give to such wars as this, the appearance of a civil contest, and not that of an hostile invasion.'[62] The forces of order – in whatever states they happen to find themselves – must join together to defend the monarchical *status quo* which is under siege in France.

By the 'publick law of Europe', he writes, 'the Potentates of Europe have ... a right, an interest, and a duty to know with what government they are to treat, and what they are to admit into the federative Society, or in other words, into the diplomatic Republick of Europe'.[63]

In his theory, the legitimacy of thrones is prior to the sanctity of frontiers.[64]

*The Laws of Vicinity and Neighbourhood*

Given Burke's substantive conception of international legitimacy, it is hardly surprising that his treatment of intervention explodes the prevailing norms and rules devised by the Rationalists of his day.[65] Consequently, to further develop his thesis that the revolutionaries have inaugurated a *civil war* in Europe, he invokes the domestic, Roman law notions of Vicinity and Neighbourhood. In his later works, he relies on these concepts of civil jurisprudence, rather than on the more conventional precepts of international law, to justify intervention.

The Law of Vicinity, as Burke explains it, is essentially the circumstance of connectedness. As shown above, Burke frequently asserts this phenomenon of vicinage for the members of the European Commonwealth. By virtue of geography, politics, economics, religion, shared history and common custom, what happened in one state of Europe necessarily had an impact on all others. The companion to this Law of Vicinage is the Law of Neighbourhood, which 'does not leave a man perfect master on his own ground' and which grants neighbours the right to protest any 'new erection, in the nature of a nuisance' to an independent judge.[66] Burke also applies this precept of Roman law to the condition between the states of Europe:

> Now where there is no constituted judge, as between independent states there is not, the vicinage itself is the natural judge. It is, preventively, the assertor of its own rights; or remedially, their avenger.... This principle, which, like the rest, is as true of nations, as of individual men, has bestowed on the grand vicinage of Europe, a duty to know, and a right to prevent, any capital innovation which may amount to the reaction of a dangerous nuisance....[67]

Therefore, the 'capital innovation' of the Revolutionaries, in the form of their contagious principles, has activated this right of vicinage for all of France's neighbours in the Commonwealth of Europe. 'What in civil society is a ground of action', he proclaims, 'in politick society is a ground of war.'[68]

In the final analysis, Burke's willingness to engage in intervention rests upon his more general understanding of state sovereignty and the requirements of international order. As Vincent noted, while observance of the procedural norm of nonintervention can contribute to the maintenance of stability in international relations, it does not necessarily exhaust the ingredients for international order. This would only hold true where states are viewed as purely autonomous and self-contained – as parts of a system rather than a society. 'Where this isolation does not obtain', he writes, 'but where various degrees of separateness and independence do, the require-ments for order are more complex'.[69] As a result, the rule of noninterven-tion will be weighed against competing imperatives.

In Burke's international theory, that competing imperative is his sub-stantive view of international legitimacy. In contrast to nonintervention-ists, who see sovereignty and nonintervention as indispensable features of international order,[70] Burke adheres to a qualified idea of sovereignty, which balances the needs of international society as a whole against the absolute liberty and independence of its individual members. In addition, because he looks beyond the confines of the state to conceive of individ-uals, groups and states as part of a wider historical and cultural 'chain of being', he claims that it is permissible to make judgements about, and to take action within, the sovereign realm of another. And finally, given his solidarist vision of the Commonwealth of Europe, which is sustained by an underlying social and cultural homogeneity, he believes the powers of Europe have both a right and an 'indispensable duty'[71] to counteract forces of disorder in any part.

To conclude with Vincent's phraseology, Burke holds the preservation of a common culture to be a *prerequisite* and not a mere requisite of inter-national order.[72] Therefore, he is prepared to override the procedural rule of reciprocal noninterference – perfectly acceptable in 'normal times' – if more fundamental components of order are threatened. In the case of the French Revolution, Burke construes the Jacobin attack on manners, reli-gion, property and dynastic right as an 'act of secession'[73] from European international society, which demands a diversion from the ordinary rules of the game.


BURKE'S LEGACY


Despite Burke's inability to influence the policy of the British Government during the 1790s, his interpretation of the French Revolution and his more general conservative philosophy have had a profound resonance. As one scholar puts it: 'One need only mention his name today to suggest an atti-tude, a stance, an entire world view.'[74] The Edmund Burke of the *Reflections* and the *Letters on a Regicide Peace* has provided a powerful image for conservatives and counter-revolutionists right up to the present day. For example, in their 'rediscovery' of Burke's thought, American conservatives of the 1950s found a welcome ideological support for their crusade against Soviet communism.[75] But what impact do Burke's ideas have on international theory today, now that the 'light and darkness' debates of the Cold War have subsided? Is Burke relevant only as a counter-revolutionary crusader, or does he speak to broader questions and issues of international relations?

## Burke and the Three Traditions

It is clear from the above analysis that Burke cannot be squarely placed in any one of the three Rs developed by Wight.[76] Though he exhibits some features of Realism, most notably its rejection of progressivism, he contests its depiction of the international system as a state of war, its mechanistic conception of the balance of power, and its denial of international morality.[77] Second, while Burke asks the same essential question as Wight's Rationalists – what is the nature of international society? – the answer he provides differs from the pluralist one associated with thinkers such as Vattel.[78] Whereas the Rationalists tend to limit their expectation of societal consensus to rules and procedures of co-existence, Burke goes a step further to demand a substantive consensus on social and cultural questions. For him, the 'obligations written in the heart' are more reliable than the 'formality of treaties and compacts'. And third, although Burke's theory of international order is based on a strong degree of homogeneity, it does not espouse the Revolutionist values of cosmopolitanism or doctrinal uniformity that are forwarded by many Enlightenment liberals. In the end, Burke's 'negative' crusade remains conservative – designed to root out an existing evil – rather than to construct a more perfect utopia.[79]

If Burke is to be placed in any tradition of international relations theory, it is only the broader notion of what has recently been referred to as an 'international society tradition'.[80] In fact, his reflections on international relations spark some of the most interesting debates within this wider camp. More specifically, Burke forces us to consider whether order is founded on the 'instrumental part' of international society – its procedural rules and institutions – or on its deeper 'correspondence in customs, manners, and habits of life'.[81]

When Hedley Bull asserts that international society is premised on some element of common *values*, he refers mainly to values about the international system as such – *pacta sunt servanda*, laws of war, or nonintervention.[82] In short, he still places international order predominantly on the shoulders of the sovereign state and on the pluralist precepts of consent and self-help. What Burke's writings draw our attention to are those political, social and cultural values which lie within the realm of the domestic, but which are nonetheless indispensable for the maintenance of international order.

Burke's ultimate marginalisation of the procedural conventions of international relations, and his treatment of the French Revolution as a *domestic* issue within the Commonwealth of Europe, make it difficult to classify him within any of the three traditions. It may also help to account for his relative neglect by scholars of international relations. But at the same time, it is only by relaxing Wight's state-centric definition of international theory to allow for a synthesis of the domestic and the international[83] that one can fully appreciate Burke's rich contribution. As Vincent pointed out, Burke tended to treat international politics 'as a branch of all politics'[84] and rejected international relations as a discrete enterprise, whether considered practically or intellectually. 'Burke's main point is that we must grasp what it is that is common to all European societies before we can gain an appreciation of the relations among them.'[85]

**Cultural Homogeneity and International Order**

Although there may be no coherent Burkean tradition which can be traced down through the centuries, his conservative arguments still find adherents. The controversy which divided Burke the crusader and Pitt the Realist is one that continues to divide theorists and practitioners of international relations, particularly in revolutionary times. Burke's answer to the perennial question of what sustains international order has been voiced by succeeding interventionists, such as Winston Churchill, John Foster Dulles, and Jeanne Kirkpatrick. Arguably, it also lies behind the self-professed neutrality of many members of the Realist school.[86] Burke's substantive conception of international legitimacy can therefore be seen as part of an ongoing discussion among conservatives on the importance of homogeneity in the maintenance of international order.

The issue of homogeneity is most obvious in a *negative* sense. When there is a clear heterogeneity of values in the international system, states are more likely to feel threatened by the example of the diverse 'Other' and the ordinary rules and procedures of international order will be more difficult to sustain. But, as Fred Halliday has recently illustrated, the theoretical importance of homogeneity goes beyond this issue of 'exemplary alternatives'. What is more interesting – and what Burke reminds us of – is the role that homogeneity plays in a *positive* sense: how it reinforces international order in times of stability. 'States are not isolated units', Halliday writes; 'they exist in an international context, and their practices, constitutions, social and economic orders derive reinforcement from the fact that other states behave like them'.[87] In other words, there is a transnational force of example through similarity as well as through difference. The international dimension is relevant not just when things break down, but is also integral to maintaining order – both between and within states – in 'normal times'.

This 'reinforcing effect' of homogeneity brings us back to the question of culture, and the relationship between John Vincent and the mind of Edmund Burke. For Vincent, as for Burke, the sources of stability in international relations were to be found not only with the sovereign state, but also with the society that existed beyond its borders.As a consequence, he advised us to 'look instead to the unity of culture for the real source of world order'.[88] Current personalities as diverse as Jacques Delors and Mikhail Gorbachev have underscored this cultural solidarity, rather than strategic balance or the forces of the free market, when accounting for unity and stability in the relations among the European states.[89] The recent attempts to enshrine a notion of 'European citizenship' reflect a similar desire to link further economic integration to the deeper, cultural homogeneity among European peoples.[90]

It is here, however, where the connection with Burke's writings and speeches becomes more problematic. The cultural homogeneity of which Burke spoke was frequently exclusive, confined to the corridors of monarchical and diplomatic power. Within his eighteenth-century context, the notion of 'the People' was an elitist one, limited to those who could and did 'travel to any part of Europe'. This emphasis on individual statesmen flows from the fact that Burke belongs to an era of politics which still champions personal responsibility and accountability.[91] Perhaps this is why so much of his international theory rests on less tangible factors – prudence, sentiment, manners – as opposed to formal rules or institutions. For him, it is not crucial to establish hard and fast Rationalist laws, for he can rely on the restraint and sound judgement of 'civilised gentlemen' to maintain order in international society. In his own writings on culture, Vincent hints at a similar divide between an elitist or diplomatic culture which unites the official representatives of states, and an international political culture, or world culture, which reaches into the societies which make up the states-system.[92]

Furthermore, the culture uniting the disparate members of Burke's international society – the Commonwealth of Europe – was dominated by the Christian religion. In today's world, there is no such common religious foundation, and only what Vincent refers to as the 'ideology of modernity' to fill the void. More importantly, this cosmopolitan culture of modernity has not been taken on board everywhere. Many are convinced that the schism between the 'West' and 'the rest' may provide the greatest fault-line for ruptures in international stability in the future.[93] The rhetoric of the Gulf War, with its frequent references to 'barbarism', suggests that cultural homogeneity will continue to affect international relations in a negative as well as a positive sense. Order among states in the present international system may increasingly be fostered by a process of 'Othering' those who are outside the parameters of 'civilisation', rather than building an all-encompassing cultural whole.

## NOTES

1.  R. J. Vincent, 'Edmund Burke and the theory of international relations', *Review of International Studies*, Vol. 10, (1984), pp. 205–18. In fact, this article was first presented in a seminar entitled 'Neglected Thinkers on International Relations', held at the Australian National University in 1983. For other commentaries on Burke, see Vilho Harle, 'Burke the International Theorist – or the War of the Sons of Light and the Sons of Darkness' in *European Values in International Relations* (London, 1990), pp. 58–79; and David Boucher, 'The character of the history of the philosophy of international relations and the case of Edmund Burke', *Review of International Studies*, Vol. 17 (1990), pp. 127–48.

2.  This was the subject of Vincent's dissertation and first monograph, *Nonintervention and International Order* (Princeton, 1974).

3.  Vincent was particularly concerned with the issue of culture in his later research. See 'The Factor of Culture in the Global International Order', *The Year Book of World Affairs*, Vol. 34 (1980), pp. 252–64.

4.  Martin Wight, 'Why is there no International Theory?' in *Diplomatic Investigations*, ed. Herbert Butterfield and Martin Wight (London, 1966), pp. 17–34 (p. 17).

5.  Ibid., p. 20.

6.  These references appear in the new edited collection of Wight's lectures. See *International Theory: The Three Traditions*, ed. Gabriele Wight and Brian Porter (Leicester, 1991). In fact, I would argue that it is Burke, rather than Grotius, who emerges from these lectures as Wight's archetype for Rationalism.

7.  *First Letter on a Regicide Peace*, in *The Writings and Speeches of Edmund Burke*, Vol. IX, ed. R. B. McDowell (Oxford, 1991), p. 240. (Henceforth, WS.) Burke also follows the Grotian/Rationalist tradition in acknowledging natural law as a source for the Law of Nations. See Hedley Bull, 'The Importance of Grotius in the Study of International Relations', in *Hugo Grotius and International Relations*, ed. Hedley Bull, Benedict Kingsbury and Adam Roberts (Oxford, 1990), pp. 78–80.

8.  *The Annual Register*, 1772.

9. Vincent, 'Edmund Burke', p. 211. In Hedley Bull's phraseology, Burke's belief in this underlying consensus places him more firmly in the 'solidarist' than the 'pluralist' branch of Grotianism. See 'The Grotian Conception of International Society', in *Diplomatic Investigations*, pp. 51–73.

10. *Reflections on the Revolution in France*, WS, VIII, edited by Leslie Mitchell (Oxford, 1989), p. 137. Alfred Cobban credits Burke with developing one of the earliest modern theories of nationality. See *Edmund Burke and the Revolt against the Eighteenth Century* (London, 1960), p. 130.

11. *First Letter*, WS, IX, p. 248.

12. Burke frequently uses the medieval term 'Christendom' when referring to Europe. This tendency to confound the newer political entity of Europe with the older cultural notion of Christendom was not an uncommon practice in Burke's time. It even found its way into the writings of more secular thinkers, such as Rousseau and Voltaire. See Denys Hay, *Europe: The Emergence of an Idea*, revised edition (Edinburgh, 1968), p. 233.

13. *First Letter*, WS, IX, p. 248. Therefore, while the different religious sects of Europe differed 'a little in the ceremonies and in the subordinate doctrines', they were all Christian and prescriptive religions. Similarly, while some states had formally cast off Monarchy, 'the spirit of Monarchy' – that form of government based on 'classes, orders and distinctions' – still survived in these self-professed republics. (Ibid.)

14. For an overview of the economic and cosmopolitan ideas of the Enlightenment, see Thomas Schlereth, *The Cosmopolitan Ideal in Enlightenment Thought* (Notre Dame, 1979), pp. 97–104.

15. Stanley Hoffmann and David Fidler, Introduction to *Rousseau on International Relations* (Oxford, 1991), p. xlvi.

16. *Reflections*, WS, VIII, p. 127. An integral part of the definition of the Commonwealth of Europe is Burke's attempt to distinguish it from the non-Europeans societies in Asia, the New World, and the Ottoman Empire. Like many of his Enlightenment peers, he uses the existence of an external 'Other' to underscore those qualities which are unique to European identity. (For further elaboration on this point, see Iver B. Neumann and Jennifer M. Welsh, '"The Other" in European Self-Definition: An Addendum to the Literature on International Society', *Review of International Studies*, Vol. 17 (1991), pp. 327–48.)

17. *First Letter*, WS, IX, p. 242.

18. Ibid., pp. 248–9.

19. Ibid., p. 249. There are parallels here with Voltaire's 'citizen of the world', born and raised on a humanist education. In contrast to the ideals of the cosmopolitanists, however, Burke's common system of manners is confined to the upper echelons of society.

20. Ibid., p. 247.

21. I am referring here to Kenneth Waltz's threefold typology for explaining the causes of war. The first image locates the origins of war in human nature; the second image looks to the nature of the state and the domestic regime; and the third image examines the nature or structure of the international system. *Man, the State and War* (New York, 1954).

22. Wight, 'Theory of International Society', in *International Theory*, pp. 41–2. This 'second image' strategy was particularly strong in the writing of

Burke's contemporaries, such as Thomas Paine and the French *philosophes*. See Felix Gilbert, 'The "New Diplomacy" of the Eighteenth Century', *World Politics*, Vol. 4 (1951), pp. 1–39.

23.  *The Correspondence of Edmund Burke*, ed. Thomas Copeland (Cambridge and Chicago, 1958–78), Vol. VI, p. 48. (Henceforth, Corr.) In particular, Burke's theory of human nature stresses the influence of the emotional rather than the rational faculties. See *A Philosophical Enquiry into the Origin of Our Ideas Sublime and Beautiful*, in *The Works of the Rt. Hon. Edmund Burke*, Bohn Edition (London, 1854–89), Vol. I, p. 37.

24.  *The Annual Register*, Vol. 15, 1772, p. 3; *First Letter*, WS, IX, p. 248.

25.  *First Letter*, WS, IX, p. 248. Burke follows the lead of the international jurists in suggesting that war should be a rule-governed activity: '[It] was a maxim generally established and agreed to ... that the rights of war were not unlimited.' See 'Speech on the St. Eustatius Affair', *The Parliamentary History of England*, ed. William Cobbett, Vol. 22, 14 May 1781, 229.

26.  Martin Wight, *Systems of States*, ed. Hedley Bull (Leicester, 1977), p. 153.

27.  This is the definition of international legitimacy advanced by Henry Kissinger in *A World Restored* (London, 1957), p. 1. As Stanley Hoffmann explains, proponents of a procedural conception of international legitimacy confine themselves to evaluating a state's external behaviour, and whether it is acceptable in terms of the standards outlined in international institutions. Heterogeneity in domestic social and political orders is tolerable, provided such procedural agreement can be reached. *Primacy or World Order: American Foreign Policy since the Cold War* (New York, 1978), p. 39. One recent study of international legitimacy, by Andreas Osiander, attempts to combine substantive and procedural elements. See *Peacemaking and International Legitimacy: Stability and Consensus in the States System of Europe*, D. Phil. Thesis, Oxford University, 1991, p. 14.

28.  According to Raymond Aron, a homogeneous international system is one in which states observe the same principle of domestic legitimacy. A heterogeneous system is one in which states are organised according to different principles of legitimacy and appeal to contradictory value systems. See *Peace and War* (London, 1966), p. 100. This notion of homogeneity has been invoked more recently by Fred Halliday in '"The Sixth Great Power": On the study of revolution and international relations', *Review of International Studies*, Vol. 16 (1990), pp. 217–19.

29.  Wight, *Systems of States*, p. 153.

30.  *Third Letter*, WS, IX, p. 327.

31.  *First Letter*, WS, IX, p. 248. There are some striking similarities between Vattel's notion of Europe as 'une espèce de république', and Burke's notion of the Commonwealth of Europe. See Emer de Vattel, *Le Droit des Gens*, Bk III, Chap. iii, para. 47.

32.  F. H. Hinsley, *Nationalism and the International System* (London, 1973), p. 71.

33.  The peace projects of Penn and Saint Pierre are discussed by F. H. Hinsley, *Power and the Pursuit of Peace* (Cambridge, 1963), and S. J. Hemleben, *Plans for Peace through Six Centuries* (Chicago, 1943).

34.  This 'medievalism' in Burke is also noted by John Vincent. See 'Edmund Burke', p. 205.

35. Wight, 'Theory of International Society', in *International Theory*, p. 42. An obvious example is the Holy Alliance of Metternich.
36. For a thorough treatment of British foreign policy during the Revolutionary period, see John Ehrman, *The Younger Pitt: The Reluctant Transition*, Vol. II (London, 1983), p. 53. The factors drawing Britain into the war in 1793 are succinctly set out by T. C. W. Blanning in *The Origins of the French Revolutionary Wars* (London, 1986).
37. *Reflections*, WS, VIII, p. 131.
38. Ibid., p. 91. Burke is especially appalled by the 'debauched' moral code of the revolutionaries, alluding to practices of sexual promiscuity, divorce, drunkenness, atheism, and even cannibalism. See *First Letter*, WS, IX, p. 247.
39. *Parliamentary History*, Vol. 30, 13 December 1792, 53.
40. *First Letter*, WS, IX, p. 199.
41. *Thoughts on French Affairs*, WS, VIII, p. 341.
42. *Third Letter*, WS, IX, p. 310. Burke finds a precedent for the French Revolutionary threat in the religious convulsions of the Reformation. At this time, Europe was divided not according to the vertical lines of sovereign states, but along the horizontal and transnational divisions of religious dogma. Ibid., p. 342.
43. As Aron suggests, such conflicts over legitimacy are also prone to extremism, as the 'adversaries of the faction in power become, whatever their stripe, the allies of the national enemy and consequently, in the eyes of some of the fellow citizens, traitors' (*Peace and War*, p. 101).
44. *First Letter*, WS, IX, p. 252.
45. Ibid., p. 239.
46. *Heads for Consideration on the Present State of Affairs*, WS, VIII, p. 402.
47. *First Letter*, WS, IX, p. 257. What is striking about Burke is the fact that he advocates military intervention from as early as January 1791. See Corr., VI, p. 211, pp. 217–19.
48. *Fourth Letter*, WS, IX, p. 50. 'To talk of the balance of power to the governors of such a country', Burke writes, 'was a jargon which they could not understand even through an interpreter.' *Third Letter*, WS, IX, p. 340.
49. *Letter to a Member of the National Assembly*, WS, VIII, p. 320.
50. *Second Letter*, WS, IX, p. 271.
51. M. S. Anderson, 'Eighteenth Century Theories of the Balance of Power', in *Studies in Diplomatic History: Essays in Memory of David Bayne Horn*, ed. R. Hatton and M. S. Anderson (London, 1970), pp. 183–98. See also Martin Wight, 'The Balance of Power and International Order', in *The Bases of International Order*, ed. Alan James (London, 1973), pp. 85–115 (p. 103).
52. Hinsley, *Nationalism*, p. 82.
53. *The Annual Register*, Vol. 15, 1772, p. 2.
54. *Third Letter*, WS, IX, p. 306; Corr., VII, p. 176.
55. A series of extracts from Vattel's *Le Droit des Gens*, complete with Burke's annotations, are included as an Appendix in an older edition of the *Thoughts on French Affairs*. See *Three Memorials on French Affairs Written in the Years 1791, 1792, and 1793. By the Late Right Hon. Edmund Burke* (London, 1797). The support for preventive intervention comes in the following excerpt from Vattel's treatise: 'If there is any where a Nation of a

reckless and mischievous disposition, always ready to injure others, to traverse their designs, and to raise domestic troubles, it is not to be doubted, that all have a right to join in order to repress, chastise, and put it ever after out of its power to injure them.' *Le Droit des Gens*, Bk II, chap. 4, para. 53.

56.   Appendix to *Three Memorials* (*Le Droit des Gens.*, Bk II, chap. 4, para. 70). In his annotations to this passage from Vattel, Burke provides the following evidence for the violation of right: 'The French acknowledge no power not directly emanating from the people.'

57.   *Le Droit des Gens*, Bk II, chap. 4, para. 56. In his letters to his son Richard, Burke advises consultation of Vattel's works on the legality of armed intervention. See Corr., VI, p. 317.

58.   *Remarks on the Policy of the Allies*, WS, VIII, p. 474. The emphasis is mine.

59.   *Le Droit des Gens*, Bk II, chap. 4, para. 56. In this section, Vattel grants the right of intervention to foreign powers in order 'to succour an oppressed people'.

60.   Corr., VII, p. 176.

61.   When counselling the émigré army gathered at Coblenz, Burke underscores the need to portray the interventionist forces as friendly European neighbours rather than foreign conquerors: 'Qu'on n'etre point comme Ennemis, mais comme Alliés et Amis – pour rendre au Roi sa liberté – remettre l'ordre, la paix ... et l'affluence ...'. See Corr., VI, p. 258.

62.   *Heads for Consideration*, WS, VIII, p. 394.

63.   Remarks, WS, VIII, p. 473.

64.   Wight, 'Western Values', p. 98.

65.   Indeed, though there is compelling evidence that Vattel supports some forms of preventive war, his language does not give licence to the kind of offensive crusade envisaged by Burke. As with Grotius, Vattel insists that fear of one's adversary is not sufficient grounds for intervention. See Michael Walzer, *Just and Unjust Wars* (New York, 1977), p. 79. Similarly, while Vattel recognises the right to intervene on the just side of a civil war, this right is not intended to endorse an 'eternal war' on behalf of a fellow sovereign (*Le Droit des Gens*, Bk II, chap. 12, para. 196). In general, Vattel's pluralist vision of the society of states is too weak to extract such extensive rights and duties of intervention from it.

66.   *First Letter*, WS, IX, p. 250.

67.   Ibid., p. 251.

68.   Ibid.

69.   Vincent, *Nonintervention*, p. 332.

70.   This noninterventionist stance is derived from two possible arguments. The first, Christian Wolff's formulation, is based on an analogy of the moral autonomy and equality of states with the moral autonomy and equality of individuals. The second contractarian argument originates in the liberal ideas of J. S. Mill. Here, the state acquires moral value by virtue of its role in protecting and expressing the rights and liberties of individuals through the medium of the social contract. For an overview of these positions, see Charles Beitz, *Political Theory and International Relations* (Princeton, 1979), p. 77. The contractarian approach has been extended in contemporary literature by the communitarian philosopher, Michael Walzer.

71. *First Letter*, WS, IX, p. 252.

72. Vincent, 'The Factor of Culture', p. 259.

73. Wight, 'Western Values', p. 98.

74. Issac Kramnick, *The Rage of Edmund Burke* (New York, 1977), p. xi. Connor Cruise O'Brien claims Burke as one of the founding fathers of modern conservatism. See 'A Vindication of Edmund Burke', *National Review*, Vol. 42, December 1990, pp. 33–5.

75. To cite one such conservative, Peter Stanlis: 'If the Commonwealth of Christian Europe is to survive and form the ethical norms of civilization throughout the world, all men, but particularly Americans, will have to learn the great lessons in Burke's philosophy.' *Edmund Burke and the Natural Law* (Ann Arbor, 1958), pp. 247–8.

76. Vincent made a similar observation. See 'Edmund Burke', p. 11.

77. As James Davidson writes, what 'saved Burke from a Hobbesian view of international affairs was his belief in the existence of a community beyond the nation capable of a moralizing influence...', 'Natural Law and International Law in Burke', *Review of Politics*, Vol. 21 (1959), pp. 483–95 (p. 491).

78. Wight himself states that while Burke is 'apparently marching sturdily along the road' of Rationalism, 'his movements are erratic'. See 'The Three Traditions', in *International Theory*, p. 15.

79. The distinction between a positive and negative crusade is drawn by Martin Ceadel in *Thinking about Peace and War* (Oxford, 1987), pp. 46–7.

80. I take this term from Timothy Dunne. See unpublished D.Phil. Thesis, Oxford University, 1993.

81. *First Letter*, WS, IX, p. 247.

82. Hedley Bull, *The Anarchical Society: A Study of Order in World Politics* (London, 1977), pp. 13–16.

83. This critique of Wight's restrictive definition of international theory is echoed by Michael Donelan in 'The Political Theorists and International Theory', in *The Reason of States* (London, 1978), pp. 75–91 (p. 90). A better definition of international theory, I would argue, is advanced by Kal Holsti: 'descriptive and explanatory statements about the structure, units, and processes of international politics...', *The Dividing Discipline: Hegemony and Diversity in International Theory* (Boston, 1985), p. 3. Under this definition, one is able to combine political and international theory, and adopt multidisciplinary tools of analysis.

84. Vincent, 'Edmund Burke', p. 205.

85. Ibid., p. 211.

86. I am particularly interested in the views of George F. Kennan. See, for example, 'America and the Russian Future', cited in Wight, 'Western Values', pp. 99–100. While not subscribing to the counter-revolutionary means of the crusaders, Realists such as Kennan often share their belief that the institutions and procedures of international order are in some sense dependent on deeper, substantive principles of legitimacy.

87. Halliday, 'The Sixth Great Power', p. 218.

88. Vincent, 'The Factor of Culture', p. 257.

89. Gorbachev's notion of the 'common European home' sought to include the countries of Eastern Europe and Russia within this cultural collective.

90.  See the report entitled *A People's Europe*, Commission of the European Communities (1989). The legal definition of a European citizen appears in the recent Treaty on European Union (Part Two, Articles 8a–8e). Interestingly enough, the freedom of movement described in these provisions coincides with Burke's observation that when a European 'travelled or resided for health, pleasure, business or necessity, from his country, he never felt himself quite abroad', *First Letter*, WS, IX, pp. 249.

91.  Burke's understanding of international morality exists most forcefully at the level of the individual ruler rather than the sovereign state. It is contained in his famous precept of political trusteeship, which appeals to the 'spirit of restraint' in such rulers and their willingness to accept the moral significance and context of their political action. Wight refers to this as a *political* morality – the 'conscientious objection of politicians'. See 'Western Values', p. 123.

92.  Vincent, 'The Factor of Culture', p. 254.

93.  Francis Fukuyama argues that the world is no longer split along East–West lines, but between 'post-historical' states who have embraced industrialisation and liberal democracy, such as the US and Western Europe, and 'historical', pre-industrial and authoritarian states, such as China and Iraq. See 'Two sets of rules for a split world', *The Independent*, 7 September 1990. Similarly, Samuel Huntington contends that the conflicts of the future will be fought not between nation-states, but between cultural units called 'civilizations'. See 'The Clash of Civilizations', *Foreign Affairs*, Vol. 72 (Summer, 1993), pp. 22–49.

# 9 Hegel, the State and International Relations
## Andrew Linklater

The English liberal, L. T. Hobhouse, had no doubt that he was witnessing the most 'visible and tangible outcome of a false and wicked doctrine' as he sat annotating Hegel's writings on freedom in his Highgate garden during a German air-raid in 1917.[1] Hobhouse's critical remarks prefigured the 'Hegel myth' in which Hegel was portrayed as a champion of state power and military force.[2] Later, Hegel, along with Nietzsche, was thought to have prepared the intellectual groundwork for the rise of Fascism, an interpretation which was stated unequivocally by Sir Karl Popper in *The Open Society and its Enemies* but debunked in the late 1960s and 1970s.[3] The impression which may prevail at present is that Hegel's writings expressed strident realism rather than proto-Fascism.[4]

But what kind of realism did Hegel's writings manifest? Friedrich Meinecke believed that Hegel gave 'the old doctrine of the interests of states' a radical twist by denying altogether the tension between power and morality which the earlier realists had stressed.[5] While it is certainly the case that Hegel often outbids past realism with his apparent exuberance for the untrammelled freedom of the sovereign state,[6] other interpretations are correct to challenge the claim that Hegel believed the state should march only to the beat of *raison d'état*. Carl Friedrich cited Treitschke's critique of Hegel to demonstrate that Hegel had less in common with the traditional champions of *raison d'état* than many have imagined.[7] More recently, Pelczynski has drawn attention to Hegel's references to a community of nations which, despite their propensity for disagreement and war, shared a common culture.[8] These references to a community of states suggest that Hegel's realism was softened by the gentler hues of Grotianism. A few observers have gone significantly further by arguing that strains of cosmopolitan thought are present in Hegel's writings. Avineri, for example, maintained that Hegel envisaged a world 'united by culture and reason' in which sovereignty would diminish and the resort to force would disappear.[9] If Avineri is correct, Hegel looked beyond the loosely organised society of states to an emerging world culture and eventual global unification.

The supposition that Kantian moral themes are present in Hegel's argument goes against the grain of most conventional interpretations. These usually point out that when Hegel maintained that those who affirmed the tension between the state and morality simply flagged their own intellectual shallowness, he had Kant's cosmopolitan doctrine of perpetual peace clearly in mind. Hegel was scathingly critical of the idea that the concrete moralities of political communities were inferior to some immutable universal morality which is anchored in every individual's mind, but he recognised that a rudimentary society or culture existed in relations between states and he believed that the elements of a European (and possibly even a world culture) were plainly visible.

Hobbesian, Grotian and, to a lesser extent, Kantian themes are combined in Hegel's writings in a curious, even unique, way. To understand their interrelations, it is important to begin with Hegel's defence of the modern sovereign state and then turn to his analysis of relations between states and the place which the latter occupies within Wight's trichotomy of traditions of international thought. The chapter concludes with some brief remarks on Hegel's influence and contemporary relevance.


THE STATE AND FREEDOM

Why was Hegel such a strong advocate of the modern state? The short answer is that he thought the state provided the sole context in which human beings could unfold their unique capacity for freedom. No other form of political organisation in world history rivalled the modern European state in this respect and in his own time, Hegel thought, no obvious challenger sat waiting in the wings. Hegel rejected the liberal argument that individuals were born with an inherent claim to freedom so that states merely protected their pre-existing rights. Contrary to liberalism, attaching value to freedom, understanding its meaning and history, and developing the institutions of the free society were all complex social accomplishments produced by struggle as much as by cooperation.

Hegel drank a toast each year to celebrate the achievements of the French Revolution although from 1796 onward, it has been argued, 'the act of liberation' meant less to him than 'the positive political and social structures of a genuine ethical community'.[10] The shift in his thinking was neither a reactionary response to the Terror, critical though he was of revolutionary excess, nor the primary manifestation of any reappraisal of liberalism. The fundamental issue was that the complexity of the origins of political community had been neglected by the liberals and the architects of the Terror alike.

For Hegel, history was a struggle for the recognition of freedom which culminated in the modern state. In the famous section on lordship and bondage in the *Phenomenology of Spirit*, Hegel argued that in the first human conflict, individuals sought recognition without reciprocity. Their conflict produced slavery in which one self-consciousness subjugated another. Hegel's analysis of the historical development of political community traced the move from the first violent struggle to the death to a civil community – a *Rechtstaat* – in which the freedom of every citizen was recognised by the rest. This powerful commitment to freedom was the social bond which gave the modern state extensive powers of social mobilisation and unprecedented global reach.[11]

Hegel did not skirt the issue that this social bond was formed in the heat of war, a crucial theme neglected in his view by liberalism.[12] His fundamental point was not that the liberals were wide of the mark in supposing that the state would be subsumed within a new international civil society but that no one would contemplate dying for the state if politics was merely about safeguarding life, liberty and property. Faced with the threat of death in war, possessive individualists would be among the first to flee.[13] War reminded peoples that the self-interested motives which were given free rein within civil society were not ends-in-themselves but ultimately subordinate to a higher collective purpose which united citizens within particular sovereign states. Hegel's observation that perpetual peace would foster the belief that civil society was absolute, whereas war was vital for the ethical health of peoples, was later cited as evidence of his crude nationalism and militarism. In fact, his remarks made the more prosaic observation that civic patriotism has a role in human affairs which the works on political economy and cosmopolitan morality have often failed to reveal.

Although he was an enthusiastic advocate of the sovereign state, Hegel did not believe that the state exhausted the moral, political and intellectual life of modern citizens, or that it was entitled to behave as it pleased in either domestic or foreign affairs. Hegel's most profound hope was that the moral and political solidarity which many of his generation had conferred upon Ancient Greece could be recovered in the modern world with its economic and political individualism and religious and ethical universalism.

He desired a synthesis of modern individualistic rights proclaimed by reason (*Moralitat*) and the strong affective ties towards specific communities (*Sittlichkeit*). Hegel believed the modern state could hold the separate economic, moral and political dimensions of human experience together: it could give the individual his head[14] – which the Ancient World had not been able to do – without placing the individual at odds with the state. Hegel's enthusiam for the state was not paid for in the currency of individual rights, and far from being a nationalist and militarist Hegel was a strong advocate of constitutional government. The Hegelian state was a *Rechtstaat* and not a *Machtstaat* realising its destiny through conquest and force.[15]

There are serious doubts that any existing state satisfied all the requirements of Hegel's ideal *Rechstaat*. Oakeshott thought that the ideal state was only 'intimated' by the states of Hegel's time; within their bounds the progress of freedom was clearly 'recognisable' but still 'incomplete'.[16] Even so, Hegel's sights were always set on shorter-term moral and political possibilities rather than on the *longue durée* which he believed was unforeseeable in any case. Since philosophy was inevitably its own time comprehended in thought, no one could leap over Rhodes to anticipate, let alone legislate for, future epochs. As for instruction, philosophy always came on the scene too late to give it, at dusk when a form of life had already grown old. With such formulations Hegel echoed Burke's hostility towards the lofty political aspirations of rootless intellectuals.

Within the constitutional framework of the modern state, individuals could also foster art, religion and philosophy, the modes of experience which contributed to the larger civilisational project which spills over national frontiers. But neither these comments on *world* history and culture (which foreshadow Marx's later comments on the world market and world literature) nor his remarks about the inherent openness of the future modified Hegel's judgement that the modern state was the highest political association of his time.

For the early critics, such as the young Marx, this celebration of the modern state was the gravest flaw in his political philosophy. Marx argued that Hegel's major work on the state was an apologia for a world replete with social imperfection and political tension, notwithstanding its proclaimed aim of overcoming contradictions in human experience. But because it was an accurate representation of the modern state, Marx added, Hegel's political thought clearly exposed the modern world's most fundamental contradictions.[17] The further observation that the Hegelian state could not satisfy the basic material needs of its own citizens was a vital theme in Marx's critique of Hegel and the backdrop to the development of class analysis. Recognising the vicissitudes of the market, and the sensitivity of modern economies to technological developments in other countries, Hegel had advocated colonisation as a simple solution to poverty and class inequalities.[18] This putative solution contained other ramifications including the destruction of indigenous peoples. Not only was the modern state structurally incapable of satisfying the economic and social needs of its population, but the measures taken to overcome its imperfections sacrificed the rights of human beings elsewhere.[19]

## THE PROBLEM OF INTERNATIONAL RELATIONS

Are there fundamental contradictions in Hegel's account of international relations? To answer this question it is useful to recall Rousseau's observations about the divided nature of the modern subject. Rousseau maintained that the modern individual is 'dragged by nature and by men in opposite directions', thereby having to 'end his life without having been able to come to terms with himself'.[20] The tension between the obligations of citizenship and the obligations of humanity was, for Rousseau, one of the deepest moral problems of international relations which his own writings had been unable to solve. In *The Social Contract*, Rousseau argued that 'all that destroys social unity is worthless; all institutions that set man in contradiction to himself are worthless'.[21] But restoring unity to modern society was purchased by sacrificing the duties which individuals owed each other as members of the larger society encompassing the whole human race.[22]

Hegel's political thought had to chart a different course if it was to remain faithful to its purpose of accommodating the claims of modern universalism. Following Schiller, Hegel came to think that the unity and coherence of the Ancient Greek polis had to break down so that higher forms of self-consciousness could develop. Hegel desired the approximation of Ancient Greek political unity within the novel social and economic context of the modern world. Neither the unreflective unity of the ancient polis, nor the neuroses of modern individualism nor a transcendent, but ultimately unrealisable, universalism but a form of social coherence which was responsive to modern ethical reflectiveness and individual rights was Hegel's goal. He believed that the balance had finally been struck by the modern territorial state.[23]

Given the terms of Hegel's own argument, the state had to recognise the claims of humanity before the proper balance could be struck. Now Hegel maintained that the principle of sovereignty implied that the state could not be brought before some higher moral bench or compelled to relinquish the right to use force to protect its vital interests, as Kant's doctrine of perpetual peace had suggested. To be complete, sovereignty required the express recognition of other states[24] and the imprimatur of international law. The system of states possessed the international equivalent of abstract right – rules governing property and the use of violence – because states attached value to order, but since there was no ethical life, no customary morality, no *Sittlichkeit* in relations between states, international law was nothing more than an 'ought-to-be' which states would disregard when it conflicted with their vital interests.[25] When states clashed violently in the international 'state of nature', good and evil were not the adversaries, but two rival conceptions of what was right. War did not decide which side was just but which of the antagonistic doctrines had 'to give way'.[26] This Hobbesian theme surfaced again in Hegel's argument that a Kantian 'League of Nations' which was authorised to settle disputes between states would inevitably bend to the particular will of powerful states rather than dutifully respect the interests of all.[27]

The conflict between right and right did not justify the state's indiscriminate use of force against the private person. War should not be 'waged against domestic institutions, against the peace of family and private life, or against persons in their private capacity'.[28] By granting that there could be justice on both sides, Hegel defended the idea of humanity in warfare much as Grotius and Vattel had done earlier. Although he argued that the rights of individuals should be respected by all states, he was opposed, as we have already seen, to the modern liberal belief that these were inherent in individuals rather than the product of society and history – the rights of man as opposed to the rights of citizens. Hegel thought largely in terms of self-contained nation-states but he recognised a sub-set of rights which devolved upon individuals and only in part because of the respect owed to their communities. There is evidence here of Hobbes tempered by Grotius.[29]

At times, Hegel could be mistaken for one of the leading lights of the British Committee on the Theory of International Politics. Consider the following observation about a European *society* of states: 'The European peoples form a family in accordance with the universal principle underlying their legal code, their customs and their civilisation. This principle has modified their international conduct accordingly in a state of affairs [i.e. war] otherwise dominated by the mutual infliction of evil'.[30] In the society of states, there are agreements about the rights of prisoners which 'depend principally upon the customs of nations'.[31] States have an 'equal right to existence' which 'entails a union of states, such as exists in modern Europe, or a condition like that of Greece, in which the states had an equal right to existence under the protection of the Delphic god'.[32] But (Wight springs to mind here) not all unions of states are the same. The European were alone in having a 'community of interest' in 'the maintenance of severalty (*sic*) – the preservation to the several states of their independence – in fact the balance of power'; and they are credited with introducing various refinements to the art of diplomacy.[33] When faced with imperial challengers, 'the nations of Europe succeeded in maintaining their individuality and independence'.[34] Hegel observed that the Europeans were keenly aware of marked differences from those people which, not having achieved statehood, could be treated as no more than 'barbarians'. The fact that such themes were developed later by Martin Wight will be noted.

## TOWARDS COSMOPOLITANISM?

Hegel thought that the development of reason in history had left its impression on relations between states because they did recognise each other's sovereignty, but he was dismissive of revolutionists, such as Kant, who argued that human reason demanded membership of a world-wide moral community (but not, it should be recalled, submission to a world state). When compared with Kant, Hegel has often been accused of failing to support the ideal of a universal community which could uphold the freedom of all humanity.[35] The criticism is that Hegel failed to acknowledge that the process of recognising the freedom of the other could be extended further than he had realised into the domain of international relations.[36] Is this in fact the case?

Some interpretations emphasise that Hegel foresaw the dialectical development of freedom in international relations. Paolucci credits Hegel with envisaging a universal international society in which all free peoples are treated as equals.[37] In some accounts, Hegel appears as a revolutionist precursor of Fukuyama. Smith's recent interpretation notes that, for Hegel, history is 'the process of mankind's progressive emancipation from those forces that inhibit the granting of respect to other individuals, peoples, and cultures'; the end of history involves the 'Westernisation of humanity, founded on the twin principles of the rule of law and Protestant Christianity'.[38] Following Kojeve, this interpretation maintains that Hegel believed the modern state would come to 'encompass the whole of humanity', thus ending *Andersein*, otherness.[39]

Does 'encompassing the whole of humanity' refer to a universal *Rechtstaat* to which all human beings belong or to the spread of modern constitutionalism across the states-system in the manner in which Fukuyama has written about the triumph of liberalism? If the latter rather than the former, did Hegel believe that a world divided between modern constitutional states would be a more peaceful world than the one which went before? The answer is certainly no. If such a family of nations ever emerged, Hegel was quick to add, it would immediately pitch itself against other states.[40] There is no ontological proof of this proposition anywhere in Hegel's writings, and every reason to dismiss it as 'hazy anthropology',[41] but it does encapsulate a crucial theme in Hegel's thought which is his critique of cosmopolitan ethics.

Hegel regarded cosmopolitanism as simultaneously a major Western intellectual achievement and a threat to its principal political accomplishment which was the modern state. On the one side, 'a man counts as a man in virtue of his manhood alone, not because he is a Jew, Catholic, Protestant, German, Italian, & co. This is an assertion which thinking ratifies and to be conscious of it is of infinite importance'; on the other hand, moral universalism 'is defective...when it is crystallised, e.g. as a cosmopolitanism in opposition to the concrete life of the state'.[42] Repeatedly, Hegel argues that because there are no permanently valid moral principles, and because the individual cannot summon the moral code from deep springs running within the self, modern doctrines of ethical individualism and universalism are vacuous when compared with the concrete moralities of particular forms of life. Throughout, Kant is the butt of Hegel's criticisms. The former expressed only 'the shapelessness of cosmopolitanism', 'the void of the Rights of Man', the emptiness of 'a world republic'. Kantian morality, *Moralitat*, leaves a long trail of 'abstractions and formalisms filled with exactly the opposite of ethical vitality'[43] which is evident in *Sittlichkeit*: those social institutions moulded by reason working in tandem with a knowledge of specific cultural traits and human needs fashioned from experience.

Hegel defended the notion that individuals should be free to prosecute their own interests within civil society and recognised the need for a sphere of individual activity within the world market. He believed that these rights should be upheld as far as possible even in times of war, but he clearly did not think they were synonymous with a living social morality, and he was certain that they were not the springboard from which the human race would eventually launch its effort to build a world-wide community. Experiments in international political cooperation were, for Hegel, limited in range within the same civilisation, and inconceivable as far as radically different social worlds were concerned. While emphasising the diverse and ever-changing nature of *social* moralities, Hegel also defended the modern demand that human practices should be justified by rational argumentation. His critique of the French Revolution aimed to reveal that society could not be remade to conform with supposedly permanent moral truths and his parallel critique of cosmopolitanism stressed that different systems of morality would never be brought under the dominion of a single rationality.

Although his remarks on humanity in warfare suggested that the state could be in breach of higher (customary) principles, Hegel evidently thought that too much had been made of the conflict between the state and humanity, the tension in particular between actual societies and the universality of reason being falsely posed. Philosophy, which came into being when unity and coherence had disappeared from social life, and which was charged with the task of overcoming powerful tensions and contradictions,[44] had no remaining business in this realm. Doing away with 'rigid antagonisms was the exclusive task of philosophy' in Hegel's view, but, he immediately adds, 'this does not mean that it is opposed to opposition and limitation as such', disunity being an essential ingredient of life.[45] The idea of 'tragedy in the realm of the ethical', which Hegel used to describe conflicts in which different sides have right on their side, captures the real import of Hegel's critique of cosmopolitanism.[46] Certain conflicts defy solution because the different parties have incommensurable starting-points and because there is no shared discourse or agreed moral framework which makes the resolution of their differences possible. Such conflicts mark the point where the outer limits upon the human potential for creating political community have been reached.[47] The existence of a society of states revealed that a loose political association could develop beyond the water's edge, yet the greatest achievement as far as the formation of community was concerned remained the modern state.

Not that political community was the only value in Hegel's mind, because beyond the state there was the realm of civilisation comprising religion, philosophy and art. The operative term here is universal history which refers to the larger cultural stock to which many different societies and epochs have made their unique donations.[48] All of these participating societies are 'restricted' when compared with the larger movement of the human spirit, yet it is states which make the largest deposits possible.[49]

Different states and cultures rise and fall in Hegel's account of history as the baton is passed to the *volksgeist* whose time has come.[50] Hegel certainly believed that certain cultures had yet to show their hand in contributing to the further development of the world spirit, America in particular being singled out as the land of the future.[51] This is the Hegelian variation on the theme of the ascent and descent of hegemonic powers which leave their impression on the larger project of the education of the human race (*Bildung*) which is the meaning and purpose of world history.

This emphasis on the evolution of world culture is different from the cosmopolitan conviction that states are ultimately answerable to universal moral principles upon which all human beings can agree, but it does imply that Hegel was a more qualified or 'softer' realist than some, including Wight, have believed. While Hegel's observations about the inevitability of international conflict clearly place him in the realist school, his remarks on the existence of a European society of states reveal Grotian leanings and his support for the civilising function of the principles of *jus in bello* reveal that cosmopolitan themes were also integrated within his argument. Unsurprisingly, given Hegel's fondness for dialectical reasoning, elements of all three traditions were interwoven in his thought in subtle and complex ways.

## HEGEL'S INFLUENCE AND SIGNIFICANCE

Largely because Hegel's enthusiasm for the modern state has been rendered archaic by the twentieth-century experience of fanatical nationalism, totalitarian state power and destructive war, there is no distinctively Hegelian perspective on world politics in modern times. Hegel failed to realise that the modern state could cancel the freedom of its own citizens, and Rousseau's invitation to the 'barbarous' philosophers, who celebrated the state's pacifying and civilising role, to read their books 'on the field of battle', reminds us that Hegel was all too complacent about war.[52] Nevertheless, echoes of important themes in Hegel's political theory can be found in modern commentaries about the unprecedented organisational capabilities of the modern state and the dynamic qualities of systems of states.[53] Many different schools of thought and approaches claim a Hegelian influence. These include two schools which Hegel would have been disinclined to accept (Hegelian-Marxist critical social theory and the Hegelianised liberalism of Fukuyama) and one approach (communitarianism) which has strong affinities with Hegel's political thought. A few comments about each approach are offered in conclusion.

On the subject of critical theory, first of all, some of Hegel's earliest but sympathetic critics believed that the great historical process traced by Hegel in which forms of life run up against insurmountable barriers to their further development and crumble under the weight of their internal contradictions would stretch far into the future. They rejected Hegel's view that philosophy should describe the 'rose in the cross of the present'. For them, the central purpose of philosophy was social criticism and the analysis of the immanent possibilities of higher forms of freedom and rationality. Some of these Hegelians welcomed the social revolutions of 1830 and defended civil, political and religious freedoms against the regimes of the Restoration. Others envisaged the absorption of the state in a religious community extending across the whole world. Many Young Hegelians, Marx included, linked the critique of religious alienation with a vision of a universal society of free individuals.[54] Frankfurt School critical theory, one of the leading manifestations of Hegelian-Marxist thought in the twentieth century, refined earlier attempts to construct a mode of inquiry which would, ideally, enable human beings to reflect upon the means of transforming their social conditions in order to achieve universal freedom. Although such themes have been slow to make their appearance in the study of international relations, the contemporary critique of realism has clearly drawn upon ideas about the historicity of knowledge and the mutability of political structures which owe a considerable debt to Hegel, although the notion of critical social theory itself owes less to Hegel than to Marx and Marxism.[55]

In a second approach, Fukuyama has argued that the demise of communism confirms Hegel's argument that, with the triumph of the modern state, history has come to an end. For Fukuyama, modern liberal-democratic societies will remain susceptible to change, therefore remaining in history in the conventional sense, but according to the Hegelian understanding of history as the struggle to be free, these societies have overcome the forms of conflict which might bring about their transformation. Reforming those social institutions which have yet to comply with the principle of freedom is their main unfinished business.

When defining the end of history in this idiosyncratic but not implausible sense, Fukuyama can properly claim an affinity with Hegel, but the additional step of portraying Hegel as a liberal ignores his trenchant criticisms of liberal-democratic theory and practice. Hegel's theory of the state preserved various individual rights within a constitutional monarchy responsible for preserving the sentimental bonds of an ethical community as opposed to upholding the contractual arrangements pertaining between atomistic individuals. At no stage did Hegel ever posit a clear nexus between liberalism and peace or argue that constitutional monarchies displayed the predisposition to associate in an ever-expanding zone of peace.[56] The premise of liberal internationalism that all individuals possessed one conception of rationality which pointed towards their eventual membership of a single cosmopolitan community was anathema to him.

Hegel's critique of liberal individualism, which has been drawn upon by perspectives as different as feminism and Fascism, has strong affinities with the third approach, contemporary communitarian thought.[57] Communitarian writers object to attempts by writers such as Rawls to determine the nature of the just society by considering the principles which rational individuals would choose if they were ignorant of their future position in society.[58] All such accounts neglect the essential truth that moral subjects develop their own identities within concrete social relations in which they have strong affinities with, and loyalties to, particular human beings. The social construction of human morality and personal identity is a theme clearly shared by Hegel and the modern communitarians. What is less clear is whether Hegel endorsed the additional communitarian theme that different systems of morality cannot be measured against some transcultural yardstick.

One objection against the communitarian argument that different systems of morality are incommensurable is that it lacks any grounds for protesting against states which promote their interests with undue force.[59] Hegel's communitarianism is not vulnerable to this criticism. His claim that human beings derive considerable meaning from belonging to bounded communities implies the need for respecting other cultures.[60] The rationalist doctrine of the equality of states, which is similar to Hegel's position, contains a similarly minimum internationalism.

There are other parallels between the Hegelian and rationalist conceptions of international society. When rationalists argue that the advocates of universalist principles of world political organisation underestimate both the state's 'positive role in world affairs'[61] and the strength of the bond which links the citizen to the state, they reiterate one of Hegel's crucial themes. When they argue that the search for the universal principles of world politics never escapes the limitations of a particular epoch or place, but add that the society of states is the clear manifestation of an important, albeit limited, consensus they bring Hegel's own themes into clearer focus. Their distrust of efforts to implement first principles, their suspicion that noble intentions may prove to be dangerous and their preference for seeking to improve existing social arrangements reflect Hegel's contrast between two moralities, *Moralitat* and *Sittlichkeit*. When they argue that the analysts of interdependence are right to stress the importance of a vast transnational society with an emerging cosmopolitan culture of modernity, but wrong to predict the demise of the nation-state, they reaffirm Hegel's observation that the state has an unchallenged role in satisfying the human need for political community. Yet the rationalists have failed to appreciate the contribution which Hegel's writings can make to their enterprise.

Some observers have argued that Hegel was wrong to rule out the possibility that supranational loyalties could become stronger within the European world of states.[62] Writing within the English idealist perspective, T. H. Green argued that the historical process of overcoming otherness could encroach upon the sphere of world politics.[63] No doubt, the expansion of international society to include non-Western societies provides some support for this vision, yet many will argue that Green's anticipated 'extension of the area of the common good'[64] has not occurred in international politics because of the continuing salience of the deeper forces stressed by Hegel. In particular, they may cite the continuing potency of national loyalties in Europe and elsewhere, and the enduring desire to create and to wield power over the other, as evidence that human beings are no more willing now than in Hegel's time to internationalise political community.

Because the desire to give expression to one's national identity through sovereign institutions has strengthened in recent times, and because the willingness to shift allegiance to post-sovereign political communities has not made real progress, one might conclude that the Hegelian era has yet to run its course. However, since current instances of ethnic fragmentation are unfolding against the backdrop of the relentless process of globalisation, it is worth recalling Hegel's comments on how the close communities of Ancient Greece gave way to the alienating world of Rome. Modern states may yet experience a similar fate. Meeting current demands for the right to express sub-national identities and managing the challenges of globalisation are problems unique to the modern world. Given its traditional hostility to demands for sub-national autonomy and its obstruction of the rise of transnational identities, the sovereign, so celebrated by Hegel, is no longer an adequate solution.

## NOTES

1. L. T. Hobhouse, *The Metaphysical Theory of the State: A Criticism* (London, 1951), pp. 5–6.
2. W. Kaufmann (ed.), *Hegel's Political Philosophy* (New York, 1970), ch. 10. See also J. Morrow, 'British Idealism, "German Philosophy" and the First World War', *Australian Journal of Politics and History*, 28, 1982, pp. 380–90.
3. Sir Karl Popper, *The Open Society and its Enemies* (London, 1945), vol. 2, ch. 12.
4. F. Northedge, 'Peace, War and Philosophy', *Encyclopaedia of Philosophy*, vol. 6, pp. 63–7 (New York, 1976).
5. F. Meinecke, *Machiavellism: The Doctrine of Raison d'Etat and its Place in Modern History* (London, 1962), p. 357.
6. When 'politics is alleged to clash with morals, and so to be always wrong', Hegel argued, 'the doctrine propounded rests on superficial ideas about

morality, the nature of the state, and the state's relation to the moral point of view', Hegel, *The Philosophy of Right*, trans. with notes by T. M. Knox (Oxford, 1952), para. 337. This would appear to be clear evidence of Hegel's realism.

7. C. Friedrich, *Constitutional Reason of State: The Survival of the Constitutional Order* (Providence, Rhode Island, 1957), pp. 92 and 97.

8. Z. Pelczynski (ed.), *Hegel's Political Philosophy: Problems and Perspectives* (Cambridge, 1971), p. 15.

9. S. Avineri, *Hegel's Theory of the Modern State* (Cambridge, 1972), p. 207.

10. See J. E. Toews, *Hegelianism: The Path towards Dialectical Humanism, 1805–1841* (Cambridge, 1980), p. 33.

11. See Hegel on the British in India: 'in India five hundred men conquered twenty thousand who were not cowards, but who only lacked this disposition to cooperate with others', *The Philosophy of Right*, op. cit., para. 327, addition.

12. *The Philosophy of Right*, op. cit., para. 324, addition.

13. Ibid., para. 324.

14. As Seyla Benhabib points out, in Hegel's writings 'women are not *individuals* ... to the same extent as men are' (author's italics). See 'On Hegel, Women and Irony', in M. L. Shanley and C. Pateman (eds), *Feminist Interpretations and Political Theory* (Pennsylvania, 1991), p. 134.

15. Friedrich, op. cit., p. 91.

16. M. Oakeshott, *On Human Conduct* (Oxford, 1975), pp. 262–3. See also Friedrich, op. cit., pp. 92–3.

17. See Marx, *Critique of Hegel's Philosophy of Right*, ed. J. O'Malley (Cambridge, 1970). On the question of reconciliation with social contradictions, see G. Lukács, *The Young Hegel: Studies in the Relationship Between Dialectics and Economics* (London, 1975), pp. 70 and 146. For an analysis of the differing views of Hegel and Marx on the subject of reconciliation with society, see M. O. Hardiman, 'The Project of Reconciliation: Hegel's Social Philosophy', *Philosophy and Public Affairs*, vol. 21, 2, Spring 1992, pp. 165–95.

18. For further discussion, see R. Plant, 'Economic and Social Integration in Hegel's Political Philosophy', in D. P. Verene (ed.), *Hegel's Social and Political Thought: The Philosophy of Objective Spirit* (New Jersey, 1980).

19. See M. Wight, *International Theory: The Three Traditions* (Leicester, 1991), pp. 53–4.

20. S. Hoffmann, *The State of War: Essays in the Theory and Practice of International Politics* (London, 1965), pp. 65–6.

21. Rousseau, *The Social Contract and Discourses* (trans. with an introduction by G. D. H. Cole) (London, 1960), p. 110.

22. For further discussion, see J. Thompson, *Justice and World Order: A Philosophical Inquiry* (London, 1992), ch. 7.

23. For further discussion, see R. Plant, *Hegel* (London, 1973) and C. Taylor, *Hegel* (Cambridge, 1975).

24. Hegel, *Philosophy of Right*, op. cit., para. 331.

25. Ibid., para. 333.

26. *The German Constitution*, in Z. Pelczynski (ed.), *Hegel's Political Writings* (Oxford, 1964), p. 210.

27. Hegel, *Philosophy of Right*, op. cit., para. 333.
28. Hegel, *Philosophy of Right*, op. cit., para. 338. In a peculiar passage, Hegel notes that the changing nature of modern technology had depersonalised conflict: this was 'no accident' because 'thought has invented the gun', ibid., para. 328.
29. 'But the idea, also reaching its apogee in the nineteenth century, that states were *exclusively* the subjects of international law, and individuals merely its objects, Grotius would have found a peculiar one', R. J. Vincent, 'Grotius, Human Rights and Intervention', in H. Bull, B. Kingsbury and A. Roberts (eds), *Hugo Grotius and International Relations* (Oxford, 1990), p. 243 (author's italics).
30. Hegel, *Philosophy of Right*, op. cit., para. 339, addition.
31. Ibid., para. 339.
32. Hegel, *The Philosophy of History*, trans. J. Sibree, (New York, 1956), p. 308.
33. Hegel, ibid., p. 431. See also the following remarks on pp. 431–2: 'The union of the states of Europe as the means of shielding individual states from the violence of the powerful – the preservation of the balance of power – had now taken the place of that general aim of the elder time, the defence of Christendom, whose centre was the papacy. This new political motive was necessarily accompanied by a diplomatic condition – one in which all the members of the great European system, however distant, felt an interest in that which happened to any one of them. Diplomatic policy had been brought to the greatest refinement in Italy, and was thence transmitted to Europe at large.'
34. Hegel, ibid., p. 432. For further discussion on these points, see H. Paolucci, 'Hegel and the Nation-State System of International Relations', in D. P. Verene (ed.), *Hegel's Social and Political Thought*, op. cit., pp. 151–66.
35. See T. O'Hagan, 'On Hegel's Critique of Kant's Moral and Political Philosophy', in S. Priest (ed.), *Hegel's Critique of Kant* (Oxford, 1987), p. 157, and J. Plamenatz, *Man and Society* (London, 1963), vol. 2, pp. 266–7.
36. On the importance for Schelling, Schleiermacher, Novalis and Schlegel as well as Hegel of 'the ethical ideal of self-realisation through reconciliation with, rather than domination of, the "other"', see Toewes, op. cit., p. 45.
37. Paolucci, op. cit., p. 165.
38. S. Smith, *Hegel's Critique of Liberalism: Rights in Context* (Chicago, 1989), pp. 164 and 169. Martin Wight called this revolutionism which is based on the value of 'doctrinal uniformity', *International Theory: The Three Traditions*, op. cit., pp. 41–2.
39. Smith, ibid., p. 227, quoting from Strauss, *On Tyranny*. Non-Western cultures are not granted the same respect however. On the question of Hegel's ethnocentrism, see W. H. Walsh, 'Principle and Prejudice in Hegel's Philosophy of History', in Z. Pelczynski (ed.), *Hegel's Political Philosophy: Problems and Perspectives*, op. cit., pp. 181–98. Smith, op. cit., p. 164 argues that the *Rechtstaat* can only be completed when the 'unification of humanity' occurs and the universal recognition of human freedom is granted.

40. Individuality implies negation, so that even if a 'family' of nations emerged, it would necessarily 'engender an opposite and create an enemy', *Philosophy of Right*, op. cit., para. 324, addition. Hegel refers to a loose *European* family of nations but there is no reason to suppose that Hegel believed that this international society would become universal. For consideration of the point that Hegel has been proven right about the tenacity of the state by the fact of its spread to all parts of the world, see C. Brown, 'Hegel and International Relations', *Ethics and International Affairs*, vol. 5, 1991, pp. 73–85.
41. See T. O'Hagan, in Priest, op. cit., p. 156.
42. *Philosophy of Right*, op. cit., para. 209.
43. Quoted by Smith, op. cit., p. 75. Kant argued that one could not universalise the maxim that it is right to steal another's property. Hegel's rejoinder was that Kant ignored the important question of whether the institution of private property is rational in the first place. For further discussion, see W. H. Walsh, *Hegelian Ethics* (London, 1969), p. 22.
44. Lukács, op. cit., p. 264.
45. Ibid.
46. Ibid., p. 417.
47. Hardimon, op. cit., pp. 175–9 argues that for Hegel reconciliation with the world meant accepting that certain aspects of human life were problematical. Being at home in the world did not mean living in a perfect community, but it did mean the absence of the tragic from the inner world of the state.
48. Smith, op. cit., p. 50. M. Riedel, *Between Tradition and Revolution: The Hegelian Transformation of Political Philosophy* (Cambridge, 1984), pp. 49–50, refers to the 'universal mind' which exists alongside the international state of nature. Hedley Bull's distinction between an international political culture and a diplomatic culture makes a similar point, *The Anarchical Society* (London, 1977), p. 317.
49. On restricted national minds, see *The Philosophy of Right*, op. cit., para. 340. G. A. Kelly, *Hegel's Retreat from Eleusis: Studies in Political Thought* (Princeton, 1978), pp. 19–20 emphasises this point about the state's location in the wider sphere of civilisation. The 1954 Hague Convention for the Protection of Cultural Property in the Event of Armed Conflict shows how this wider sphere of civilisation can give rise to international obligations. See A. Roberts and R. Guelff (eds), *Documents on the Law of War* (Oxford, 1989).
50. Hegel, *The Philosophy of Right*, op. cit., para. 347.
51. Hegel, *The Philosophy of History*, op. cit., pp. 86–7.
52. Rousseau, *The State of War*, in M. Forsyth, *et al.* (eds), *The Theory of International Relations: Selected Texts from Gentili to Treitschke* (London, 1970), p. 174.
53. E. Gellner, *Thought and Change* (London, 1964), ch. 7 and Michael Mann, *The Sources of Social Power*, vol. 1 (Cambridge, 1986), esp. ch. 7.
54. For a discussion of each of these moves within Hegelian thought, see Toews, op. cit., pp. 133–4, 138–40 and 361.
55. R. W. Cox, 'Social Forces, States and World Orders: Beyond International Relations Theory', *Millennium*, 10, 1982, pp. 126–55 emphasises the significance of Vico for this line of argument, and M. Hoffman, 'Critical

Theory and the Inter-Paradigm Debate', *Millennium*, 15, 1987, pp. 231–49 focuses on Horkheimer and Habermas. A. Linklater, *Men and Citizens in the Theory of International Relations* (London, 1990), chs 8–10, draws significantly on Hegel's philosophical history.

56.  Kant rather than Hegel is the thinker with the greater affinity with Fukuyama's belief that there is an intimate connection between liberalism and peace.

57.  On feminism, see M. Herrera, 'Equal Respect Among Unequal Partners: Gender Difference and the Constitution of Moral Subjects', *Philosophy East and West*, 42, 1992, pp. 263–75. On the other hand, Hegel's argument about the conflictual nature of international politics can be read as a gendered account of the states-system. See R. Grant and K. Newland (eds), *Gender and International Relations* (Buckingham, 1991), esp. chs 1–3. For a discussion of Hegel's impact on communitarian thought, see S. A. Schwarzenbach, 'Rawls, Hegel and Communitarianism', *Political Theory*, vol. 19, 4, 1991, p. 540.

58.  M. Sandel, *Liberalism and the Limits of Justice* (Cambridge, 1982); M. Walzer, *Spheres of Justice* (Oxford, 1983); A. McIntyre, *After Virtue* (London, 1981).

59.  Thompson, op. cit., p. 20.

60.  Although respect was largely confined to the European world.

61.  H. Bull, 'The State's Positive Role in World Affairs', *Daedalus*, 108, 1979, pp. 111–23.

62.  Walsh, op. cit., p. 57.

63.  For further details, see T. H. Green, *Prolegomena to Ethics* (Oxford, 1906) and P. P. Nicholson, 'Philosophical Idealism and International Politics: A Reply to Savigear', *British Journal of International Studies*, vol. 2, 1976, pp. 76–83.

64.  T. H. Green, *Prolegomena to Ethics* (London, 1906).

# 10 Friedrich Gentz, Rationalism and the Balance of Power
Richard Little

Friedrich Gentz was a quintessential rationalist who lived through a period of revolutionary change and unheaval in Europe. From the start of the French Revolution to the consolidation of the Concert of Europe in the aftermath of the Napoleonic Wars, Gentz was passionately involved with the action unfolding on the European stage, initially as an observer and commentator, but later as a minor participant. He achieved fame in his lifetime, becoming known as the Secretary of Europe, when he acted as the Secretary-General for the Congress of Vienna, but he has been relegated to no more than a footnote in the history of the era. Writing incessantly about the developments in European politics as they occurred, he believed not only in the importance of theorising about international politics but also in the inextricable link between theory and practice. His name remains familiar to students of international relations as an ardent defender of the balance of power, although his views have never been identified as either seminal or particularly influential.

It is not the intention of this chapter to try to recover Gentz as an important and original theorist of international relations. Such an endeavour would necessarily fail. Gentz was very much a man of his time and his thinking about international relations derived from a common stock of knowledge. He formulated no new theories and recommended no innovative practices; instead, he articulated, albeit with great conviction, assessments of international politics which he knew would find a receptive audience. Indeed, his audience, as it happens, paid him to provide justifications for the policies they were already embarked upon. But Gentz was not simply a propagandist. He chose his paymasters because they were pursuing policies he believed in, and his justifications were built upon theoretical foundations which he considered to be true.

While Gentz does not repay further investigation as an original thinker, he does help to illuminate Wight's traditions of international theory. Gentz is lodged at the very centre of the rationalist tradition. Far from Europe being made up of adversarial states locked in perpetual conflict, as portrayed by the realists, Gentz depicted the continent as an organic whole. He devoted his life to ensuring that what he liked to refer to as the body of Europe was preserved from the disease of revolution. Gentz remains of interest, therefore, because he illustrates with such great clarity how a rationalist contends with the practical effects of revolutionary forces.

Attempts have been made to chart the sources of influence which helped to ground his rationalist frame of reference. In his youth, his views were very fluid, but as he matured, he came to adhere to a limited number of fundamental principles which guided his rationalist response to the flux of daily events. He studied under Kant at Königsberg, and was undoubtedly influenced by some aspects of Kantian thought in later life, although he was never a philosophical thinker, and throughout his life was primarily interested in the political consequences of what was happening in the world around him.[1] The influence of Burke was, arguably, to become much more significant than Kant's.[2] Gentz, however, was never an unquestioning conservative; he acknowledged the need for change but at the same time, he manifested the rationalist's deep suspicion of attempts to move any complex international situation to an extreme outcome. Although unrelentingly opposed to the Revolutionary and Napoleonic regimes, because of their endeavours to overthrow the established European order, he saw no inconsistency, after the defeat of France, in opposing the restoration of an absolute monarch and recommending that Napoleon should continue to govern. He favoured a constitutional form of government for France because that was what the people wanted. He acknowledged in 1815 that circumstances had irrevocably changed during the years since 1789, when the Revolution began, and that it was dangerous to attempt to turn back the clock. 'Legitimacy', he argued 'is born in time; it can therefore be considered not in an absolute, but only in a relative, sense; and from time to time, like everything human, it must be modified.'[3]

Because Gentz occupies such a central position in rationalist thought about international relations, it is perhaps unsurprising to find that analysts of a rationalist predisposition in the contemporary discipline have evinced more interest in his writings than analysts working in either of the other two traditions. Rather more surprising is the fact that contemporary rationalists have reached competing assessments of Gentz's theoretical position. This debate throws an interesting light on the proposition that rationalism provides a *via media* between realism and revolutionism.[4] Necessarily, it will be argued, rationalism is both more complex and more ambiguous than the other two traditions. It will be argued, further, that contemporary rationalists have tended to underestimate the complexity of the rationalist tradition. An important dimension of the tradition has been persistently obscured. This has led to a rather confused debate in the analysis of contemporary rationalists. It will be concluded that recent developments in the international system have made it easier to expose the hidden dimension within the rationalist tradition.

Before proceding with this analysis, however, a brief historical sketch of Gentz will be provided, not only because he is now a somewhat shadowy historical figure, but also because his political analysis is so closely bound up with the role he was playing in the diplomatic arena.

## A BRIEF BIOGRAPHY[5]

Friedrich Gentz was born into a Prussian burgher household in 1764, although he was destined to spend almost half of his life in the rarefied world of the Austrian aristocracy. The desire to become part of that world was intense, and when Gustavus IV awarded Gentz the Swedish Order of the North Star in 1804, and he was elevated to Friedrich Von Gentz, his elation was unconcealed.

Gentz's father was government official who eventually became the director of the Royal Mint in Berlin and it seemed, initially, as if the son too would spend his life as a public servant in Prussia. But from an early stage, he displayed a keen interest in political ideas. As a young man, his encounter with Kant left a lasting impression, although he was then quickly drawn to the more empirically based, utilitarian ideas of the Enlightenment thinkers in Berlin. Like many of his contemporaries, Gentz was influenced by Montesquieu; he also learned English, and became acquainted with Adam Smith. His interest in economic thought was to stand him in good stead; an astute analysis of the British economy brought him sometime later to the attention of Pitt. He is also considered to have been deeply influenced by Cicero.[6]

When the French Revolution broke out, Gentz initially praised the event, as providing the 'first practical triumph for philoooophy'.[7] But as the ønoossus of the Revolution became apparent, Gentz's position quickly began to shift. His Kantian belief in progress became tempered by a growing recognition of the requirements of history and tradition. In 1793, he translated Burke's *Reflections on the Revolution in France*, and he appended some of his own essays on the events in France at the end of the text; the publication immediately established his reputation as one of the most important political commentators in Germany. Interest in his role as a government official in the General Directory, the pricipal administrative agency in Prussia, quickly palled and he began, with the benign acquiesence of his superiors, to devote increasing amounts of time to publishing.

Initially, his commentary was compatible with Prussian policy. He accepted, for example, in 1795, that Prussia should withdraw from the war with France. He took over a journal at this time and then in 1799 he founded the anti-revolutionary *Historisches Journal* with the support of the Prussian government. The enterprise was endorsed by the foreign office, it was subsidised by the audit office, and Gentz was relieved for a year of his official duties by his superior so that he had the time to organise the journal. Unable to find suitable articles to publish, he proceeded to write all the entries for each monthly issue until the journal was eventually closed the following year. During this period, Gentz became increasingly disaffected with Prussian policy which was veering way from Britain and towards a reconciliation with France. In his articles, not only did he praise British policy, but he also began to demand the intervention of Prussia into the war with Republican France. Britain was compared to a 'dependable squire' while France was likened to 'a daring gambler' prepared to risk everything for the chance of world domination.[8]

Gentz's journal was given a very mixed reception. Prussian ministers, on examining the journal, became increasingly unhappy when they realised that they were subsidising a journal which was failing to endorse Prussian foreign policy. In 1800, the King, unsurprisingly, refused to appropriate further funds to subsidise the journal. Gentz, who was already in financial difficulties, tried to make contingency plans. He turned to another of his readers, the British Ambassador in Berlin, for financial support to maintain the journal. The Ambassador, Lord Carysfort, had often drawn on Gentz's analysis in his reports, and he also recognised the importance of attempts to influence public opinion in Prussia; he willingly conveyed Gentz's request to London. The British foreign secretary, Lord Grenville, thought the proposal impractical, but he did agree to provide Gentz with upto £200 'for services abroad'.[9] In a separate move, Gentz had also started to send secret memoirs to the government in London via a British agent.[10] From this time on, although with some very inconvenient lapses from the standpoint of Gentz's endlessly precarious financial situation, he became a frequent recipient of payments from the British government. Between 1806 and 1809, for example, he received £4500, rather more than an Under-Secretary of State in London would have received at the time.[11]

The articles in *Historisches Journal* were also read in France. A member of the French Foreign Ministry, Count Hauterive, described by

Hinsley as 'perhaps the earliest director of a modern ministry of information',[12] wrote, anonymously, *The Situation in France at the End of the Eighth Year* in 1800 to counter the arguments being advanced by Gentz who was seen to be 'instructed and probably paid' by Great Britain.[13] According to Hauterive, it was not the French, but the British, who were primarily responsible for destabilising Europe. Britain was the state with global aspirations which had unsettled relations among the European states long before 1789. Gentz had little alternative but to respond to the challenge and he did so in *On the Political Situation in Europe Before and After the Revolution*. The book defended the British and called for yet another Coalition to be mounted against France. The Prussian censor demanded that the production of the book should be halted. But the book had lost much of its sting by March 1802 when the British signed the Treaty of Amiens with the French. Europe was to experience a respite after a decade of war.

Gentz's persistent failure to perform his official duties, however, led in April 1802 to a request for his resignation. In conjunction with intractable personal and financial problems, he eventually fled from Berlin, two months later, leaving a wife and a string of debtors. He was never to return; almost all his remaining years were to be spent within the Austrian Empire. The flight to Vienna took place after Count Stadion, the Austrian ambassador in Berlin, had been persuaded that Gentz could be of use to the Austrian Government. Gentz had come to the attention of Stadion as the result of an article in *Historisches Journal* proclaiming the innocence of the Austrian Government, incorrectly, it materialised some years later, after a group of French delegates had been assassinated following an abortive peace congress at Ranstatt. But when Gentz arrived in Vienna he was given a less than enthusiastic reception by the Emperor. After some vigorous lobbying, by Stadion and the young Metternich, whom Gentz had recently encountered, the Emperor was eventually persuaded to give Gentz a pension of 4000 florins a year, the title of Imperial Counsellor and an undertaking that 'he continue to write for the Good Cause'.[14]

The 'Good Cause' of defeating, first revolutionary France, and then Napoleonic France, had been and remained Gentz's principal priority in life. Although dependent upon foreign governments for his finance, Gentz rarely compromised his own views or deviated from his basic aim of encouraging the defeat of France. Napoleon, he observed, 'this wanton, blaspheming, villainous bandit has become an obsession with me'.[15] In his more reflective moments, however, Gentz adhered to a somewhat more elevated assessment of his own role and activities. Later in life he commented, 'I hold it of the utmost importance that in politics especially there should be a group of writers whose fixed ideal is the highest political good, who assume that every important governmental measure is directed towards this end, and who treat the subject always as though in the final analysis real philanthropy, wisdom and virtue *must* underlie all endeavour.'[16] Metternich noted in consequence that Gentz was 'sure only of fundamentals' and that 'like all scholars he was impractical'.[17] As Gentz became more closely involved in the process of decision-making, he came to acknowledge the politician's need to temporise and to moderate demands, but in the process he also accepted that he had lost the ability to act as a political commentator. He was incapable of sustaining the necessary illusions; statesmen, he came to believe, were only capable of acting on the basis of narrow sectarian interests. 'When one has reached this condition', he concluded, 'one can no longer exert a wholesome influence on the public.'[18] It was some time yet, however, before he would become closely enmeshed in what he called 'the workings of the machine'.[19] For several more years he was still to be preoccupied with analysing and reporting on political events from the sidelines.

After his arrival at Vienna, he found himself repeatedly at loggerheads with his new political masters. Indeed, he was convinced that Austria would only agree to join a coalition against Napoleon when the foreign minister, Cobenzl, had been replaced. He made the argument strenuously in his reports to England. But Gentz was still very far from participating or even understanding the inner workings of the cabinet in Vienna.[20] Unbeknown to Gentz, in July 1804, Cobenzl formed a secret military alliance with Russia and Britain, helping to produce a Third Coalition against the French. Gentz was happy to revise his opinion of Cobenzl, however, when he eventually realised that the Austrians were willing to go to war with France. Military engagements began in September 1805 and Gentz was convinced that on this occasion Napoleon had overreached himself.[21] In response to a request by Cobenzl that he should awaken popular enthusiasm for the war, Gentz set to work on *History of the Balance of Power in Europe*, a book designed to extol the European order which he believed Napoleon wished to destroy. But the initial conception of the book never reached fruition. With Austria's ignominious defeat by the French at Ulm, Gentz, terrified at the prospect of being captured by the French, made a hasty departure from Vienna, eventually coming to rest at Dresden within the relatively safe neutral haven of Saxony. Thoroughly disillusioned, Gentz went on to publish what he had written, in the heady days before Austria's defeat, as *Fragments Upon the Present State of the Political Balance in Europe*. Within months it had been translated and published in England.

From a political perspective, the next three years were gloomy ones for Gentz. Exiled in Prague, without the Austrian pension, he was even put under police surveillance by Stadion, the new foreign minister, as part of a concerted Austrian effort to seek favour with the French. But when the Austrians decided to move once more on to the offensive, Gentz was summoned back to Vienna in February 1809. The return was brief, war merely brought further disasters to Austria, with Gentz once again fleeing from Vienna. In the subsequent peace negotiations, only stubborn resistance by Austria's negotiators prevented the country from being divided into three. Gentz came to the unhappy conclusion that five or six years of peace, giving time for complete recovery, was essential, if France was ever to be defeated. This assessment coincided with the views of Metternich who had become the foreign minister in the aftermath of the war; Gentz was eventually to become his closest adviser.

Initially, again out of deference to the French, Metternich felt it advisable for Gentz to continue living in Prague. But over the next five years, despite frequent political disagreements, Metternich and Gentz developed mutual admiration for their respective abilities. After the defeat of France in 1814, Metternich was established as the President of the Congress of Vienna with Gentz operating as his secretary; and it was Gentz who was given the task of drawing up the final treaty. But he was unimpressed by what he saw and noted that 'The magniloquent phrases about "restitution of the social order", the "recovery of European politics", and "enduring peace based upon a just apportionment of power", and so on were trumped up only to quiet the masses and to confer on the Congress some semblance of import and dignity. But the real sense of the gathering was that the victors should share with one another the booty snatched from the vanquished.'[22] His services were appreciated, nevertheless, and the possibility was even mooted of establishing him as a permanent secretary-general of Europe,[23] although the idea was quickly buried by Metternich. But he did act as secretary for all the subsequent Congresses at Paris, Aachen, Carlsbad, Troppeau, Laibach and Verona. He continued to work in close cooperation with Metternich until 1828, proffering advice which was designed to maintain the structure of the system, established at the Congress of Vienna. Thereafter, his influence faded, and he died in 1832.

## RATIONALISM, REALISM AND THE BALANCE OF POWER

Gentz was not an original or philosophical thinker. His primary interest was to ensure that the European states-system was preserved intact. When analysing developments on the European stage, he drew upon an established body of ideas, focusing, in particular, on the balance of power. Given the centrality of the concept in Gentz's frame of reference, it may seem strange, at first sight, to insist on categorising him as a rationalist because the balance of power is almost invariably identified as the touchstone of realist thought. There is, however, an overwhelmingly strong reason for defining Gentz as a rationalist. He identified Europe not as an anarchic arena but as a union or federation of states, a states-system, with all states having a responsibility to maintain the integrity of the system. And from Gentz's perspective, the balance of power played a crucial role in preserving the integrity of Europe.

This then raises the question of how realists and rationalists both manage to give the balance of power such a position of prominence in their thinking. Wight moved some way towards answering this question by insisting that the balance of power is used very differently in the two traditions.[24] When realists refer to the balance of power they are drawing attention to the way that states endeavour to manipulate the prevailing distribution of power to promote their own interests. By contrast, for rationalists, the balance of power is associated with the preservation of a just equilibrium. He quotes Gentz, who argued that the balance of power represents 'that constitution subsisting among neighbouring states ... by virtue of which no one among them can injure the independence or essential rights of another without meeting with effectual resistance on some other side, and consequently exposing itself to danger'.[25]

Although Wight took some initial steps towards clarifying this distinction between the realist and rationalist approach to the balance of power, his ideas on this topic were not worked out systematically and, moreover, they only appeared recently, almost two decades after his death. Although others have independently arrived at a similar conclusion,[26] the potential for understanding the balance of power in terms of competing theoretical traditions is still largely unrealised. Although it may be true to argue, therefore, that Gentz was not an original thinker, it becomes of interest to investigate how his thinking about the balance of power fits into the rationalist tradition.

His approach to international relations, unsurprisingly, has not been subjected to systematic scrutiny with any frequency. But two analysts, Hinsley[27] and Forsyth,[28] both of a rationalist persuasion, have subjected his debate with Hauterive to a careful review. Indeed, it could be argued that everything of any significance about Gentz's thinking on international relations has already been identified and evaluated in their discussions. On further inspection, however, it is possible to observe an important division of opinion about Gentz in the analyses offered by Hinsley and Forsyth. Their debate has been left unresolved and it opens up questions not only about how Gentz actually viewed the balance of power but also what role the concept plays in the rationalist tradition.

**Competing Rational Assessments of the Balance of Power**

According to Hinsley, the debate between Gentz and Hauterive revolved around competing assessments of Europe prior to the French Revolution. In summarising Hauterive's position, Hinsley identifies first the argument that long before the onset of the French Revolution there had been general disorder in Europe and any conception of a federal union had ceased to exist. This breakdown was attributed to the rise of Russia as a dominant actor in Europe; the attempts by the European states to counter the growing power of Prussia; and, of primary importance, the destabilising effects of Britain's expanding colonial and commercial system. Hauterive is then seen to have argued that France's new-found strength could be used, first, to provide a bulwark against Britain, and second, to regulate and maintain an equilibrium among the European states. On this basis it would then be possible to restore a universal and perpetual system of public law in Europe. Hinsley associates this line of argument with an attempt to combine the frustrated hopes for French hegemony in Europe with the early-eighteenth-century desire for Europe to form a single state.

Hinsley then turns to Gentz and focuses initially on his denial that Europe had ever had a political and federal constitution. Gentz insists, moreover, that such a constitution could never emerge in Europe because it would be impossible to establish a treaty which satisfied all the divergent interests of the European states. Indeed, even if such a treaty could have been formed, Gentz insists, it would not have survived because the European states inevitably change and grow at different and unanticipated rates. Europe's public law during the eighteenth century had in consequence undergone persistent modifications to accommodate changing circumstances. Gentz accepted that the rise of Russia had been a source of conflict in Europe, but he insisted that public law had been maintained because the growing power of Prussia had had a balancing effect. By the same token, the growing power of Britain had provided 'a new weight in the general balance'.[29] From Gentz's perspective, therefore, the Revolution had interrupted the progressive development of Europe. And far from improving conditions in Europe, the growing power of France under Napoleon had created the danger of universal dominion. It was accepted that there had been imperfections in the states-system which had operated in Europe prior to the Revolution, but as Gentz saw it, these imperfections had been in the process of being eliminated.

Hinsley goes on to suggest that it is important to understand that in his analysis Gentz was drawing on two different conceptions of the balance of power. One conception, signified by the need to combine against hegemony, stretched back to the time when the threat of a universal monarch had existed. The other conception, which evolved during the eighteenth century, referred to the idea of an equilibrium with the European states collectively acting as counterweights for each other. In 1802, Gentz was relying on both of these meanings, but Hinsley argues that the balance of power came to be associated exclusively with the latter conception. Indeed, after the Napoleonic Wars, when the Congresses were being held, Gentz even suggested that the balance of power generated by competing alliances was in the process of being replaced 'by a principle of general union, uniting all the states by a federative bond under the direction of the 5 principal powers'.[30] But the second conception of the balance of power was insinuated back into the system by the acknowledgement that the persistence of a federal union depended upon the existence of an equal distribution of power among these five states.

Forsyth provides a very different assessment of the debate between the Frenchman and the Prussian to the one offered by Hinsley. The divergence in interpretation is most apparent in the case of Hauterive, who draws, Forsyth argues, on the argument first developed in France in the middle of the eighteenth century, that the European balance of power was being threatened by the British who were seen to be using their sea-power to achieve economic hegemony and ultimately to establish a universal monarchy. This thesis, according to Forsyth, provides the foundations for Hauterive's distinctive and highly original interpretation of the circumstances surrounding the French Revolution.

Hauterive starts by providing an elaborate explanation of how the French Revolution had been the inevitable consequence of social instability precipitated by the evolution of the commercial system. The Revolutionary Government had been unable to resolve the sources of tension within France, but an equilibrium had been restored by Napoleon. France was thus depicted as a source of stability in a highly unstable international system. Hauterive identifies colonial and maritime expansion as the root cause of the problem because they had been omitted from the system of public law established at the Treaty of Westphalia which had provided the foundations of the continental federative system. Subsequent attempts to bind colonial and maritime issues into the public law of the continental system had been unsuccessful. At first, Hauterive argues, this had not mattered. But after the Treaty of Utrecht, Britain had more insistently used its advantageous geographical position to monopolise the commercial and maritime systems beyond the reach of the continental system of public law. Hauterive argued that the governments on the continent had failed to recognise the link between maritime and continental commerce or between general commerce and public power. He identified, in particular, the indissoluble connection between English commerce and English power, recognising that its dominance of overseas trade enabled it to organise a vast network of credit across the continent. The extraordinary position of power achieved by Britain had effectively eroded the system of public law established at the time of Westphalia. To restore the European states-system, therefore, it was essential for the continental states to ally in order to reestablish the balance of power between continental and maritime interests.

From Forsyth's perspective, Hinsley fails to give sufficient credit to the force of Hauterive's argument; and he suggests Hinsley has been misled by the summary of Hauterive's argument given by Gentz. Once the significance of Hauterive's argument is taken on board, Forsyth asserts, it becomes necessary to acknowledge that Gentz and Hauterive are *both* working within a balance-of-power framework. But they are relying on very different conceptions of the balance of power. Forsyth here is not making reference to the distinction drawn by Hinsley. On the contrary, Hinsley's distinction is incorporated into the broader framework mapped out by Forsyth. It is suggested that the distinction drawn by Hinsley occurs because Gentz is forced to shift gears during the course of his analysis.

Initially, Gentz is working from an ideological perspective and it is argued that faced with an ideological foe who wishes to overthrow the system, there is no alternative but to adopt an 'unnatural' coalition, which he distinguishes from a 'natural' alliance. This distinction corresponds to the two meanings attributed to the balance of power by Hinsley. The unnatural coalition relates to what Hinsley sees as the older formulation of the balance of power. As Gentz put it, a 'temporary, urgent and truly common interest may suspend every usual federative relation, and unite all nations in the prosecution of a common object, without regard to the similitude or diversity of their permanent views'.[31] But Forsyth goes on to show how Gentz then reverts to Hinsley's second meaning of the balance of power to justify why France, now divested of its revolutionary zeal, must still be regarded as a threat, requiring collective action. Again, Gentz develops the argument very clearly. 'It is a leading maxim in every rational system of practicable politics, that every power is dangerous to the rest, which possesses the means of disturbing the general peace, and wants nothing but the will to use them. If we depart from this maxim, we no longer find any fixed point whatever in the whole sphere of politics; there remains nothing then but the vague suppositions and wavering hypotheses, uncertain options of personal characters, and loose probabilities, which one movement presents and the following destroys.'[32]

Forsyth, therefore, has no difficulty identifying the two conceptions of the balance of power put forward by Hinsley. But he insists that the debate between Hauterive and Gentz is founded on the much more fundamental division between the idea of a continental balance of power which raises military and territorial concerns and a commercial balance of power which depends on financial, trading and colonial considerations. Since Forsyth's argument subsumes Hinsley's, it would seem that he has said the last word on the subject. But it is possible to argue that neither completely comes to terms with the complexity of Gentz's position. To understand his position, it is necessary to look much more closely at how Gentz's assessment of the balance of power fitted into his broader conception of the world.

## Gentz on the Balance of Power

It was fitting that Gentz should have become the secretary for the European Congresses, because he identified himself first and foremost as a European. He believed, moreover, that it was essential for all Europeans to put the interests of Europe ahead of the interests of any individual state; the very survival of Europe as a federative entity depended upon such an attitude. It should not be assumed, however, that Gentz operated from a Euro-centric position. In fact, he was very conscious that Europe was part of a broader and rapidly changing system. He was preoccupied, in particular, with the growing power of Russia and the United States. He noted in 1818, for example, that 'The progressive extension of the territory of the United States is in my opinion the greatest political fact of our time; here lies concealed the seed for events that will entirely change the face of the world not in a hundred, but in twenty years.'[33] Gentz went out of his way to promote trade between Austria and the United States, and to secure the appointment of Erich Bollmann as the American consul to Vienna.[34] It has been recorded that Bollmann silenced his Viennese aristocratic hosts on one occasion when he talked of the 'marvels' of the United States. One of the listeners records, 'This whole country had become remote from us because of the long maritime war, but still more remote was the idea of a republic as a fabulous, nay, even an alarming example of how ordinary citizens can establish power and importance to a degree that we in Europe are still in the habit of associating only with the nobility and with royalty.'

The writer goes on to observe that 'Gentz was as though crushed by the weight of the thing.'[35] The writer assumed that Gentz was concerned about the success of republicanism. But it seems more likely that Gentz was pondering the consequences for the balance of power in Europe of this emerging great power on the other side of the Atlantic. He had always been of the opinion that a legitimate government could take any political form; the only consequence of any significance was what effect the government would have on the power of the state.

During the Revolutionary and Napoleonic Wars, however, the United States had no more than a marginal effect on events in Europe. But during that period Gentz was concerned about the growing power of Russia, although he also wished to contest Hauterive's argument that the rise of Russia had destroyed the federative system in Europe. Gentz distinguished Russia from the other European states because he regarded it as a Eurasian state and not part of European civilisation. Nevertheless, he acknowledged that a process of civilisation was taking place in Russia and he argued that this process represented the greatest event in world history since the discovery of America.[36] He argued that it would provide an entry for Europe into Asia, while at the same time effectively eliminating any threat from the Asiatic barbarian tribes which had threatened Europe in the past.

Despite the process of civilisation, Gentz could not deny that Russia had played a vital role in the partition of Poland, a key event which Hauterive used as evidence to support his argument that the federative system of Europe had broken down before the onset of the French Revolution. The partition of Poland was, in fact, an issue Gentz returned to repeatedly in his writing. Because the principal virtue of the balance of power for Gentz was the way that it preserved the independence of the members of the states-system, the partition of Poland was extremely troublesome. He regarded the action as an abuse of power and 'one of the most odious and pernicious events of the eighteenth century'.[37] Gentz was particularly disturbed by the fact that the partitioning powers used the balance of power to justify the partition, so that 'while they inflicted upon its spirit the most frightful wounds, they borrowed its attire, its form and even its language'.[38] The irony was also not lost on Gentz that Poland had been deprived of its independence not because of conflict between the Great Powers, but because of their willingness to cooperate. He argued, therefore, that the partition of Poland was 'incomparably more destructive to the higher interests of Europe' than previous acts of violence, because, for the first time, states had been willing to collaborate to destroy a member of the states-system.[39] The balance of power had thereby been subverted.

Gentz refused to admit, however, that this event justified the claim that the Westphalian system had collapsed. He made his case on a number of different grounds. In the first place, he drew a comparison between the system of a mixed constitution within the state and the balance of power in the international system. In both cases, the potential for collaboration rather than balancing exists in order to deal with extraordinary situations where a common danger exists to the freedom of the system. An unavoidable problem exists, however, because although 'the divided powers must necessarily act in concert for good and salutary purposes, they can also, in extraordinary cases, voluntarily combine for bad ones'; and Gentz accepts that this represents a 'danger which baffles all human skills to avoid'.[40] There are, Gentz seems to be saying, unavoidable flaws in any system of government.

Gentz goes on to argue that Poland was an exceptionally fractious and weak state with extremely powerful neighbours. In an earlier era, he asserts, Poland's independence would also have been lost. But the destruction would have been wrought by a 'dreadful war' and the territory would have been absorbed by a single conqueror. Instead, Poland had been 'divided by an arbitrary but peaceful treaty and a new balance of power has been established on its ruins'.[41] Gentz, while deploring the act, insisted that it had not damaged the European balance of power, and that the manner of the partition did represent a degree of progress on previous eras.

Nevertheless, Gentz remained very wary of Russia. When he was endeavouring to promote the idea of a coalition between the European powers, he insisted that Russia should not be allowed to come to the forefront of this process, but should be held, in reserve, on the periphery of the European arena. For this reason, he also saw an alliance between Prussia and Austria as essential. Throughout the period, moreover, he was concerned that Russia might take advantage of the situation in France to enhance its own position.

The inability of the Europeans to overcome Napoleon made Gentz increasingly concerned about the possibility of an alliance being formed between France and Russia. He argued that 'of all political combinations this would be the most ruinous' and he went on to assert that 'if European politics still retained even a shred of concern for its honor, its aims and its duty it would oppose this final and most terrible of all evils with its last breath'.[42] When the Treaty of Tilsit was signed, in 1807, cementing just such an alliance, Gentz's worst fears appeared to have become a reality. His concern was that these two 'colossal powers' would set about partitioning Europe. Indeed, he believed that they could dominate not only

Europe, but Africa and Asia as well, destroying the power of Britain in the process. The example of the Polish partition provided an ominous precedent. In apocalyptic terms, he argued at the time that 'this unnatural, outrageous duumvirate, will eventually come to the same end as others of their sort'. Drawing a comparison with the conflict between Octavian and Mark Antony, he concluded that 'This barbarous struggle over the question whether the world is to belong to one tyrant or two brings to a close the eighteen-year-old drama whose theme was universal freedom!'[43]

Although Gentz saw Russia and France as the major threats to the stability of the states-system, he was convinced that, by means of a coalition, stability could be restored. It is important to recognise that, while simultaneously endeavouring to undermine Hauterive's position, he did not, in developing his thesis, completely deny Forsyth's argument that the balance of power can take divergent forms, although he certainly contested the idea that Britain could be extracted from the continental balance of power on the grounds that it monopolised the distinctive forms of maritime and commercial power.

He argued, in the first place, that the distribution of power was constantly shifting and that, as a consequence, the distribution of power upon which a federal constitution was founded will inevitably change over time. Foreign trade, however, was only 'one of the many and various springs which set this great machine in motion'. Moreover, no state had been an 'idle observer' of this process; all had become involved in the commercial system. So, although all states had not gained equally by their involvement, it was untrue to suggest that the Westphalian system had been destroyed by the emergence of the commercial system. Gentz accepted that those states which had first developed commerce and colonies had an initial advantage, and, furthermore, that there had emerged a 'new and distinct balance of the maritime and commercial states'.[44] There had been no question of 'dangerous preeminence' developing as a consequence of this development because there were a variety of states equally involved in the commercial system. He identified, in particular, Britain, Holland and France. As Gentz saw it, 'That commerce of the world should be divided between three, nearly equal favoured nations, was the most fortunate circumstance others could have desired'; it prevented any abuse of power. Even more important, it meant that because there existed 'a counter-balance of a distinct nature' then it could be used to contend with any serious threat to the general or continental balance of power.[45]

Even before the French threat to the stability of Europe had diminished, Gentz was already looking ahead to identify other potential dangers. Of central concern was Germany. He argued that 'The independence of

Germany is Europe's primary political need and conforms to the supreme best interest of Europe as a whole.... It is certain that if the much promised *eternal peace* should ever cease to be a shadow picture, it must be brought to mankind by this road and this road alone.'[46] And Gentz was in no doubt that to achieve that end, Germany must serve as the foundation for a European balance of power.[47] What Gentz meant by this was that the states which made up the confederation of Germany needed to be independent but separate. He believed that the emergence of a single Germany at the centre of Europe would destabilise the entire European system.

## Gentz, realism and rationalism

A review of Gentz's thinking about the balance of power highlights a number of distinctive features which help to delineate the rationalist tradition. These features, moreover, are reinforced when examined in conjunction with Gentz's debate with Hauterive. In the first place, it is clear that analysts working within the rationalist tradition are well aware that the balance of power can be subverted by states operating on realist premises. There is, as a consequence, a clearly discerned need to dissociate realist and rationalist conceptions of the balance of power. Gentz, conscious of working within a tradition of thought which yielded a distinctive conception of the balance of power, viewed the balance of power as an institution which was designed to ensure that the European states respected each other's existence, observed the rules and conventions which they formed with each other, and moderated their demands on other members of the system. He did not associate the balance of power with the attempt to maintain what he called an 'equipoise'. In so far as it was possible to visualise his conception of the balance of power in terms of a set of scales, he saw it in 'constant alternate vacillation' and through the application of counterweights, the scales would be prevented from 'passing certain limits'.[48] He had to think of the balance of power in these very dynamic and fluid terms because he recognised that the power capabilities of states undergo constant change.

Gentz did not presuppose, however, that states had any clear conception of the precise distribution of power at any point in time. As he saw it, '*the fear* of awakening common opposition, or of drawing down common vengeance must of itself be sufficient to keep everyone within bounds of moderation'.[49] From this perspective, then, the balance of power would become increasingly effective as more centres and sources of power were added to the system. These could act as additional counterweights and decrease the likelihood that any state could take an untoward action without incurring some kind of response. By the same token, any concentration of power would have the reverse effect. It was for this reason that he was alarmed by the expansion in power within France and Russia and why he did not wish to see the unification of Germany. These developments inevitably encouraged what Wight identifies as a realist approach to the balance of power. The worst scenario which Gentz can envisage has Russia and France maintaining a balance between them and operating a policy of divide and rule across the globe. A realist approach to the balance of power is seen to encourage such an outcome. Gentz clearly recognises the possibility of states cooperating with each other and pursuing balance-of-power tactics at the expense of other states in the system. But it is also apparent that he is very alarmed by this realist subversion of the balance of power.

Gentz, therefore, identifies two very different conceptions of the balance of power which can be found in the realist and rationalist traditions. It is worth noting that Hauterive also draws a similar distinction and that both he and Gentz see themselves operating within the rationalist tradition. Their different positions arise because whereas Hauterive sees Britain pursuing a realist strategy, endeavouring to manipulate the balance of power in its own favour, Gentz considers that it is France which is adopting the realist posture. Despite their different assessments, both accept that a distinction needs to be drawn between what is being identified here as a realist strategy which is designed to manipulate the established balance of power so as to benefit an individual state and a rationalist strategy which aims to protect the overall system.

A second feature of Gentz's analysis of the balance of power which helps to delineate the rationalist tradition relates to his conception of power itself. Power is not simply expressed in military terms. Gentz makes very clear that there is a distinct role for economic power. From this perspective, economic power does not simply underwrite military power. Instead, it operates as a separate and significant force in the relations among states. Hauterive adopts a very similar position. The divergence between Gentz and Hauterive does not relate to the importance attached to the independent role played by military power but rather to their assessment of the effects of economic power on the European scene. Gentz argued that economic power was balanced between a variety of states and was thereby reinforcing the overall balance. By contrast, Hauterive insisted that economic power inside and outside the European arena was being monopolised by Britain. As a consequence, the balance of power was being subjected to a serious challenge. The challenge was seen to be all the more serious because of its insidious nature. The effects of

Britain's growing economic power were much less apparent than the growth in the military power of a state. In any event, both Gentz and Hauterive make very clear that economic power has a major and independent role to play in international relations and the balance of power.

A third feature of the rationalist tradition which emerges through an analysis of Gentz's discussion of the balance of power relates to the structure of the international system. At first sight, it could be argued that Gentz's position is highly Eurocentric but this is an over-simplification. While there is no doubt that Gentz focuses his attention on Europe, it is equally clear that he sees Europe operating in a global system. Although much of his attention was focused on the threat to Europe posed by the French, it is also apparent that he was anxious to ensure that contact with the wider world did not weaken or undermine the bonds which held Europe together. From Gentz's perspective, for example, the balance of power was a European institution which allowed the European states not only to co-exist but to develop progressively more civilised relations with each other by, among other things, an evolving network of rules. Gentz recognised that by using realist strategies, the balance of power could be extended to the global arena, but this would inevitably occur at the expense of maintaining and developing civilised relations within the European states-system. Although the issue is not discussed directly, it would appear that Gentz approved of the idea of economic links, in the first instance, being extended to the extra-European arena. It is unclear how he envisaged the long-term relationship, but it is evident that at that period, the rationalists saw a coherent union of European states operating in the context of a much broader, more disorganised and potentially highly dangerous world system.

## GENTZ, RATIONALISM AND REVOLUTIONISM

In the wake of the Napoleonic Wars, Gentz believed that the Great Powers 'are nothing more than the most important and most natural protectors of the general order' and that, as a consequence, 'the smallest sovereign state is as independent as France, England or Russia within its own territory and in the domain of its own laws'.[50] But while international relations seemed to be extraordinarily stable at this time, Gentz became increasingly concerned about the growth of revolutionary forces within the European states. The situation was seen by Gentz to be doubly dangerous because of the closely–knit character of the European states-system. As a consequence, 'no member can be mutilated, wounded or poisoned without the harm penetrating more or less deeply into all the others'.[51] During this period, therefore, Gentz was inclined to describe the European states-system in horizontal rather than vertical terms. Confronted by what he saw as a universal revolutionary movement, Gentz stressed the need for solidarity on the part of the monarchs. From a rationalist perspective, therefore, the cosmopolitian character of revolution left the sovereign leaders of the European states with no alternative but to adopt a collective and interventionary response.

There is an obvious inconsistency in the position adopted by Gentz. On the one hand, he is arguing that the stability of the European states-system secured the independence of all states, whereas on the other, he is suggesting that the danger of revolution creates a general right of intervention. Other rationalists quickly highlighted this inconsistency. Castlereagh, for example, denied categorically that the Great Powers had any general right to intervene. He endeavoured to restrict the right of intervention to situations where the balance of power was under threat.[52] Disputes about the right of intervention have persisted and have remained highly contentious amongst defenders of the rationalist position.

The resulting ambiguity in the rationalist position has, perhaps inevitably, encouraged a degree of inconsistency in the response of revolutionist critics of rationalism. For example, Cobden argued on the one hand that Gentz's idea of a closely-knit union of European states was a 'chimera' while, on the other hand, he attacked the willingness of the leaders of European states to intervene and defend each other against revolutionary forces.[53]

## CONCLUSION

This brief study of Gentz tends to endorse the idea of the rationalist traditions forming a *via media* between realism and revolutionism and it also throws fresh light on disputes among contemporary analysts working within the rationalist tradition. Wight has portrayed rationalism as a 'broad middle road'[54] running between realism and revolutionism. Gentz found himself being pulled at different times towards policies which were tempered by both realist and revolutionist thinking. Confronted by an expansionist power pursuing realist strategies, Gentz felt that there was no alternative but to advocate the formation of an 'unnatural' coalition which moved the international system away from the fluid power positions which operate under normal circumstances and towards a rigid power confrontation based upon an essentially realist conception of the situation. At the other extreme, when faced by a universal revolutionary force, Gentz believed that there was no alternative but to dissolve all differences between states' leaders and pursue a collective strategy. At both extremes, then, Gentz reveals how rationalists are required to react to the other two traditions by adopting some of their characteristics and thereby reducing to some extent the coherence of their own tradition. There is little doubt that Gentz would, on the one hand, have endorsed the revolutionary response of the US in the 1940s when confronted by the perceived global and revolutionary threat from communism and, on the other, the essentially realist response to the threat posed by Saddam Hussein in the 1990 Gulf Crisis.

At a more theoretical level, Gentz also throws an interesting light on the dispute among contemporary rationalists about whether to distinguish between an international system and an international society. Bull and Watson have drawn a sharp distinction between the two and they argue that the European society of states steadily extended outwards during the nineteenth and twentieth centuries to embrace increasing portions of the globe which was made up of regional international systems.[55] A system exists whenever states interact with each other; a society emerges when these interactions are constrained by an agreed set of rules. James[56] has argued that this distinction cannot be sustained. He argues that if states are interacting, then they must be doing so within an established body of rules; human interaction presupposes rule-governed behaviour. Whatever the sociological and linguistic merits of this argument, an analysis of Gentz reveals that it runs at odds with the tradition of rationalist thought. Gentz depicts Europe as a rule-governed system operating and endeavouring to survive within a global system. Gentz is clearly very concerned about the possibility that Europe's interaction with this wider system will have deleterious effects on the European states-system. In contrast to realists who depict the global arena as an anarchic and dangerous state of nature, and where every state has to look out for itself, the rationalists have traditionally depicted Europe as a haven of civilisation operating within a wider and more dangerous system. There is no doubt that this is a highly ethnocentric picture of world politics. But it does seem to be an important feature of the rationalist tradition of thought which has often been under-played. It is only relatively recently that attention has been drawn to the existence of two sets of rules in the historical development of world politics, one guiding relations among European states, and another guiding relations between European states and the outside world.

It has become much easier to identify and expose this feature of the rationalist tradition since the demise of the Soviet Union and the end of the Cold War. In searching for new ways to characterise the evolving structures of world politics, increasing attention is being paid to a centre–periphery model, which depicts a set of stable, developed and peaceful liberal states operating at the centre of the system and another set of unstable, underdeveloped and potentially violent states operating at the periphery.[57] If realism reigned in the era of the Cold War, then it seems likely that rationalism could well hold centre-stage in the post-Cold War era.

## NOTES

1.   The influence of Kant has been noted by several authors. See, for example, Golo Mann, *Secretary of State: The Life of Friedrich Gentz, Enemy of Napoleon*, trans. W. W. Woglom (New Haven: Yale University Press, 1946). He states, 'Kant's rigid ethics, his categorical imperative, and his idea of a league of nations can still be traced in the manifestoes with which Gentz summoned the world twenty years later to concerted effort against Napoleon' (p. 10).

2.   There are competing assessments of Burke's influence on Gentz. M. Forsyth argues that the influence was considerable. See 'The Old European States-System: Gentz versus Hauterive', *Historical Journal*, 1980, 521–38, p. 524. Paul R. Sweet, *Friedrich Von Gentz: Defender of the Old Order* (Westport, Conn.: Greenwood Press, 1970 [1941]) argues, by contrast, that the shift from Kant to Burke would have involved an 'intellectual somersault' which is not in evidence when his writings are examined closely. In fact, there seems little doubt that Gentz was influenced by both writers. He absorbed ideas in a very eclectic manner and used them in a very pragmatic fashion.

3.   Sweet (fn 2), p. 203.

4.   See Timothy Dunne, 'Mythology or Methodology? Traditions in International Relations', *Review of International Studies*, Vol. 19, No. 3, 305–18, p. 307.

5.   I have relied primarily in this section on Mann (fn 1); Sweet (fn 2) and Paul F. Reiff, *Friedrich Gentz: An Opponent of the French Revolution and Napoleon*, University of Illinois Studies in the Social Sciences, Vol. 1, No. 4, 1912.

6.   See Reiff (fn 5) who develops the argument that Cicero was the primary influence on Gentz, pp. 30–52.

7.   See Mann (fn 1), p. 47.

8.   See Sweet (fn 2), p. 49.

9.   Ibid., p. 51.

10.  Mann (fn 1), p. 46.

11.  Ibid., p. 152.

12.  F. H. Hinsley, *Power and the Pursuit of Peace: Theory and Practice in the History of Relations between States* (Cambridge: Cambridge University Press, 1963), p. 186.

13.  Ibid., p. 73.

14. Sweet (fn 2), p. 68.
15. Mann (fn 1), p. 101. He goes on to note that Napoleon referred to 'a miserable scribe called Gentz, one of those dishonourable men who sell themselves for money', p. 139.
16. Ibid., p. 207.
17. Ibid., p. 178.
18. Ibid., p. 207.
19. Ibid.
20. Sweet (fn 2), pp. 101–15.
21. Mann (fn 1), p. 111.
22. Ibid., p. 213.
23. Sweet (fn 2), p. 203.
24. M. Wight examines the balance of power from the perspective of the three traditions in chapter 8 of *International Theory: The Three Traditions*, ed. G. Wight and Brian Porter (Leicester and London: Leicester University Press, 1991).
25. F. Gentz, *On the State of Europe Before and After the French Revolution; Being an Answer to L'etat de la France a La Fin de l'an VIII*, trans. J. C. Herries (London: J. Hatchard, 1802), p. 55.
26. See, for example, R. Little, 'Deconstructing the Balance of Power: Two Traditions of Thought', *Review of International Studies*, Vol. 15, No. 2, 1989, pp. 87–100; and P. W. Schroeder, *Review of International Studies*, Vol. 15, No. 2, 1989, pp. 135–54.
27. Hinsley (fn 12).
28. Forsyth (fn 2).
29. Hinsley (fn 12), p. 192.
30. Hinsley (fn 19), p. 197.
31. Gentz (fn 25), p. 56.
32. Forsyth (fn 2), p. 535.
33. Sweet (fn 2), p. 238.
34. Ibid., p. 199.
35. Mann (fn 1), p. 222.
36. Gentz (fn 25), p. 17.
37. Ibid., p. 364.
38. F. Gentz, *Fragments Upon the Present State of the Political Balance in Europe*, trans. unknown (London: M. Peltier, 1806), p. 77.
39. Gentz (fn 25), p. 76.
40. Gentz (fn 38), p. 72.
41. Ibid., p. 365.
42. Mann (fn 1), p. 143.
43. Ibid., p. 144.
44. Gentz (fn 25), pp. 49–50.
45. Ibid., pp. 55–6.
46. Sweet (fn 2), p. 152.
47. Mann (fn 1), p. 164.
48. Gentz (fn 38), p. 63.
49. Gentz (fn 38), p. 63.
50. C. Holbraad, *The Concert of Europe: A Study in German and British International Theory 1815–1914* (London: Longman, 1970), p. 19.

51.  Ibid., p. 21.
52.  D. L. Hafner, 'Castlereagh, the Balance of Power, and Non-intervention', *The Australian Journal of Politics and History* 26, 1980, 71–84.
53.  Holbraad (fn 50), p. 154.
54.  Wight (fn 24), p. 15.
55.  H. Bull, *The Anarchical Society. A Study of Order in World Politics* (London: 1977), pp. 9–13; and A. Watson, 'Hedley Bull, States-systems and International Societies' *Review of International Studies*, Vol. 13, No. 2, pp. 147–54.
56.  A. James, 'System or Society?', *Review of International Studies*, Vol. 19, No. 3, pp. 269–88.
57.  B. Buzan, 'New Patterns of Global Security in the Twenty-First Century', *International Affairs*, Vol. 67, 1991, pp. 431–52, and J. M. Goldgeier and M. McFaul, 'A Tale of Two Worlds: Core and Periphery in the Post Cold War Era', *International Organization* 46, 1992, pp. 467–91.

# 11 Vattel: Pluralism and Its Limits

## Andrew Hurrell

The place of Vattel in both the narratives of international society and in the doctrinal histories of international law appears relatively clear and uncontested. For the theorists of international society, such as Martin Wight, Hedley Bull and John Vincent, Vattel stands full square in the pluralist camp. He upholds the idea that there can indeed exist an international society of states – 'the great society established by nature between all nations', as Vattel calls it. But it can only be a limited and pluralist society constructed around the goal of coexistence and embodying an ethic of difference. It is a society different in kind from that which exists within domestic society and is based on what Vattel calls the 'natural liberty of states' or what Andrew Linklater has labelled 'state libertarianism'.[1] It provides a structure of coexistence, built on the mutual recognition of states as independent and legally equal members of society, on the unavoidable reliance of self-preservation and self-help, and on freedom to promote their own ends subject to minimal constraints. Its dominant values are, to quote Vattel once more, 'the maintenance of order and the preservation of liberty'. Similarly, for Terry Nardin the concept of a society of states that emerged for the first time in the eighteenth century can be understood in terms of a 'practical' and opposed to a 'purposive association' – 'an association of independent and diverse political communities, each devoted to its own ends and its own conception of the good'. For Nardin, a '[P]ractical association is a relationship among those who are engaged in the pursuit of different and possibly incompatible purposes, and who are associated with one another, if at all, only in respecting certain restrictions on how each may pursue his own purposes'.[2] Such views stand in clear contrast to a more truly Grotian or solidarist conception of international society in which the interests of the whole form the central focus rather than the independence of the states of which it is made up; in which the domestic analogy is at least partially accepted; and in which international society is about more than the provision of the necessary framework for the minimalist goal of continued coexistence between states and embodies a far broader degree of solidarity and consensus.[3]

Vattel's position in the doctrinal histories of international law does not differ radically from this view. He is widely viewed as having brought international law much more firmly into line with the actual practice of states and as having contributed to the delineation of what was to become the mainstream conception of western international law: a law in which states are the principal actors and the units around which international order is to be constructed; in which there is a clear distinction between international and municipal law; in which participation is based on the mutual recognition of state sovereignty; in which the international legal system is universal and incorporates all full members of international society; and in which there is an increasingly clear distinction between the law on the one hand and politics and morality on the other. In both the substance and the style of Vattel, then, it is possible to see a decisive move away from what David Kennedy has called primitive legal scholarship, with its view of the state as only one actor within a broader *jus gentium*, with its overriding concern with the just war, and with its determination to incorporate international law into an overarching moral and political framework.[4] Although he prepared the ground for the decisive shift towards positivism that was to dominate international legal thought for the next century-and-a-half, Vattel's own position is seen as ambivalent in that he 'was unable or unwilling to free himself from the traditional lore of the *jus naturale*'.[5] Finally, for many international lawyers, it is Vattel's emphasis on the absolute independence of states that was the most significant characteristic of his writing – the 'principle of legal individualism' as Brierly labels it[6] – a characteristic widely applauded in the nineteenth century but increasingly criticised in this century.[7]

This chapter does not seek wholly to overthrow this conventional picture of Vattel. But it does want to unsettle it and to argue that the emphasis on 'state libertarianism' and untrammelled sovereignty has been overdone to the neglect of Vattel's broader moral purpose and the weight given in his work to the norms of the necessary natural law. The first section brings together the main features of Vattel's system of international law and exposes the foundations on which Vattel's pluralism is grounded. The second section then examines three countervailing arguments: first, that natural law obligations and the 'offices of humanity' continue to play a central role in Vattel's writing; second, that sovereignty is limited both by Vattel's acceptance of the legality of humanitarian intervention and by other limits on the kinds of states and state behaviour that can be tolerated within international society; and third, that the conventional narratives of international law and society misrepresent the histori-

cal context within which Vattel was writing and underplay the degree to
which he was working with intellectual assumptions and resources very
different from those which underpin the textbook image of the classical
European state system. Indeed, re-examining Vattel challenges the all-
too-common assumption that, once upon a time, there was a neat
'Westphalian model' in which understandings of sovereignty and norms of
non-intervention were stable and uncontested. The concluding section
examines two common charges made against Vattel, first that of complacency, and second that of intellectual incoherence.


## THE FOUNDATIONS OF PLURALISM

The foundations of Vattel's system of law are suggested in the sub-title of
his work: the 'principles of the law of nature applied to the conduct and
affairs of nations and sovereigns'. Acknowledging his debt to Hobbes,
Barbeyrac (Grotius's translator) and, above all, Christian Wolff, the foundations of Vattel's argument are developed in three stages. In the first place
he accepts the analogy between the natural liberty of states and the natural
liberty of individuals in the state of nature. 'Nations, or sovereign states,
are to be considered as so many free persons living together in a state of
nature'.[8] Although begging many questions, this analogy has been enormously powerful in Western liberal thought and there can be no doubt that
Vattel's writings contributed considerably to its influence, plausibility, and
apparent 'naturalness'.

Second, Vattel stresses the differences between states and individuals:

Individuals are so constituted, and are capable of doing so little by
themselves, that they can scarcely subsist without the aid and the laws
of civil society. But, as soon as a considerable number of them have
united under the same government, they become able to supply most of
their wants; and the assistance of other political societies is not so
necessary to them as that of individuals is to an individual (p. xiv).

Or again: 'Social bodies or sovereign states are much more capable of supplying all their wants than individual men are; and mutual assistance is not
so necessary among them, nor so frequently required' (p. 135). In this
Vattel once more follows Hobbes, who, after having famously argued that
states 'are in continual jealousies, and in the state and posture of gladi-
ators', went on to remark: '[B]ut because they uphold thereby, the industry
of their subjects, there does not follow from it, that misery, which accompanies the liberty of particular men.'[9]

The third step is to conclude from this that the natural law that applies to states will be different in kind from that which applies to individuals. It gives rise to different kinds of rights and duties and to a much looser form of society than that which is necessary within domestic life. Thus we find the central idea in Vattel of a 'necessary change in application': 'that the rules and decisions of the law of nature cannot be purely and simply applied to sovereign states, and that they must necessarily undergo some modifications in order to accommodate them to the nature of the subjects to which they are applied' (p. x).

On the basis of these steps, Vattel locates three categories of law. First, the necessary law of nations, 'pure' natural law as seen within the context of the law of nations. This law establishes objective principles of justice and provides a normative measure against which the positive law of nations can be judged. Its central feature is a general duty to behave in a social manner and to do everything that will contribute to the happiness of others. It is an immutable law, 'always obligatory on the conscience' but one which, as we shall see, cannot be enforced directly in the relations between states. Second, there is the voluntary law of nations, the modified law of nature as applied to the society of states. These essential alterations 'are deducible from the natural liberty of nations, from the attention due to their common safety, from the nature of their mutual correspondence, their reciprocal duties, and the distinctions of their various rights, internal and external, perfect and imperfect' (p. xv). Vattel believed that civil society arises primarily from need for both individuals and states to protect themselves and procure what is necessary for self-improvement and security. The cornerstone of this voluntary law is therefore self-preservation and here he follows Hobbes in tending towards a minimalist view of natural law as 'but conclusions, or theorems concerning what conduceth to the conservation and defence of themselves'.[10] It is this view of natural law and this change of application which underpins Vattel's critical distinctions within the voluntary law between perfect and imperfect rights and duties. Third, there is the arbitrary law of nations which 'proceeds from the will and consent of nations' (p. xvi) and which is established either 'by express engagements, by compact and treaties' (p. xvi); or by custom to which states have given their tacit consent – 'certain maxims and customs, consecrated by long use and observed by their mutual intercourse with each other as a kind of law' (p. lxiv).

It is certainly the case that Vattel's system lays great emphasis on independence and self-preservation. According to the 'applied' or voluntary law of nature, states have a strong right to independence. 'Nations being free and independent of each other, in same manner as men are naturally free and independent, the second general law of their society is that each nation should be left in the peaceable enjoyment of that liberty which she inherits from nature' (p. lxi). International law and cooperation are still possible but will be based not directly on natural human sociability, but rather on rational self-interest and on concern for the general welfare and safety of the society of states as a whole.

It is also the case that the flexibility of the voluntary law, its central focus on the liberty and independence of states, and its recognition of the necessity of self-help mean that the benefit of the doubt is often on the side of the individual state – for example, in deciding when treaties have to be broken, what constitutes 'innocent passage', how far the 'offices of humanity' should be a constraining force on state behaviour, or in determining what is the correct balance between means and ends in the conduct of war. As Vattel puts it: 'As a consequence of that liberty and independence, it exclusively belongs to each nation to form its own judgement of what her conscience demands of her, – of what she can and cannot do, – of what it is proper or improper for her to do: and of course it rests solely with her to examine and determine whether she can perform any office of humanity without neglecting the duty which she owes to herself' (p. lxi).

The pluralist and limited character of Vattel's conception of international society therefore rests partly on a view of natural law that lays great emphasis on self-preservation and partly on his argument that, when it comes to state practice, the necessary law could no longer be considered decisive:

> The necessary and the voluntary laws of nations are therefore both established by nature, but each in a different manner; the former, as a sacred law which nations and sovereigns are bound to respect and follow in all their actions; the latter, as a rule which the general welfare and safety oblige them to admit in their transactions with each other (p. xv).

It is voluntary law that is central to the political existence of international society. It is concerned with those obligations without which that society could not exist, concerned with the 'mere existence of society' – a society in which order is based on mutual forbearance and mutual respect of each others' sovereignty. It is the law that can be practically enforced, for, as Vattel argues, to try and enforce the necessary law of nations, 'would be to prescribe a medicine far more troublesome and dangerous than the disease'. Or again: 'It is therefore necessary, on many occasions, that nations should suffer certain things to be done, though in their nature unjust and condemnable; because they cannot oppose them by open force, without violating the liberty of some particular state, and destroying the liberty of their natural society' (p. lxiv).

But, as developed in more detail in the next section, to focus solely on self-preservation, on the independence of states, and on the practical limits of the voluntary law would be to neglect Vattel's broader moral scheme and his theory of moral obligation. Although the emphasis on the will and consent of states does indeed point in a positivist direction, Vattel is still deeply concerned with 'the immutable laws of justice, and the voice of conscience'. Moreover it is also important to note that he does not equate the positive law solely with arbitrary law. He is very clear that the 'Positive Law of Nations' is made up of the voluntary law together with conventional and customary law. There is, therefore, a twofold movement: on one side he seeks to move from pure natural law to applied natural law; but on the other side, he wants to maintain a clear connection between the particular practices and customs of states and this applied or modified natural law. In the Preface he argues – not without a degree of ambiguity – that 'the natural law of nations ... produces between nations even an *external* obligation wholly independent of their will'.[11] Although, as a matter of fact, international law was increasingly manifest in actual agreements and particular practices, Vattel sought to argue that its core propositions could be derived logically from natural law assumptions about the character and rational interests, propositions to which states could be understood to have given their tacit or presumed consent (Prelims 27, p. lxv).[12]

On these foundations, three features of Vattel's system of international law can be briefly noted.

(1) *A Law between Equal States*   The scope of law is narrowed to that between sovereigns, in clear contrast to sixteenth- and seventeenth-century natural lawyers who were concerned with a broader society that included both individuals and a world society or *civitas maxima* and in which there was little clear distinction between *jus inter gentes* and *jus gentium*. For Vattel, international law is the law between states – 'The law of nations is the law of sovereigns' (p. xvi) – and one in which individuals have no direct place (for example the duties of humanity towards outsiders are devolved on to the state). Indeed one of Vattel's most notable arguments is to reject Christian Wolff's conception of a great republic. Wolff had seen the existence of the mass of concrete agreements as reflecting the existence of a great republic (a *civitas maxima*) 'instituted by nature herself, and of which all the nations of the world are members' (p. xiii). For Vattel this is an impossible fiction: 'This idea does not satisfy me; nor do I think the fiction of such a republic either admissible in itself, or

capable of affording sufficiently solid grounds on which to build the rules of the universal law of nations, which shall necessarily claim the obedient acquiescence of sovereign states.... Nothing of this kind can be conceived or supposed to subsist between nations. Each sovereign claims, and actually possesses an absolute independence of all the others' (p. xiii).

For Vattel, international law is directly focused on the legal regulation of a plurality of independent states and centrally concerned with establishing the conditions for coexistence: the constitution of the units and rules for membership; the elaboration of the basic rules of coexistence and communication in times of peace (as in the codification of the law of diplomatic practice or the creation of means of dispute settlement by mediation, conciliation or arbitration); and the establishment of war as a formal legal state (see below). The state is placed at the centre of his view of international relations and there is an acceptance, even endorsement, of its self-regarding nature. This is based partly on an awareness of evolving international practice, but also on the argument that pluralism and respect for difference is a positive good: 'To this we may add, that independence is even necessary to each state, in order to enable her properly to discharge the duties she owes to herself and to her citizens, and to govern herself in the manner best suited to her circumstances' (p. xiv). International society needs to be based on a respect for difference, as, for example, in his discussion of religion: 'the differences of religion is a thing absolutely foreign to them.... Their common safety requires that they should be capable of treating with each other, and of treating with security' (p. 195).

Within this framework, Vattel is the first writer on international law to elucidate clearly the principle of sovereign equality, that all states possess equal rights – or an equal capacity for rights (as opposed to equal substantive rights). This he proclaims most notably in his famous quotation: 'A dwarf is as much a man as a giant; a small republic is no less a sovereign state than the most powerful kingdom' (p. lxii). It is worth noting that, in this, Vattel was not merely reflecting existing practice, given the degree to which formal precedence remained a central feature of diplomatic practice (ending only in 1815 at the Congress of Vienna).

(2) *War and the Balance of Power* Vattel stands for a distinct approach to the problem of war in international relations. On one side, the central importance of the concept of just war remains. Within the context of the necessary law war can, and should, be judged as just or unjust. But on the other side, the imperatives of self-preservation make it difficult to incorporate the concept of the just war into the voluntary law of nations, or to act upon notions of justice and injustice in the practice of international

relations. Instead the emphasis is shifted towards regulation of the conduct of war (*jus in bello*, the law of war as procedure). The laws of war are developed in a far more systematic fashion and apply to both sides as a consequence of the existence of a legal state of war. Equally the concept of neutrality is sharpened and there emerges for the first time the idea that neutrality requires strict impartiality. This, of course, follows from Vattel's argument that 'regular war, as to its effects, is to be accounted just on both sides'. Finally, the emphasis on order and stability lead him to propound in modern form the doctrine of prescription.

The tension between power politics and a system of law that seeks to regulate the resort to force is manifest most clearly in Vattel's discussion of the balance of power. Here he recognises openly the tension which his natural law predecessors had been unwilling to acknowledge and which his nineteenth-century successors often sought to exclude from the realm of law, namely that the prevention of hegemony is fundamental to the very existence of international society.[13] The right of a state to secure itself and the tendency of powerful states 'almost always' to oppress their neighbours make it both inevitable and justifiable that the sovereign should act upon outward signs of threat and base policy on prudence and suspicion.[14] In the absence of what we would now call a functioning system of collective security, Vattel recognised that the balance of power must have logical as well as political primacy over international legal attempts to regulate the resort to force. It is a small step (but one that Vattel did not take) to abandon the idea of the just war altogether and to accept that international law, as William Hall put it, 'recognizes war as a permitted mode of giving effect to its [a state's] decisions'.[15]

(3) *State and Nation*     Vattel defines states in terms of political societies in which sovereignty belongs essentially to the people. 'It is evident that men form a political society, and submit to laws, solely for their own advantage and safety. The sovereign authority is thus established only for the common good of all the citizens' (p. 12). In addition Vattel repeatedly emphasises his opposition to the patrimonial conception of state (the 'source of all those disastrous wars undertaken from ambition, restlessness, hatred or pride'). He thus points towards a right to resist tyranny and an end to the bartering of territories between rulers and to international acceptance of a right of conquest (although, perhaps typically, he is still able to accept partitions and the transfers of territory based on a notion of implied consent). Finally, there is an emerging idea of states, not just as political associations, but as distinct communities whose government should take into account their distinct character, although, as with Rousseau, his patriotism is still largely civic in character.

Thus we find in Vattel a particularly clearly expressed account of the foundations of the idea of international society which had become well established by the mid-eighteenth century: that states are less vulnerable than individuals and have less fear of sudden death; that they are unequal in power and resources; and that, if they are rational, they will be less tempted to destroy each other than will individuals in a state of nature and will be able to develop at least minimal rules of coexistence based on self-interest and rational prudence.

## THE LIMITS OF PLURALISM

The weight of Vattel's argument, then, does indeed tend towards a pluralist and limited conception of international society in which state sovereignty and self-preservation are emphasised. But that pluralism is not unlimited and the idea that Vattel propounds a simple notion of untrammelled sovereignty is mistaken. Taken together the limits to pluralism are substantial and the arguments important, both because of what they tell us about Vattel, but also because they help to establish the boundaries of subsequent political, legal and moral discourse.

*Duties beyond borders* In the first place, it is important to remember that Vattel was not solely concerned with the strict rules of international law, but also with the broader moral context within which those rules could be judged and assessed. For Vattel, as for other natural law theorists, the law of nature is not concerned with law narrowly defined as a system of formal positive rules, but provides the theoretical principles from which the legal and moral rights and duties of states and sovereign princes can be derived.[16] Vattel's positive law includes conventional law rooted in state practice, but seeks to derive general principles that are binding on all states irrespective of the particularities of state practice.

Thus the necessary law of nations is not jettisoned, but remains a central element of Vattel's system. As we have seen, the necessary law 'is the principle by which we may distinguish lawful conventions or treaties from those that are not lawful, and innocent and rational customs from those that are unjust or censurable' (p. lviii). It is needed 'in order that we may never confound what is just and good in itself with what is only tolerated through necessity' (p. xv). In Book II Vattel makes it clear that the idea of common duties and the 'offices of humanity' need to be upheld even though they do not fit easily with notions of *raison d'état*. As he remarks, 'The following maxims will appear very strange to cabinet politicians; and such is the misfortune of mankind that, to those refined conductors of nations, the doctrine of this chapter will be a subject of ridicule' (p. 133). Vattel is obviously aware, then, that morality and power politics sit uneasily together. But, in marked contrast to his nineteenth-century positivist successors, he insists that both need to be discussed together and, despite the seductive appeal of positivism, that the law/morality distinction will always remain blurred and uncertain.

Thus we find Vattel arguing for a strong duty to assist others: 'one state owes to another state whatever it owes to itself, so the other stands in real need of its assistance, and the former can grant it without neglecting the duties it owes to itself' (p. 135). For example, Vattel considers the need to assist those attacked: 'Thus, when a neighbouring nation is unjustly attacked by a powerful enemy who threatens to oppress it, if you can defend it, without exposing yourself to great danger, unquestionably it is your duty to do so' (p. 135). He also discusses the need to relieve famine and reaches similar conclusions.

Vattel certainly provides a powerful picture of how the actual scope for these offices of humanity is limited by the constraints of power politics:

> Melancholy experience shews that most nations aim only to strengthen and enrich themselves at the expense of others, – to domineer over them, and even, if an opportunity offers, to oppress and bring them under the yoke (p. 140).

In the first place, the scope of such activities is mitigated by the need for circumspection, and prudence dictates that states should be careful in helping potential enemies (hence, for example, his defence of the Navigation Acts in England). Second, Vattel argues that individual morality cannot be simply transferred to sovereigns or statesmen who must uphold an ethic of responsibility. Thus a prince or statesman might privately believe that more should be done, but cannot always act upon this belief 'because it is not his private interest that is in question, but that of the state – that of the nation that has committed herself to his care' (p. 140).

Vattel's prudentialism underlines the limits of morality in a world of power politics. But it does not deny the reality of a broader social context in which there are duties beyond borders and in which there is agreement on the content of moral standards and the nature of moral behaviour. For some critics, '[T]he concept of an imperfect obligation, so vital to Vattel's thought, immediately weakens the moral framework which holds together the natural society of nations'.[17] Yet the distinction between perfect and imperfect obligations is perhaps better viewed as one way of dealing with the inevitable conflicts of interest that arise in any moral community.

Moreover the limits to moral behaviour are not as constraining as sometimes suggested. According to Koskenniemi, for example, Vattel believes that 'no state is obliged to aid another State if it would endanger its own self-perfection'.[18] Yet Vattel argues that assistance should always be given unless such action would place the state in great or imminent danger. Or consider the critical subject of the balance of power. Vattel does not adopt a militarist position in which the resort to force is accepted as inevitable and perhaps even beneficial. He is very clear that the aggrandisement of a neighbouring power does not in itself provide sufficient grounds for fear and justify a resort to force. His prudentialism forces him to recognise that formal notions of just and unjust war may have to be displaced and that, in the last resort, threats must be subjectively defined. Yet, at the same time, he is anxious to provide criteria for that calculation, however rudimentary: what can be 'reasonably presumed', the 'degree of probability of attack', the 'seriousness of the evil threatened' and 'clear evidence of unbridled power and ambition'.

Vattel, then, provides a picture of law and morality that stays close to the practice of states, that seeks to go with, rather than against, the grain of power politics. It does not deny that there is a shared moral standard against which state action and international law can and should be judged. The problem is not that there is 'an absence of consensus about international ethical standards',[19] but rather deep scepticism as to how far those standards can be applied politically. Vattel's prudentialism therefore stresses the propensity of international relations to frustrate grand progressive schemes for peace and progress and highlights the difficulties of escaping from the realist logic of recurrence and reproduction. It is a constrained and ultimately pessimistic picture of law and morality, but it is not one that focuses exclusively on the absolute rights of states, nor one that, as Brierly argued, denies the existence of a social bond between states.

*The limits of tolerance* A critical measure of the absoluteness of understandings of sovereignty concerns how far domestic tyranny can be the subject of international action. For Vattel there are indeed limits to the norm of non-intervention and he is willing – again cautiously – to countenance external intervention against tyranny. That there should be a presumption *against* outside intervention should by now be clear:

> It is an evident consequence of the liberty and independence of nations, that all have a right to be governed as they think proper, and that no state has the smallest right to interfere in the government of another. Of all the rights that can belong to a nation, sovereignty is, doubtless, the most precious....

However, given his belief that '[T]he public authority is therefore established merely for the common good of all citizens', Vattel is also clear that the abuse of power cannot be hidden behind the veil of sovereignty.

> But, if the prince, by violating the fundamental laws, gives his subjects a legal right to resist him, – if tyranny, becoming insupportable, obliges the nation to rise in their own defence, – every foreign power has a right to succour an oppressed people who implore their assistance (p. 155).

Knowing what constitutes insupportable tyranny is, of course, far from easy. Vattel, foreshadowing a long tradition of legal thought on the matter, lays emphasis on the existence of civil war: 'Whenever, therefore, matters are carried so far as to produce a civil war, foreign powers may assist that party which appears to them to have justice on its side' (p. 156). The same pattern of thinking is applied to the suppression of freedom of religion. Religion normally provides no right to intervene or interfere, for, as he puts it, 'What rights have men to set themselves up as the defenders and protectors of the cause of God?' (p. 158). In normal circumstances the suppression of freedom of religion would create at most a right to intercede on behalf of co-religionists. But again there are limits: unless the persecution be carried to an intolerable excess: then, indeed, it becomes a case of manifest tyranny, in opposition to which, all nations are allowed to assist an unhappy people' (p. 159).

Remec is no doubt correct to argue that 'Vattel does not recognize any general right to punish crimes for the sake of human society in general.'[20] But the absoluteness of sovereignty is not unlimited and can be overridden in cases of 'intolerable persecution' and 'evident tyranny'.

*The limits of international society*    The creation of international society and, especially, the successful consolidation of an increasingly dense international society in particular parts of the world, leads naturally to divisions between insiders and outsiders. If there is an international society, what are its limits? Does it incorporate the entire human race or is it limited to a particular area? If it is limited, what are the principles of inclusion and exclusion? To what extent is such a division a source of instability and insecurity? International society writing has attached considerable importance to the evolution of conceptions of this division, tracing, on the one hand, those doctrines and ideas that rested on principles of exclusiveness, based on being Christian, being European or being 'civilised'; and on the other hand, the powerful counter-current in Western thought that has maintained the existence of a universal community of mankind and that has drawn its primary inspiration from the long tradition of natural law.

Vattel tends towards an inclusive conception of international society, acknowledging the rights of political communities in many parts of the world. In contrast to the natural law tradition reaching back to Vitoria, he implies that non-European communities have the right to deny freedom of trade to the Europeans (the right to trade is only with those 'who are *willing* [my emphasis] to correspond with such intentions' and trade can be declined if it is dangerous or disadvantageous). More generally he is critical of European imperialism in the Americas: 'Those ambitious Europeans who attacked the American nations, and subjected them to their greedy dominion, in order, as they pretended, to civilize them, and cause them to be instructed in the true religion…' (pp. 136–7).[21] He dismisses the idea of Grotius that sins against nature such as cannibalism should be punished by force of arms because such justifications 'open a door to all the ravages of enthusiasm and fanaticism, and furnishes ambition with numberless pretexts' (p. 137).

For Vattel, however, there may still be political communities whose refusal to accept the ground-rules of international society places them, quite literally, outside the pale. One example concerns the case where 'the maxims of a religion tend to establish it by violence, and to oppress all those who will not embrace it' (p. 195). In those cases, international society should unite 'to repress such outrageous fanatics, who disturb the public repose and threaten all nations' (p. 195). Similarly, the sovereign who does not even try to justify their violation of promises and treaties 'deserves to be treated as an enemy of the human race' (p. 230). A similar attitude is adopted towards those who resort to force without reason or pretext: 'All nations have a right to join in a confederacy for the purpose of punishing and even exterminating those savage nations' (p. 305).

What we see then as the apparent licence granted to all states is in fact only to be granted to those states that fall within certain limits: one category of limits has to do with domestic political arrangements, denying the protection of sovereignty and the norm of non-intervention to those states which are obviously tyrannical or oppressive. A second category has to do with states that refuse to accept the shared goal of coexistence and toleration. It is certainly true that these limits are relatively narrow – both because pluralism is in itself valuable and because of the clear danger of abuse if the presumption of non-intervention is not steadfastly upheld. But taken together they provide the foundation for a modified pluralist vision of international law and morality (such as that proposed by John Rawls) in which rights to mutual respect and independence are balanced only by the protection of certain minimum standards of human rights and by the need to uphold the overall structure of coexistence.

*Vattel in Context*    The final difficulty with the view of Vattel as the exponent of an extreme pluralist conception of international society is that it distorts the historical and intellectual context in which he was writing. There are two important points to be made. First, it is important to set Vattel's insistence on the rights of states against the shared awareness of belonging to a *grande république* based on a common diplomatic language, a common culture and a common civilisation. Thus in Vattel the untrammelled freedom of states is balanced both by a still very strong belief in the obligations and restraints derived from natural law and by the perception of Europe as a single moral, and still to a real, if by now limited extent, political, community. This community was based on what Gibbon called in 1770 'the general ressemblance of religion, language, manners' and was accepted both by those such as Vattel who sought to perfect the practice of eighteenth-century diplomacy and by those such as Rousseau who decried its failings.

Second, and more important, Vattel was writing within a context in which the modern idea of a society of wholly sovereign and autonomous states had barely begun to emerge and in an intellectual universe dominated by the moral language of the natural lawyers of the seventeenth century and especially of the tradition of thought that runs from Grotius to Hobbes and Pufendorff.[22] The search for origins makes it easy to pre-date changes. This is true of international lawyers who, as David Kennedy has argued, 'use historic texts either to demonstrate that the authors' contemporary vision is fully present, if in nascent form, or that modern doctrinal and systemic developments are foreshadowed in the historic texts'.[23] But it is also a serious difficulty with the theorists of international society whose work is founded on the claim that there is constant and coherent tradition of thought that runs from at least the time of Grotius down to the present day. Although the idea of a state *system* can perhaps be located earlier, it was only in the period from around 1740 to 1790 that understandings on the various core elements of the emerging *society* of states began to stabilise. This is true of the emergence of the concept of the balance of power as a shared and well-understood principle of international order.[24] It is also true of more general understandings of the concepts of war and peace. As Hinsley has argued, a great deal of the writings of the early peace-planners (certainly up to the Abbé Saint Pierre, whose peace project appeared in various versions between 1712 and 1729) looked *back* to the restoration of a unified and peaceful Christendom rather than *forward* to the progressive establishment of international peace in a recognisably modern sense.[25] Indeed the terms of the modern debate on war and peace only become well-established towards the end of the eighteenth century in the writings of, for example, Kant and Bentham.[26]

Vattel is writing, then, during a period in which the conception of Europe as a collection of Great Powers and nation-states was coming to replace an earlier idea of Europe still heavily influenced by the collective memory of the unity of Christendom. He recognises and seeks to respond to the aggression and acquisitiveness of foreign policy and to the ever-increasing emphasis in state practice on the autonomy of individual states and on the primacy of *raison d'état*. But he had by no means broken free from the ideas of those thinkers still very much concerned with the restoration of the unity of Christendom and whose conception of Europe was fundamentally backward-looking.

This is particularly true of the two writers whose works Vattel was most concerned to develop and to popularise, Leibniz and Christian Wolff. Vattel's first work was a defence of Leibniz (*Défense du système leibnitzien*, written in 1747) and Leibniz's essentially medieval vision of European 'international relations' is clear both from his earlier writing on international law and from his comments on Saint Pierre's peace plan written in 1715. In these comments Leibniz argues for a reformed papacy and empire as the best foundations for peace among the states of Europe and as the only viable form of pacific federation.[27] Of still more direct influence on Vattel, Christian Wolff continued to view the regulation of states in terms of a reformed and strengthened Holy Roman Empire and derived his conception of the voluntary law of nations from the existence of a *civitas maxima*.[28] It is possible to argue, then, that there is a critical discontinuity in understandings of international relations and international society in the second half of the eighteenth century, and that Vattel was at least as closely associated with the political language and intellectual assumptions of early-modern Europe as he was with the 'modern' notion of a European society of sovereign states.

Thus, despite recurrent conflict and despite the pluralism and fragmentation of the emerging state system, there was still a deep-rooted belief that these separate states constituted a political and moral unity. Europe was still viewed as a single interdependent system and as a kind of single republic in which political disunity coexisted with cultural unity and interdependence. Vattel is struggling with the need to combine a universal foundation of law and morality with the increasingly divisive and conflictual political realities of his time. In this he reflects the tension between identity and difference, between pluralism and unity, that was common to so many aspects of Enlightenment thought – the degree to which faith in universally valid moral and scientific laws was being challenged by growing recognition of political and cultural diversity; by growing emphasis placed on local climate and history (as in

Montesquieu); and by a new sense of history and time (as in Vico and Herder). Vattel's international law lays emphasis on both the rights of separate states and the continued existence of duties to others, to humanity at large. Moreover he continues to reflect the outlook of Leibniz and Wolff in being unable to conceive of, let alone accept, a clear choice between political fragmentation and moral relativism on the one hand and a universal or cosmopolitan morality on the other. He believes that individual state interest can be reconciled with a universal morality and wholly rejects Rousseau's agonised (and to many far more modern) question of whether 'in joining a particular group of men, we have really declared ourselves the enemies of the whole race'.[29]

## CONCLUSIONS

Vattel's success has never been in doubt. His work was enormously popular, becoming one of the most influential international law texts of all times. There were 20 new editions of *Le Droit des Gens* between 1758 and 1863, 29 printings of the English edition in that period, and 19 in the United States, where its influence was perhaps greatest of all.[30] As van Glahn puts it: 'It can seriously be maintained that despite the vital contribution of Grotius, no single writer has exercised as much direct and lasting influence on the men engaged in the conduct of international affairs in the legal sphere, at least until very modern times, as did Vattel.'[31]

The success of Vattel in large part resulted from his style. Comparing Vattel to his predecessors, Robert Ward noted in 1795 that 'he has thoroughly cleared them from the cumbrous ornaments which were supposed to adorn them, and had rendered the way into the interior less difficult and obscure'.[32] *Le Droit des Gens* is indeed a strikingly modern text, written in a language that we can understand and laying out the features of an international system that is still very much with us. Its tone is very much that of the Age of Enlightenment: secular, pro-scientific, humane, even democratic (with its stress that government should be based on consent of the governed). It filled a clear gap as an elevated manual of diplomatic practice written by a professional international lawyer when, for the first time in European history, such a phrase had begun to take on meaning. On the other side it has often been noted that his success derived as much from the ambiguities and inconsistencies of his text as from his clarity of expression. As Martin Wight notes, 'it is part of his charm (and no doubt of his lasting influence) that he contains inconsistent arguments that can be used to support contradictory policies'.[33]

Yet, despite the great influence of his work, Vattel's intellectual stock has never stood very high. It is widely argued that he was not a great nor original thinker but rather someone who clarified and applied contemporary ideas on the law of nations to the realities of his age – 'a witness as well as a lawyer' as Sir William Scott put it. He was writing at the time when international law was becoming increasingly formalised and collected together (for example the Abbé de Malbly's *Droit Publique de l'Europe fondé sur les Traités* published in 1747) and when there was a notable expansion in the laws of war (agreements on prisoners, on military hospitals, etc.). Personally not an especially interesting figure, Vattel is candid in admitting his debt to Christian Wolff and that his central aim was to make Christian Wolff's abstract theorising more concrete and comprehensible. Damning with the faintest of faint praise, de Lapradelle noted: 'Grotius a du génie, Vattel du talent'. He was an 'adapteur élégant et fin, mais plus agréable que solide, et plus délicat que puissant'.[34] Bentham was far more severe and direct, describing Vattel as 'old womanish and tautological'.

There are two persistent criticisms. The first touches on the tone of Vattel's writing and attacks his complacency. It is clear that Vattel did stay close to the political realities of his age, thereby opening himself to Kant's charge that he was no more than an apologist for power politics, a 'sorry comforter', for whom law is little more than *Realpolitik* translated into a different idiom. He moved with the times in permitting and prohibiting what governments of the time wished to see permitted and prohibited. He drew the line in the right place and his work is never in radical contradiction to the realities of his age: in terms of units, ends and conduct of international relations.

For those who view the eighteenth century international system in terms of balance and restraint, as one in which enlightened rulers and skilled diplomatists manoeuvred for position, and where the existence of war did not undermine the continued reality of a 'single republic', such a position need not pose any great difficulty. Adam Watson, for example, argues that:

> The eighteenth century European *grande république* stands out amongst states systems and phases of systems as exceptionally successful. It was well managed by the conscious co-operation, or at least restraint, of its member states ... the level of creative statecraft of the European eighteenth century is so outstanding that many of its concepts and much of its machinery continue transmuted in the present very different global system, and much of the wisdom which was then acquired remains relevant to other international societies including our own.[35]

But for many others, such a view is altogether too rosy. Thus, although his own position rested heavily on Vattelian assumptions and often tended in a basically pluralist direction, Bull disliked Vattel's complacency and his unworried view of international law and morality. He argued that Vattel never gave the impression of having looked over into the abyss of international anarchy.[36] There was nothing of Grotius's impassioned reaction to the devastation of the Thirty Years War; nor of the grim awareness that the international anarchy is fundamentally problematic – the sense that we get from Rousseau and Kant. This criticism is in large measure justified. Vattel's work does indeed give rise to charge of complacency and, despite his talk of the dangers of war, the shades of Pangloss lurk in the pages of *Le Droit des Gens*: that all is for the best in this best of all possible worlds, or as Pope put it in the *Essay on Man*: 'One truth is clear, WHATEVER IS, IS RIGHT.' Vattel's attempt to reconcile law and power politics does often appear too easy and his repeated argument that duties to other states will in fact be in a state's interest betrays a complacent belief in the workings of the hidden hand of providential nature. Certainly, Vattel's image of European international society stands in marked contrast to those of his contemporaries who railed against the brutalities of war and against the monarchs who sought to gain from it: Voltaire's attack on the supposed gentlemanly and honourable character of war in *Candide*; or Rousseau's bitter denunciations as, for example, in his letter to Malesherbes in 1760:

There are only wars which are in nobody's interest which desolate the whole world, immense standing armies in times of peace which are without use or effect in times of war, ministers always occupied doing nothing, mysterious treaties without purpose, alliances that take a long time to negotiate and which are broken the following day, finally subjects that become all the more miserable as the state becomes rich and all the more despised as the prince becomes powerful.[37]

The second charge is of incoherence or intellectual feebleness. Thus Nussbaum notes the '[S]triking ambiguity of his formulas and the inconsistency of his conclusions'.[38] Lauterpacht talks of his 'elegant use of evasion'.[39] Similarly Esther Brimmer has argued: 'Repeatedly Vattel would establish a definition consistent with natural law and then undermine it by yielding to exigencies of state liberty.'[40] Linklater argues that '[T]hese different perspectives cannot be accommodated within a single theory'.[41] Yet such criticisms run the risk of underestimating the tensions and ambiguities inherent in the idea of international society itself and their susceptibility to theoretical or political resolution. Vattel is not a profound thinker and did not always succeed in avoiding internal inconsistency; but his underlying ambitions were not misconceived or self-deluding.

What these representatives of Enlightenment jurisprudence sought to achieve was precisely a distinction between themselves and their classical predecessors without having to ratify whatever it was sovereigns wished to do. They defined voluntary law to consist of the interpretations and 'modifications' which States have introduced into necessary natural law in order to apply it in practice. It was subjectively based and thus avoided the accusation of abstract utopianism (which Vattel threw at Berbeyrac [*sic*], Hobbes and Grotius). But it was not apologist, either, as it was still natural law and maintained its connection with an objectively constraining morality. It was a mediating device to avoid, partially and temporarily, the immediate objections that contemporaries (and successors) directed upon pure naturalism (too objective) and pure positivism (too subjective).[42]

Put another way, the tradition of international society represents a sustained attempt to understand the relationship between the power political order on the one hand and the normative legal and moral order on the other, and to argue that no account of order in international life can ignore the complexities and ambiguities that lie at the heart of this relationship. Kant was correct in his assessment of Vattel as one of the 'sorry comforters' [*lauter leidiger Tröster*] for whom international law is substantially about developing a framework of coexistence in a world of independent states and for whom the place of morality is heavily constrained. As Kant implied, Vattel could not look beyond a world in which power politics is an inevitable condition of international relations and in which international law does indeed often come dangerously close to justifying the power games of states. But, as this chapter has sought to argue, he is far more than a complacent and simple-minded exponent of state libertarianism or legal individualism. Vattel stands as one of the abidingly important 'classical theorists of international relations' because of his attempt to hold law, morality and power politics together. He remains the *locus classicus* for a limited conception of international society in a world where might rather than right will all too often predominate, in which pluralism and the respect for diversity have a moral value, but in which there are also moral bonds that stretch between states and across societies.

## NOTES

1. Andrew Linklater, *Men and Citizens in the Theory of International Relations* (London: Macmillan, 1982), chapter 5 'Vattel's Society of States', p. 86.
2. Terry Nardin, *Law, Morality, and the Relations between States* (Princeton: Princeton University Press, 1983), p. 9 and, for his discussion of Vattel and eighteenth-century international society, pp. 60–8.
3. The distinction between pluralism and solidarism is developed in 'The Grotian Conception of International Society' in Butterfield and Wight (eds), *Diplomatic Investigations* (London: Allen and Unwin, 1966). Some confusion has arisen because Bull used the term 'Grotian' in two senses: firstly to describe the doctrine that there is such a thing as international society; and, secondly, to contrast the Grotian solidarist conception of international society from the more pluralist Vattelian conception. See Bull, *The Anarchical Society* (London: Macmillan, 1977), p. 322.
4. David Kennedy, 'Primitive Legal Scholarship', *Harvard International Law Journal*, 27, 1 (Winter 1986).
5. Percy Corbett, *Law and Society in the Relations of States* (Yale: Yale University Press, 1951), p. 29.
6. J. L. Brierly, *The Law of Nations* (Oxford: Oxford University Press, 6th edn, 1963), p. 40.
7. Cf. Brierly's criticism: 'By teaching that the "natural" state of nations is an independence which does not admit the existence of a social bond between them, he makes it impossible to explain or justify their subjection to law ... by cutting the frail moorings which bound international law to any sound principle of obligation he did it an injury which has not yet been repaired'. Brierly, *The Law of Nations*, p. 40. Van Vollenhoven's idealist critique is harsher still: 'If Grotius is the apostle of the *rights* of Nations, perhaps the prophet of an ultimate League of Nations, Vattel is the absolute negation of both the Law of Nations and League of Nations'. C. van Vollenhoven, *The Three Stages in the Evolution of the Law of Nations* (The Hague: Martinus Nijhoff, 1919), p. 31. For a strong statement of the continued relevance of Vattel, see Peter F. Butler, 'Legitimacy in a States-System: Vattel's *Law of Nations*', in Michael Donelan (ed.), *Reason of States* (London: Allen and Unwin, 1978).
8. Emerich de Vattel, *The Law of Nations*, trans. Joseph Chitty (London: Stevens and Sons, 1834), p. lvi. [All subsequent references are to this edition.]
9. Thomas Hobbes, *Leviathan* ed. John Plamenatz (Glasgow: Collins/Fount, 1983), pp. 144–5. Note the extent to which Locke follows a similar argument. To quote Richard Cox; 'But separate commonwealths are, at least in principle, much more nearly self-sufficient bodies. They possess a united force capable of defence of the body politic and its members. The state provides for the relative peace and security of the members, protects their properties, and establishes the conditions which conduce to industry and the production of plenty. Consequently the incentive which individuals have to leave the state of nature is lacking in the case of independent commonwealths.' Richard H. Cox, *Locke on War and Peace* (Oxford: Clarendon Press, 1966), p. 137.

10.  Hobbes, *Leviathan*, p. 168. For background on the development of ideas of natural law and natural rights, see Richard Tuck, *Natural Law Theories. Their Origin and Development* (Cambridge: Cambridge University Press, 1979).

11.  For a critical assessment of this strategy of reconciliation, see Martti Koskenniemi, *From Apology to Utopia. The Structure of International Legal Argument* (Helsinki: Finnish Lawyers' Publishing Company, 1989), p. 94.

12.  It is often suggested that there is a decisive shift towards positivism in the period after Vattel, as for example in the works of J. J. Moser and G. F. von Martens. (See, for example, Murray Forsyth, 'The Tradition of International Law', in Terry Nardin and David R. Mapel (eds), *Traditions of International Ethics* (Cambridge: Cambridge University Press, 1992), p. 35.) Yet Vattel's attempt to mediate between naturalism and positivism remains influential well into the late eighteenth century. See, for example, D. H. L. von Ompteda, *Literatur des gesammten sowohl natürlichen als positiven Völkerrechts* (Regensburg, 1785).

13.  Compare with Grotius: 'Quite untenable is the position that according to the law of nations, it is right to take up arms in order to weaken a growing power which, if it becomes too great, may be a source of danger'.

14.  The success of Vattel's ideas make it easy to forget that they were by no means universally accepted among international lawyers. For an opposing contemporary position, whose title was to resonate so strongly in the nineteenth-century peace movement, see J. G. Justi, *Die Chimäre des Gleichgewichts von Europa* (1758).

15.  William Edward Hall, *A Treatise on International Law*, 8th edn (Oxford: Clarendon Press, 1924), p. 81.

16.  Compare Rawls's notion of the law of peoples: 'Finally, I note the distinction between the law of peoples and the law of nations, or international law. The latter is an existing, or positive, legal order, however incomplete it may be in some ways .... The law of peoples, by contrast, is a family of political concepts with principles of right, justice, and the common good, that specify the content of a liberal conception of justice worked up to extend to and to apply to international law. It provides the concepts and principles by which that law is to be judged.' John Rawls, 'The Law of Peoples', in Stephen Shute and Susan Hurley (eds), *On Human Rights* (New York: Basic Books, 1993), p. 51.

17.  Linklater, *Men and Citizens*, p. 84.

18.  Koskenniemi, *From Apology to Utopia*, p. 91.

19.  Linklater, *Men and Citizens*, p. 89.

20.  Peter Remec, *The Position of the Individual in International Law according to Grotius and Vattel* (The Hague: Martinus Nijhoff, 1960), pp. 231–2.

21.  Vattel does not oppose all European colonialism. On the one hand, he draws a clear distinction between South America where the rights of political communities were abused and North America where the indigenous peoples had failed to exploit their land: 'Those who still pursue this idle mode of life occupy more land than they would have need of under a system of honest labour, and they may not complain if other more industrious Nations, too confined at home, should come and occupy part of their lands' (p. 138).

On the other, he is able to reconcile the continued existence of political community with many forms of imperial control. For a discussion see C. H. Alexandrowicz, *An Introduction to the History of the Law of Nations in the East Indies* (Oxford: Oxford University Press, 1967), pp. 151–3.

22. See Richard Tuck, 'The "modern" theory of natural law', in Anthony Pagden (ed.), *The Languages of Political Theory in Early-Modern Europe* (Cambridge: Cambridge University Press, 1987).

23. Kennedy, 'Primitive Legal Scholarship', p. 2.

24. See, in particular, Paul W. Schroeder, *The Transformation of European Politics 1763–1848* (Oxford: Clarendon Press, 1994).

25. See F. H. Hinsley: *Power and the Pursuit of Peace. Theory and Practice in the History of Relations Between States* (Cambridge: Cambridge University Press, paperback edn, 1980), chapter 8; and *Nationalism and the International System*, pp. 69–71.

26. See Martin Ceadel, *The Origins of War Prevention: The British Peace Movement and International Relations, 1730–1854* (Oxford: Clarendon Press, forthcoming 1995).

27. These are reprinted in Patrick Riley (ed.), *Leibniz. Political Writings* (Cambridge: Cambridge University Press, paperback edn, 1992), pp. 176–84.

28. See Francis Stephen Ruddy, *International Law in the Enlightenment. The Background to Emmerich de Vattel's 'Le Droit des Gens'* (New York: Oceana, 1975), chapter IV.

29. J. J. Rousseau, 'Abstract of the Abbé de Saint-Pierre's Project for Perpetual Peace' (probably written between 1756 and 1758 and published in 1761), reprinted in Stanley Hoffmann and David P. Fidler (eds), *Rousseau and International Relations* (Oxford: Clarendon Press, 1991), p. 54.

30. Details of translations, editions and citations of Vattel's work are given in Arthur Nussbaum, *A Concise History of the Law of Nations*, revised edition (New York: Macmillan, 1962), pp. 161–4; and A. de Lapradelle's introduction to *Le Droit des Gens* (Washington, DC: Carnegie Institution, 1916), pp. xxvii–xxxiii.

31. Gerhard van Glahn, *Law Among Nations*, 4th edn (New York: Macmillan, 1981), p. 50.

32. Robert Ward, *An Enquiry into the Foundations and History of the Law of Nations in Europe* (London: J. Butterworth, 1795), volume II, p. 626.

33. Martin Wight, 'Western Values in International Relations' in Butterfield and Wight (eds), *Diplomatic Investigations*, p. 119.

34. de Lapradelle, 'Introduction', p. xliii.

35. Adam Watson, *The Evolution of International Society* (London: Routledge, 1992), pp. 212–13.

36. Lecture series, 'Theory and Practice of International Relations, 1648–1789' Although in his early writings Bull argued strongly in favour of a pluralist conception of international society, he came to adopt a much more critical position. In his lectures he argued that Vattel's acceptance that the doctrine of the natural liberty of states could be used to override international obligations was 'sinister'; and, in the Hagey Lectures he argued: 'It should be clear that whatever case might have been made out at earlier periods of history for such a doctrine of the natural or inherent rights of sovereign states or of independent political communities it cannot be acceptable

now.... The rights of sovereign states, and of sovereign peoples or nations, derive from the rules of the international community or society and are limited by them.' Hedley Bull, *Justice in International Relations*. The 1983–84 Hagey Lectures (Waterloo, Canada: University of Waterloo, 1984), p. 11.

37. Given this view it is not surprising that Rousseau provides one of the sharpest (and almost exactly contemporary) critiques of international law in *L'Etat de Guerre* probably written in 1757/58:

As for what is commonly called international law, because its laws lack any sanction, they are unquestionably mere illusions, even feebler than the law of nature. The latter at least speaks in the heart of individual men; whereas the decisions of international law, having no other guarantee than their usefulness to the person who submits to them, are only respected in so far as interest accords with them.

In Hoffmann and Fidler (eds), *Rousseau on International Relations*, p. 44.

38. Nussbaum, *A Concise History*, p. 159.
39. Hersch Lauterpacht, *The Function of Law in the International Community* (Oxford: Clarendon Press, 1933), p. 7.
40. Esther Brimmer, 'Emer de Vattel's *Le Droit des Gens*', Oxford, unpublished M. Phil. thesis, 1985, p. 65.
41. Linklater, *Men and Citizens*, p. 89.
42. Marti Koskenniemi, 'Theory: Implications for the Practioner', in Philip Allott *et al. Theory and International Law: An Introduction* (London, 1991), p. 28. This argument is developed at greater length in Koskenniemi, *From Apology to Utopia*, pp. 85–98.

# 12 Conclusion
## Ian Clark and Iver B. Neumann

The theorists presented in this volume have not been engaged in a conversation like the theorists once memorably assembled by Michael Donelan at
The Perpetual Peace. On that occasion, Kant chaired a discussion in which
participated, among others, Aristotle, Augustine, Hobbes, Locke,
Rousseau and Hegel, with important interventions from the chairman
himself. In that device, Donelan presented the notion of political theory as
timeless dialogue.[1]

The contributors to this book have not started with any such assumption. It has been their task to place their writers in historical context, to
outline the main elements of their thinking, and to assess their contribution
to the development of thought about international relations. However, in
doing so, they have indeed pointed to the affinities with, and differences
from, other patterns of thought: the elaboration of classical traditions, and
the location of writers within them, is a recurring motif of this work.

By this means, an indirect conversation has taken place and we are
driven to return to the historical preconditions for, as well as the legitimacy of, this procedure. The introductory chapter discussed at length the
advantages and disadvantages of using traditions as pegs on which to hang
an exposition of the main themes in theoretical reflection about the
subject. What more can be said about this at the volume's end? Can texts
be treated in such a dialogical way?

When Wight constructed his canon of traditional perspectives, he did so
in an intellectual atmosphere where the very idea of a canon was under
challenge in other intellectual guilds. His comment that 'classification
becomes valuable, in humane studies, only at the point where it breaks
down' may be seen as sensitivity to the dangers of reifying and closing
traditions.[2] But what also seems to be at issue here is Wight's lack of
belief in dialectical progress.[3] The kind of breakdown he seems to have
in mind is not a dialectical *Aufhebung*, an instance which makes
classification superfluous by uniting previously discrete and contradictory
elements into a synthesis, but rather the collapse of the classificatory
scheme itself when confronted with the richness of the ideas inherent in
and between the various texts.

Wight's solution to this problem is decidedly not dialectical but dialogical, or to be more precise, trialogical. Whereas Wight is usually seen as a totalising thinker, there is also in his work an affinity to the idea of timeless dialogue, as celebrated by writers such as Mikhail Bakhtin.[4] Writing inside Stalin's Soviet Union, in what was proclaimed to be the end-result of historical dialectics and, as a practical consequence, the end of dialogue, Bakhtin developed a philosophy of textual and timeless dialogue. Texts exist concurrently not only in the sense that one of the texts to be found in this volume carries on a dialogue with the texts quoted, but also in the sense that a reader who has already read *Leviathan*, can hardly turn to a reading of *The Peloponnesian War* without actualising a dialogue between the two texts. Thus, once *Leviathan* was written, it transformed the way *The Pelopponesian War* would be read in the future. It is a corollary of this view that all texts are only actualised in dialogue: a timeless dialogue of texts is not only a possibility, but a necessity. Following this logic, Wight's traditions should be reimagined as a polyphony of textual voices, some louder than others, but where even the most subdued may, at a future time, have a more assertive part to play. This may offer some consolation to the many authors not represented in the present volume.

The identification of traditions in international-relations thinking has recently received some stout defences, the force of which may even be increased if looked at in the light of Bakhtin's argument. Timothy Dunne regards them as remaining 'an important element of the international theorists' craft'.[5] Yet at the same time, he is anxious that the proliferation of categories may lead to 'coherence' being 'displaced by a Babel of contending voices'.[6] In Bakhtinian perspective, the defence stands but the worry is superfluous. Pierre Hassner seems to question the efficacy of a trialogue at the present time when he asks, plaintively, 'where are the three traditions now that we need them?' but actually then proceeds to investigate the nature of the post-Cold War world on the basis of them.[7] Common to both defences is an insistence that it is no part of their value that the traditions be presented as reified schemes which rigidly divide the debate and the contributions to it: the importance of devising such intellectual schemes lies precisely in the potential for creative synthesis which is afforded.

Such an approach is unanimously endorsed by the contributions to this book. Virtually all have difficulty in 'pigeon-holing' their particular subject within a specific tradition, the only exception being Gentz, who is deemed to be the 'quintessential rationalist'. In all other cases, our contributors reach a mixed and qualified judgement. This is as might be expected. More importantly, however, in the majority of cases the commentators see the inability to assign their writers to one tradition exclusively, not as an analytic weakness, but as a fruitful outcome: the value of the distinct traditions lies precisely in their drawing of our attention to the diverse elements which make up an individual theorist's position. The main sceptic is Fidler, who injects the dissenting note that analysing Rousseau against the three traditions produces 'more confusion than clarity'. Otherwise, our essayists seem to be persuaded of the enriching effect of assessing each writer against the traditions: it enables them to illustrate the 'internal' debate among the traditions in which each theorist is engaged and out of which each develops a unique composition of diverse elements.

This theme emerges clearly from the findings of the majority of our contributors. For example, and in summary form, Vitoria is found to have realist and rationalist aspects but, simultaneously to be the 'first revolutionist', largely on the basis of his emphasis on human rationality and equality. Navari's Hobbes is by no means the definitive realist: our view of him, as of the elephant, depends upon which part we touch. Smith is wrenched from his comfortable association with the liberal internationalists and demonstrated to have salient realist characteristics. Kant, according to Williams and Booth, has not been well-served by Wight's assigning to him of revolutionist camp-followers and, certainly, needs to be 'rescued from the Kantians'. Rousseau manifests major departures from the realism with which he is commonly, if mistakenly, associated. Finally, Hegel is shown to combine elements of all three traditions in his own distinctive way. If, as noted, Gentz can be lined up with the rationalists without demurral, the effect is nonetheless to displace the complexity of his position into the heart of rationalism itself. In all cases, our understanding of these writers has been sharpened by this emphasis on the dynamic tensions which co-exist within them.

There are three other conclusions which emerge from this collection. They relate to the inferred distinction between political theory and international theory; to the scope of the international theory agenda; and to the significance of the contribution, and subsequent impact, of the theorists who have been included in this volume.

There is little support for the notion, embedded in Wight's argument, that political theory and international theory constitute distinct fields of endeavour. Indeed, in many respects the most powerful theme to emerge from these studies is the emphasis placed by our theorists on the integral nature of the political and ethical issues associated with our dual lives as 'men and citizens': the quest for the good life is inescapably bound up with our international arrangements and there is a reciprocal effect between what is desirable domestically and internationally. To this extent, the volume reinforces Steve Smith's summary judgement that 'political and international theory share the same concerns and imperatives and are part of the same theoretical enterprise...'.[8]

With varying emphases, this theme can be discovered in all the contributions but is best illustrated in the discussions of Rousseau, Kant and Hegel. Fidler makes the strenuous argument that the international is but one of the links in the chain constraining human freedom: there can be no good life without resolution of the moral contradictions entailed by international relations. There is a synergistic relationship among the three problems to be overcome, namely, the corruption of human nature by civilisation, oppressive conditions under tyrannical government, and the nature of the international system itself. These problems are not soluble in separation from each other. Likewise, the denial of separate realms of theory is fundamental to the claim that Kant is a theorist of world politics. Kant's preoccupation, as with Rousseau, is with the tripartite dimensions of human nature and moral potentiality, the status and form of government within the state, and the conditions for perpetual peace. While it is commonplace to see Kant's contribution as the association between republican government and the good international society, Williams and Booth see this as only a partial reading unless it is remembered also that human nature is a necessary cause of peace. In such an intermingling, separate domestic and international discourses on political theory can have no foundation. And finally, Linklater's Hegel, as might be anticipated, synthesises the two realms of theoretical endeavour. For all his association with the state, Hegel did not believe that the state 'exhausted the moral, political and intellectual life of modern citizens'. Given the elements of universalism to which Linklater then draws our attention, it would seem that political and international theory are essentially one and the same enterprise.

If this book springs out of a recognition that international relations scholars would do well to stop delineating their discipline in opposition to political theory, then it is equally the case that political theorists could spend more time theorising the borders of the *polis*. One of their number recently asked, 'A politics *sans* sovereignty: is it possible? What would it look like?' This reminds us that modern political theory has acquired its name exactly because its concern is with a *polis* whose borders have been seen as fixed, whereas we may now be in a position where this is changing.[9] To specify a point made in the introduction, if we are now at an historical juncture where the social construction of sovereignty is undergoing a radical transformation, texts from the classical canon which deserve close attention are those written the last time such a radical change occurred. In the words of John Vincent:

> it may be helpful to compare Grotius' treatment of the emergence of the states-system with our contemporary preoccupation with its actual or potential decline... to consult Grotius not merely as a defunct publicist, someone who ran his lap long ago, but as a scholar who has thought deeply about the tension between the attachment to a local community and the more abstract obligation to world society as a whole.[10]

If classical theory does have a secure place in the heterologue about international relations, may it also be seen to make a contribution to the wider meta-theoretical agenda which occupies so much contemporary attention and is outlined in Chapter 1? An early commentary on Wight's traditions had already suggested that there was a wider set of issues lurking beneath the formalised Wightian scheme of thought. It noted the following of the traditions:

> And because they link theory with history, because they transcend the distinction between international and all other forms of politics, and because they comprehend competing worldviews and are intimately related to values, they represent the sort of theory of which the times we are entering would appear to stand peculiarly in need.[11]

More recently, Dunne has seen the strength in the employment of traditions in theory to reside precisely in its transcendence of the 'distinctions between theory and practice, philosophy and context'.[12] Furthermore, Adam Watson's self-proclaimed evolutionary perspective on international society shows how it may be applied to broader historical sequences than that of the modern states-system. Watson too cautions us against the 'danger that our categories may come between us and reality'.[13]

Some of our contributors echo these suggestions in pointing to the broadened scope of theory to be discovered in the classical texts. Over and above their discussion of the obvious substantive matters of the classical agenda, they raise fundamental questions about the role of theory itself. Kant may suffice to illustrate the point but without any claim to his being representative of the others. Part of Kant's significance is deemed to lie in his discussion of epistemology and ontology. Above all, he asserts the primacy of the normative and the idea that theory is the foundation of practice. By this intellectual route, according to Williams and Booth, the Kantian approach is inescapably concerned with the meta-theoretical agenda.

Finally, it is necessary to offer some brief assessment of the overall contribution and impact of these sundry theorists. Individually, who has done most to influence the development of international relations theory? Any such attempt is inherently problematic and, in most respects, ill-conceived. If we accept that each author is in dialogue with the reader, and with the other texts, we are led to conclude that there is no Archimedean standpoint from which such a determination might be made: to privilege a certain text, is to risk imposing an agenda upon the subject and to close down the range of contributions to it. In any case, the reputations of our various theorists have waxed and waned as they have been responded to, or neglected, by subsequent generations: the perceived significance of each cannot be judged from the arbitrary perspective of the present.

It would be invidious to conduct any Oscar-presentation ceremony of this kind with a declared winner. If it were to be done, some criterion would need to be set out. It would not be sufficient to rest reputation on quantity of output alone because the scale of the contribution in all cases is modest. However, the standard comment that political theorists have only addressed international issues as peripheral to the domestic, itself rests on the validity of the distinction between international and political theory which has already been denied. If that distinction is disallowed, the corpus of their writings becomes that much more impressive. We might then move towards awarding the prize on the basis of the *range of the contribution to a unified world politics.* Even if this remains an imprecise and contested measure, it would yield a prize worthy of the name.

On this basis, we can certainly identify those who would not be included in the final nominations. For all their fine qualities, Vitoria, Grotius, Vattel, Smith and Burke would not make the short-list. Gentz is eliminated by Little's dismissal of him as neither important nor original, however sophisticated his practical insights into the workings of the European balance of power. Of those represented in this volume, we are left with Hobbes, Rousseau, Kant and Hegel. Despite the acuity with which Linklater traces Hegel's resurrection in critical theory, 'end of history' theories, and communitarian normative theory, he does concede that the state has gone so badly off the rails in the twentieth century, with totalitarianism and war, that there is now no distinctively Hegelian perspective on world politics. Hobbes has a major reputation in the field but Navari usefully reminds us that this reputation is a recent, and certainly a twentieth-century, acquisition. Moreover, that for which he is most often cited, namely the analysis of the state of war, is extremely brief in the original. Perhaps his nomination must also fail.

This leaves us with Rousseau and Kant. The case for award of the prize to Kant is the one pressed most vigorously in these pages. Williams and Booth accept Chris Brown's judgement that Kant is 'the greatest of all theorists of international relations'. But perhaps we should not accede simply on the strength of this advocacy. Let the prize be shared, even if this runs the risk of seeming to reduce all classical theory to the oft-noted, and equally often criticised, permanent dialogue between these two dominant figures.

## NOTES

1. 'The Political Theorists and International Theory' in Donelan (ed.), *The Reason of States* (London: Allen and Unwin, 1978).
2. Wight, *Traditions*, p. 259.
3. H. Bull, 'Introduction: Martin Wight and the Study of International Relations' in M. Wight (ed. Hedley Bull), *Systems of States* (Leicester: Leicester University Press, 1977).
4. See, for example, M. Holquist, *Dialogism: Bakhtin and His World* (London: Routledge, 1990).
5. 'Mythology or Methodology? Traditions in international theory', *Review of International Studies*, Vol. 19, No. 3, July 1993, p. 318.
6. 'Mythology', p. 307.
7. 'Beyond the Three Traditions: the philosophy of war and peace in historical perspective', *International Affairs*, Vol. 70, No. 4, Oct. 1994.
8. 'The Self-Images of a Discipline' in K. Booth and S. Smith (eds), *International Relations Theory Today* (Oxford: Polity Press, 1995), p. 9.
9. Jean B. Elstein, 'Sovereignty, Identity, Sacrifice', *Social Research*, Vol. 58, 1991, p. 560.
10. 'Grotius, Human Rights, and Intervention' in H. Bull, B. Kingsbury and A. Roberts (eds), *Hugo Grotius and International Relations* (Oxford: Clarendon Press, 1990), pp. 252–3.
11. B. Porter, 'Martin Wight's "International theory"', in Donelan (ed.), *The Reason of States*, p. 73.
12. 'Mythology or Methodology?', p. 318.
13. *The Evolution of International Society* (London: Routledge, 1992), p. 10.

# Index